Four years ago this man gave thousands of readers a tremendously vital message in *Three Magic Words*. And literally thousands of readers wrote to him to say that they had changed the tone of their lives from negative to positive by following his teaching. "My whole life is changed. It is the most inspiring book I own," was a typical letter.

Now in *The Secret of Secrets* he delivers another tremendously vital message, one that will lead to mastery over circumstance and life. To the "three magic words" of his first book he now adds the "four steps" of the method for converting the realization of an indwelling God into a richer, fuller life.

U. S. Andersen has developed his inspiring, dynamic philosophy during a very active life. He learned about the psychology of winning when he was a football great. In World War II he served as a Naval officer and in the heat of battle learned that evil is the great illusion and that sin is error. In recent years as a successful Los Angeles businessman, he has learned that the secret of success is to create rather than to compete.

Three Magic Words gave the key to power, peace and plenty. His second inspirational book, *The Secret of Secrets*, shows how to use the mystic powers of the mind to gain mastery over oneself and one's environment.

This new book by the author of the best-selling *Three Magic Words* carries forward the hopeful message of that inspiring book: *It is no longer necessary for modern man to lead a life of quiet desperation. He can do something about his dilemma. The secret waits....*

What *is* this secret? And how can one discover what it is and learn to use it?

U. S. Andersen calls it THE SECRET OF SECRETS because, strangely enough, it is within each man and yet can set him free. It is a secret that is making itself known over the face of the earth. It has become the common meeting ground of all religions. *Sri Aurobindo* says "It is the one secure and all reconciling truth which is the very foundation of the universe. "It is this truth and its application to your own life that is the theme of THE SECRET OF SECRETS.

There is in man, below the level of his consciousness, a vaster mind, a mind of enormous power and knowledge, a mind universal in scope, common to all men but exclusive to none. U. S. Andersen furnishes ample proof that this mind exists and that you can tap it. Wise men have learned that the human mind is a magnificent machine with an infinite reservoir of power still untapped by the mass of men.

The magic moment when you learn to link with this power is the moment when the secret of abundance becomes yours ...

the spiritual equivalent of having a money tree in your own back yard.

This book is divided into twelve chapters. Each chapter is packed with illuminating case histories to make every idea clear. At the close of each chapter there is a "Meditation"... beautifully phrased and meticulously compact summing up what has just been discussed.

Every chapter makes thrilling reading. "Health and Well-Being" is an attack on the negative prompters which make egos sick ... the prompters which make people say, "I don't feel well," "I'm not very smart," "I'm ugly," "I'm lonely." Each physical and mental ailment has its counterpart in a spiritual ailment, the author shows; cure that and the physical and mental ailment is also healed.

The chapter on "Loving and Being Loved" is one of the wisest and frankest discussions of this important subject that has appeared in print.

The chapter on the mystic powers of the mind deals with thought transference and other manifestations of the universal mind or what is known to science as extrasensory perception.

These are but three of the twelve chapters that can help you recapture control over your inner and outer life. The seeds of all possibilities exist within you if you would only learn this SECRET OF SECRETS.

THE SECRET
OF
SECRETS

U. S. Andersen

Melvin Powers
Wilshire Book Company

12015 Sherman Road, No. Hollywood, CA 91605

TO
ANN ANDERSEN
With Love

FOREWORD

This book is intended to show how the spiritual realization of an indwelling God may be applied to the various problems of everyday living. My previous book, *Three Magic Words,* ended with the revelation that man's consciousness is God's consciousness in process of becoming. *The Secret of Secrets* begins with this premise, then lays down a method by which such awareness may be used for the practical end of a richer and fuller life.

This method is somewhat like Yoga. It was indicated by Sri Aurobindo in summing up the *Bhagavad-Gita* when he wrote, "The secret of action is one with the secret of life. Life is not for the sake of life alone, but for God. Action is for self-finding and not for its external fruits. There is an inner law of all things dependent on the supreme as well as the manifested nature of the self; the truth of works lies there. The largest law of action is therefore to find the truth of your highest and inmost existence and live in it. Only by discovering your true self can your doings be perfected in a divinely authentic action. Know then yourself. Know your true self to be God and one with the self of all others."

The method offered for mastery over life is to make a sacrament of every thought and deed, giving each to the Lord and Master of creation without attachment to results. By such a procedure a man gradually frees himself of the limitations of personal ego and comes to understand that a larger power, a greater self may be unloosed through his own nature. He sees that it is God who thinks in him, God who wills in him, God who acts through him, and a new spiritual center of gravity is established. The ego dissolves, God-consciousness comes, and a man's peace and power are immensely enhanced because he moves in tune with the infinite.

On the surface this appears a contradiction to the generally accepted premise that positive thinking can change one's life, but in fact that premise is developed here far beyond such psychological limitations. Positive thinking alone is not the key to attainment, else there never would be a confident failure. Man is not bigger than God, and in the end it avails him only heartache to impose his ego-will on God's will. Yet man is far more than a puppet; he is God Himself in process of becoming, and it is by seeking out the nature of this real self that he prospers. This, however, he cannot do without first having a positive viewpoint of life. He must believe in his own immortality, in the assured ends of truth, justice, beauty, and brotherhood on earth; and when at last he has laid aside ego and glimpsed the limitless dimensions of his true spiritual being, then he sees that nothing is impossible to him. He achieves divine consciousness, his word is law, his thoughts rule the universe.

Such is his destiny. To that end may this book lead you.

CONTENTS

THE SECRET
OF
SECRETS

1 THE CORE OF THE PROBLEM

God dwelleth always right where thou art
Shed thy ego and thou wilt soon see
Hidden within thy most secret heart
A plan that is perfect for thee

WE PUNISH OURSELVES

Alex was a middle-aged man in a midwestern city. His history was an astonishing record of failure. Whatever he turned his hand to eventually crumbled about him. There came a time when he could not even find a job. He and his family were destitute.

His wife said, "I can't understand it. Alex is the kindest man I've ever known. He's a hard worker, and I know he's smart. Other men, smaller, meaner men, are successful, but poor Alex, all his luck is bad."

"Does he think so?" she was asked.

She nodded. "He believes God is punishing him."

It took a long time to pursuade Alex that God punishes no one. His guilt complex was so deeply rooted that he was dangerously passive. He felt compelled to be kind to others because of this guilt, but he expected nothing but misfortune in return. His personality was so involuted that he lived as if in a funnel; he was all turned in on himself. Only when he began to sense finally the infinite spiritual presence of

13

God did his ego start to dissolve. Then he began to see other people for the first time, not as extensions of his own personality, but as living embodiments of God. His sense of personal worth grew as he gained humility. One day he was offered a job by a chance acquaintance; today he is a vice-president in that company. The president says of him, "Alex inspires confidence. Something looks out of his eyes and says, 'I like you. Let's be partners.'" God-consciousness indeed has remade the life of this one-time failure.

SEEDS OF DESTINY

Each of us carries within him the spiritual causes that determine his destiny. Sometimes these causes are not so much spiritual as psychological "prompters," and when they become twisted through fear, hate, bitterness, or resentment our lives can be driven calamitously. But psychological prompters, no matter how deeply buried in the subconscious, can be overcome by spiritual understanding. This understanding may be arrived at by intellectual grasp, by suffering, or simply by humility, very often by all three, but once arrived at it is as a new birth of the soul. That which you fancy yourself to be you never have really been, for it is a thing that changes with the seasons and alters with the tides. What you truly are is a permanent thing, changeless, with its foundations planted in eternity. To let go of the old self and cleave to the new is the essence of spiritual growth. This new birth, without which, Jesus said, a man cannot enter the Kingdom of Heaven, completely alters the world.

He who views the world through the ego sees all things as existing outside himself. He feels separate, isolated, and the world appears to him as a series of unrelated things and objects all possessing certain inherent dangers to his own being. He feels small, harassed, unloved, to him the world seems cruel and unjust. Yet when he awakens to his true spiritual self, all the old fears and hates and resentments dissolve. He then sees his kinship with all things, attains to spiritual identification with them, grows into a spiritual oneness with all creation that no longer leaves room for his personal ego and its wounds and vanities. By letting go of his small self he attains to a vast self, a self that encompasses all things. Then at last he recognizes with Walt Whitman, "The whole theory of the universe is directed to one individual—namely to You."

SPIRITUAL REBIRTH

It is through spiritual rebirth that we overcome all things. It is through our growth into the spiritual image of God that the purpose of life itself is fulfilled. For that purpose did spirit first become involved in matter, to that end shall it one day be free.

We are such materialists in this age of electronics and atom bombs that there is often much scoffing about the "spiritual" existence of man. Many there are who state that man is body only, that he comes into existence as a machine destined to run a certain length of time, that the apparent director within him is only an illusion fostered by the machine's acquisition of rational habit patterns. What a desert of mind and soul such a belief must be! What else can the holder of such a belief do but spin out his futile existence in a web of frustration and resentment? Look into the eyes of your loved ones and you know at once the living presence of spirit. It need not be weighed, measured, and counted; it is there, and you recognize it. All the mathematics and logic in the world can neither prove nor disprove it, but you know it just the same. Spirit recognizes spirit, for it is the same in each of us, invisible and indivisible.

This knowledge, though it exists in the intuitive center of every man, nevertheless needs some logical justification before it can break through the mental barriers of this materialistic age. "It is all well and good," says the materialist, "to talk of feelings and intuitions but you must admit that they cannot be proved or disproved. What religion needs is something concrete, a fact, something provable." Well, feelings *are* provable. All of us recognize an act of bravery, an act of love, an act of kindness, why then must there always be so much doubt over the validity of the conduct of a man who claims to know God? All actions spring from feelings, many of them from the most spiritual feelings, and if it were not for these intangibles, which no one can weigh, measure, or even classify adequately, this world would be as still and silent as a tomb.

MASTER OF CREATION

It is spirit, soul, consciousness that is ever first cause, master and mover of creation, alpha and omega of existence. It is God stuff, infinite, eternal, changeless, arrested but a moment in form, manifesting its myriad appearances as a dancer might display infinite numbers of costumes, but remaining always one, indivisible and changeless.

This is God, not a giant-sized man, not even a god as we might imagine in our minds and make an image of, but a power, a presence, a being, an infinite intelligence pervading all and creating all yet remaining unaltered amongst the ever-changing.

A professor at a western university was illustrating to his class examples of deductive and inductive reasoning. "Deductive reasoning," he stated, "is to reason from an effect to a cause. For example, I know I exist. I did not make myself or the world I live in, therefore I deduce that someone else did. This someone I call God. Now inductive reasoning, on the other hand, is to reason from cause to effect. For example, I know that I think and that this thinking increases my knowledge. Inductive reasoning, therefore, tells me that I may increase knowledge of my Creator through taking thought. That, gentlemen, in a nutshell, is all that is going on in the world." Wise man, he knew God through mind, but truth to tell, he also knew him through his heart.

SHEDDING THE EGO

Now the core of the problem of existence is this. Most of us believe ourselves to be creatures of circumstance, pushed around by the whims of fate and buffeted on all sides by forces over which we have no control. When we do manage to persuade ourselves that we can exercise control over our inner and outer lives we often do so with a magnified ego that has convinced us of our power through fostering the illusion that we are better than others. Obviously such a delusion is doomed to short life. We attain to mastery neither through magnified ego (the worst of all possible solutions) nor through an involuted ego that brings a sense of personal worthlessness. We take the first and most important step to mastery by shedding the ego altogether and identifying ourselves with God.

While the foregoing may be read by many, it will be the rare reader who at once penetrates its meaning. For to let go of personal self is to suffer a kind of death. To shed the ego means to attain to a state of personal abstraction wherein we can view ourselves with detachment, neither condoning nor condemning, aware of our personal existence neither more nor less than we are aware of the existence of our fellows. It is this state of consciousness that teaches us to love our neighbors as ourselves, not necessarily through an increased love for our neighbors, but more through a less personalized and more detached regard for ourselves. In this state we learn to identify ourselves with a greater consciousness, a vast intelligence. We feel it underlying our existence, buoying us up, supporting us, giving us our awareness. Little by little we expand to meet it, until that which we were, our ego, begins to recede, until at last we view our personal existence as through the inverted end of a telescope. Now we begin to see what we truly are and to let go of what we never really have been. Now the world is changed. It has no more resemblance to what it was before than we have to what we were before, for, in the words of Evelyn Underhill, "We behold at any specific moment not that which is but that which we are."

THE INFINITE POWER

God, first cause, unlimited consciousness, infinite intelligence, involves Himself in matter and manifests in myriad forms, not to prove anything, not to fight anything, not to overcome anything, not to separate right from wrong, but only for the pure joy of expression; and this, as we know it, is the beginning of things, of the manifest world, of the stars, of the planets, of life. God Himself becomes involved in matter, and what He becomes, while infinitely less than Himself in form and substance, nevertheless *is* Himself, true and entire, in spiritual potential. Nothing can become this or that but God; God is all, there is nothing else.

And so consciousness is arrested in form, in being, spun out in space and time as a man or a woman, calling itself by a name, peering outward at a world that seems to dwarf it, overcome by problems because it assumes itself to be contained within that world rather than perceiving the truth, which is that the world is contained within *it*. This is man, who has isolated himself with his developing ego, cut himself off from the roots of his power which are firmly placed in the reaches of space and time.

> Strong is the soul, and wise, and beautiful
> The seeds of godlike power are in us still;
> Gods are we, Bards, Saints, Heroes, if we will.
> —Matthew Arnold

SOMETHING DEEP INSIDE

Joe McAdams was a strong, husky young man, a flyer in World War II. Joe had a vast appetite for life. He played and fought and laughed and frolicked, and in general comported himself like an enthusiastic bear cub. Then one day his plane was shot down. Joe was wounded in both legs, but managed to parachute from the flaming ship. He landed in the sea, where he floated for hours in his life jacket. Sharks attacked him. Joe fought them with his knife. When he finally was picked up he barely was conscious and had nearly bled to death. Both legs were so badly damaged they had to be amputated. Joe, intensely physical, joyous Joe, faced life as a cripple. He went into a state of shock. Though conscious, he would talk to no one. He had to be force-fed.

The plain fact was that Joe no longer wanted to live. He apparently had taken the mental stand that if he couldn't be whole in body he wanted nothing further to do with life. He grew gaunt and pale. His skin hung lifelessly on his mangled body. Yet he did not die. Some spark within him resisted. For many months he seemed to hover on the very brink of death, then he began to recover. First sign was a return of color to his face, then his eyes grew brighter, then one day he smiled; after that he rapidly regained his strength. With a zest he entered into the rehabilitation program, learned how to be expert with his new artificial legs, set about studying hard so that he eventually was accepted at one of the East's finest engineering schools. Today Joe holds a responsible job with one of the nation's leading manufacturers. Those who know and love him realize that a great change has been wrought in this young man, a change far greater and deeper than that undergone by his scarred body. There has been a subtle but deep change in his entire personality, in his very character. He is still the vital, energetic Joe everyone knew, but now around all his actions and words there hangs a new aura, a kind of otherworldliness, a spiritual quality that the old Joe McAdams never showed. Joe was asked about this.

"I guess it's pretty obvious I've changed," he said, "inside, I mean, where it really counts. And it's more than just a change. The old Joe McAdams died out there on that Pacific atoll where he lost his legs. I'm the new Joe, and I was born on that same Pacific atoll. I was born one day when I realized that everything in life changes and fades away and the only thing that stays is something inside you, something that is you and yet is not you and is big and powerful and always there. It's God, I think. That's what really changed me."

SPIRITUAL REALIZATION

Do you assume for one moment that some freak of circumstance, some coincidental arrangement of atoms and molecules, some bizarre chance from among an infinite number of chances has caused you to exist? Have you not looked inward on yourself and become startled beyond all possibility of recovery by the tremendous and sudden awareness that *you* are *you?* There are no words to express the true miracle of this self discovery. That the world exists, the planets, the stars, the mountains, oceans, seas, is a workaday thing, the substance of life, the backdrop against which the play is staged. But suddenly to realize that you, that unique and individual you, are here, are witness, are called into being, this is to know God, fully and surely. Such a realization forever lays to rest all materialistic philosophy, all atheism, all agnosticism. God is, you are, God is in you.

One evening a professor of mathematics, a forceful experimenter and a questing man, was told of such spiritual revelation. "You say you experience this thing," he answered, "so I believe you. All right, let's accept it. God manifests himself in myriad forms through the mere joy of His being, and what He becomes is less than Himself for a moment but truly Himself in eternity. What's the point? Surely you recognize that people suffer. Many people you must have known have gone through anguish because they had not resources to cope with some worldly situation and thus were forced to suffer. Who suffered then, these people or God, and if either or both, why? Surely God is no masochist, enjoying self-punishment, yet why does He become less than Himself and literally frustrate and torture Himself?"

"It is not God who suffers, or even the people," he was told. "It is only the mask God has donned that suffers and this does not truly exist, but is only illusion."

"Is it illusion when a man is dying of cancer and he cannot even withhold his screams at the pain?"

"That which suffers is an illusion, bound to illusions, fed by illusions. This is ego, the sense of personal isolation from God. When an individual surrenders his ego he then identifies himself with God and no longer can suffer, nor can he die. Cancer cannot kill him, for cancer is an illusion, even as that which it preys upon is an illusion."

"You would have a most difficult time explaining that to the American Medical Association," the professor answered.

"There is even a difficult time explaining it to those already convinced that spiritual causes precede physical causes. But that does not alter its validity. A whistle can be made that sounds a note so shrill that only the rare human ear can hear it. To the great majority of mankind the whistle is silent, but that does not mean it does not sound its note. There are those who hear the whistle; there are those who perceive God and thus are free of the sufferings of the ego."

"Then it is your belief that disease is just one of the sufferings of the ego?"

"Yes."

"What, in your opinion, causes disease?"

"The distortions of the ego—fear, hate, bitterness, resentment, jealousy, guilt, and their cousins. These work on the subconscious, call into existence physical counterparts to match the suffering ego."

"And what is the cure?"

"Shedding the ego and making a spiritual identification with God. Failing that, see your doctor."

He laughed. "I shall see mine first, thank you."

He didn't however. Since that evening our professor has come a long way in spiritual discovery. His naturally inquisitive mind has led him down many roads, but now he is vigorous in his contention that all physical manifestation has a spiritual cause and that disease itself is just one more evidence of man's being out of joint with his spiritual source.

LIFE AGAINST LIFE

It is indeed difficult to shed feelings of separateness and isolation, for it almost seems that these are foisted upon us by the very nature of life. We look about us and on all sides we see living things preying on living things. The oft repeated picture of a number of fish, each successively larger than the next and simultaneously swallowing each other, seems to give us our most apt picture of life, "The eater, eating, is eaten." It is from this observation of what Darwin termed, "the survival of the fittest," that we perhaps develop our submerged hostilities and general cynicism toward the underlying lovingness of God. It is from this observation that we perhaps even develop our atheism, our spiritual hopelessness, our existentialism, our feelings that life is "against" us. What we fail to perceive is that God is all, that nothing is ever lost, strayed, or unredeemed. No one falls but what another takes his place, and no one truly falls and no one truly wins, for each is God. Do you think for a moment that God wins victories over himself?

Yet the plain and irrevocable fact is this—life feeds on life. In the drama unfolded by master intelligence manifesting itself in myriad forms through the mere joy of existence, the procession of movement through time and space and matter is accomplished through one form being destroyed and replaced by another better and more serviceable and therefore truer form. Thus life feeds on life. It is almost as if God is thinking and each of his thoughts manifests a form and then another truer thought absorbs the old one, making a new form, and so on.

GOD BECOMING

Now, of course, we come to the standard shout of dismay. "How can it be," the egoist moans, "that a just and loving God would conceive such a method of unfolding Himself, a method that visits untold suffering upon His children as they are forced to struggle, to suffer pain, be defeated, and finally die?" And the answer to this question is that it is illusion that we are separate from God, it is illusion that we are children of God, for each of us in his true nature is God Himself, whole and entire, and God does not suffer pain, defeat, or death. Only the ego suffers pain, is defeated and dies. And the ego is illusion only and never exists at all.

Why does God don this illusion then? Why, in each of His separate existences, does He not know Himself as God instead of as some individual person? The answer to that is the answer to the riddle of existence. When the infinite becomes the finite, it forsakes the inherent perception of the infinite, and its understanding becomes that of the thing it has become. Thus God, becoming a thing, no longer knows Himself as God, but only as the thing He has become. The thing He has become is the ego of the thing. It does not in any way alter the nature of God, nor is it even truth in itself, but simply exists as a consciousness to fit the form. Yet always underlying it is the consciousness of God, infinite, eternal, with vast reservoirs of knowledge and power seeping ever upward, molding the thing ever better, molding always through strife between ego and ego, yet underlying all with love.

> Though the mills of the gods grind slowly,
> Yet they grind exceedingly small;
> Though with patience stands He waiting
> With exactness grinds He all.
> —Elizabeth Barrett Browning

MIRROR ON THE WORLD

Mt. Whitney is the highest peak in the Sierras. From its slopes it is possible to look eastward on a clear day into the vast reaches of rugged Nevada. Nowhere, as far as the eye can see, is there sign of another human life. You can look upward, focus on a pinpoint in the blue, look outward, and the land undulates to a level horizon, look downward, and the earth seems remote, detached, the habitat and handiwork of another race. Here you can sense yourself as the very center of the universe. All lines of force and purpose pass through you. Move and the center moves with you. All things meet and resolve themselves here. You are the center of an unimaginable circle whose circumference is nowhere and whose center is everywhere, so that anyone, no matter who or what or where he may be, sensing the circle, senses himself as the center. This is God's universe; it is infinitely one.

No matter our spiritual dedication, however, material life continually forces itself upon us. Daily we meet tensions, competitions, exertions, emotional peaks and lassitudes, so that it is almost as if we were riding a roller coaster over bounding forces that we do not and cannot control. We feel isolated in our fleshy prisons and long for the touch and contact of another hand, the consolation that someone else exists and feels the same as we, alone also, reaching out. We are constantly beset by feelings of inferiority and personal unworthiness so that we adopt standards that are all based on our comparison with others. People are better looking, worse looking, smarter, dumber, taller, shorter, thinner, fatter, poorer, wealthier, stronger, weaker, healthier, sicker, more talented, less talented, always in reference to ourselves. We hold up a mirror to the world, and the mirror is our ego. We see everything through it, and everything is colored accordingly.

YOU SEE ONLY WHAT YOU ARE

Henry David Thoreau wrote, "What a man thinks of himself, that it is which determines, or rather indicates, his fate." It is this peculiarity of the ego, that it can only see what it already is, that blinds us to the vast possibilities of our lives. If the ego feels unloved, it finds only an unloving world. If it hates, the world hates it. If it is bitter and cynical, it knows only a bitter and cynical world. Rare is the man and wise who perceives that all possibilities are right where he is. He need only change his perception to see them. He doesn't create them by changing his perception. He only becomes aware that they are there; they existed all the time.

It is this spiritual and psychological law, that all change much first be wrought in consciousness before it can be perceived in the outer world, that gives life its exciting possibilities. Each of us can, by an act of mental decision, alter his consciousness and thus alter his life. This is not to say, for example, that by some miracle you one day can be incapable of comprehending higher calculus and the next understand it perfectly simply because you have decided to understand it. Decide to understand it and you remove the *barriers* to understanding it. You first may have to learn arithmetic, algebra, plane and solid geometry, and a number of similar tools, but if your decision is made firmly, one day you will find yourself understanding calculus. The seeds of all possibilities exist within you. There is nothing too great, too vast, too undreamed of that you might not aspire to it and in time have it grow into the image of your dream.

THE POWER OF DECISION

A few years ago a young man came to Hollywood in an empty boxcar of a freight train. He had no money and only the few clothes on his back. He washed the dirt from his face in the restroom of a gas station and went immediately to the gates of 20th Century Fox Studios where he requested an audience with Mr. Darryl Zanuck, production head of the studio. The gateman took in his soiled clothes, his lack of coat and tie. His face clouded with outrage. "Get out of here!" he shouted. "No bums or panhandlers allowed!"

The young man left, crestfallen. He had been so sure that his confidence, his very brash hopefulness would gain him the audience he sought that he had not even considered the possibility of failure. He could not even get through the gates of a studio! He was so shaken that he couldn't bring himself to try another, but that night he came to a decision. He would be an actor no matter the hardships and disappointments. He would let nothing daunt him. He would work, he would learn, he would study, and in the end, he made this solemn resolve, he would be an actor.

Next day he found a job washing dishes in a restaurant. He discovered a school for young actors, complete with theatre. He did well in a tryout, and when it was discovered he was short of funds he was given a job as custodian of the building in return for his tuition fees. He was also allowed to sleep in the theatre. He spent three years in this manner, working, intent on his resolution. Then one day as he was walking down the street, he was stopped and asked if he were an actor. He answered he was. He was offered a screen test. After the test came a contract, then a small part, then a larger one, then a starring role. Today he is one of Hollywood's biggest stars, secure at the top of his profession because he knows his job so well.

Many will insist that our young man would have been stopped on the street and asked if he were an actor regardless of whether he had spent those years working and studying to prepare himself, but we must insist otherwise. It was no coincidence that he was stopped. The quality of his consciousness attracted this circumstance to him, and his consciousness had been tempered to that quality by the years of training and discipline he had subjected himself to. Thus it is that always we call into existence around us those images that we visualize in the depths of our being, and any man, by the power of his decision, has the capacity to change his consciousness and thereby change his life.

It is by expanding our consciousness, then, that we may influence and even control our destinies, and the tool with which we are able to accomplish this is by forsaking the ego and identifying ourselves with God. It is obvious that an all-wise and omnipotent God is aware of all things, past, present, and future. It is similarly obvious that the will of a person or individual ego imposed upon the will of God is not going to change God's plan. It is through such realization that we become aware of the futility and the suffering caused by the exertion of ego-will, but it is also through this realization that we run up against one of the greatest snags in the doctrine of free will as against that of predestination. For our contention is that despite the fact that all things in the future are known to God, man himself is possessed of free will, freedom to determine the events and happenings of his life.

FREE WILL AND PREDESTINATION

Some contend that if God knows what is going to happen that particular thing *must* happen and man cannot alter it and therefore he is a mere puppet and does not have free will. But the mistake that these contenders make is that they are thinking of man as ego rather than as a part of God, or even God Himself. Man is not separate from God. It is only the illusion of his ego that makes him appear so. And God is not deluded. Therefore He does not recognize man as man or individual men as individual men. When there is a thing to be done in the plan that He holds, He knows that He Himself in one of His myriad forms will do it. He does not concern Himself whether this particular form has the illusion that it is Bill Jones or Ed Brown. He only follows the law of His nature, and the consciousness best suited to the thing accomplishes the thing. Thus it is that as individual egos we have complete freedom, freedom to change or alter or improve the quality of our consciousness so that it will be best suited to the thing we want to do. When the consciousness has been so altered the thing to be done is inevitably attracted; this is God's law.

It is therefore through the alteration of consciousness and not through exertion of will that all things come to us. Ego-will is for one thing only and that is to impose discipline upon itself. The power to make a decision lies in the power to discipline the ego, and it is here and only here that ego-will may be and even must be exerted. Ego-will never can be exerted over things, over people. To attempt to do so only creates the opposite reaction. Confine your use of will power to yourself, to self-discipline, self-control. Develop in yourself the power to make clear-cut and firm decisions, to stick to them no matter the obstacles. In that manner you will expand your consciousness to meet the goals you have set for yourself.

FORSAKING EGO-WILL

In all things other than self-discipline we must learn to forsake ego-will and subject ourselves to the will of God. This is not the subjection we might first think it to be, for all we are doing is forsaking the ego, which is illusion anyway, and attuning ourselves to the will of our greater Self, which is God. By subjecting ourselves to the will of God we recognize Him not only in ourselves but in the world around us, in the people we meet, in the objects and things and circumstances of our days. We begin to see things as a whole, and we begin to find our places in that whole according to the quality of our consciousness, a consciousness that now is taking on greater and greater powers because it has begun to identify itself with God. In all things we see the master hand, and in many things the hand of the Master becomes our own.

Strike, Thou the Master, we Thy keys,
The anthem of the destinies!
The minor of thy loftier strain,
Our hearts shall breathe the old refrain,
Thy will be done!
                    —John Greenleaf Whittier

One sometimes hears it said by those who have buried three-fourths of their natures that there is nothing in this world worthwhile except those things that have proven they are facts by taking form. A tree, they say, is a fact. It exists as a tangible thing and bears its own testimony to its existence, so that nothing more need be said about it. Even the kinds of trees, elm, birch, fir, cedar, etc., can be recognized without difficulty so that no debates, arguments, or theories need be postulated about them. All ideas, emotions, and feelings, say these materialists, are merely reactions of individual natures to a world full of things that are facts but which individual natures attempt to disguise in order to make them conform to personal desires. This last thesis, however, certainly smacks a good deal of an idea in itself and perhaps defeats the entire contention. In any case, defeated it is. For nothing in the world is more impotent than a thing in itself, and nothing in this world is more potent than an idea in itself.

FORM OUT OF IDEA

Follow the process of creation and you will see that the idea always precedes the thing and the thing is never the whole embodiment of the idea but only a partial manifestation of a vision dimly seen and partially understood. This particular conclusion not only may be applied to art, music, literature as the obviously creative fields, but as easily can be applied to the worlds of medicine, physics, chemistry, and electronics. A Tolstoy bringing forth from the recesses of his subconscious those ideas which took the concrete form of *War and Peace* is still no more a creator than Newton pondering the falling apple and from it arriving at the law of gravity. Each entertained an idea, each gave it form.

It is this power of decision, this law of form out of idea that is at once our salvation and our undoing. Sensing it, we sense all power within ourselves, but at the same time we build a wall around it that encysts it into the small thing the ego is. We can be anything we wish to be, take any stand we wish to take, the decision is ours. But as long as such decision or stand is motivated by the ego, it can have no greater power than that of the ego, which is scarcely any power at all.

ATTUNEMENT

If there is one thing in all life that is an unavoidable conclusion it is that all things are the manifestation of some Directing Intelligence with an absolute purposefulness of design. Life is going somewhere, is unfolding something, has a definite goal, and these things, even the most egoistic of us must admit, are in the hands of no man, or even group of men, but rather rest in the lap of the Intelligence that created all. Once we understand this, once we have complete faith in the existence of this Master Intelligence, once we know God, we no longer desire to change the world but immediately sense that our salvation as individuals lies in *attuning* ourselves to it.

No man, living in pride and vanity, can do this simple thing. Whether his ego is bloated because of his sense of superiority or whether it is involuted because of his sense of inferiority, it is one and the same. He has cut himself off from the roots of his being and no longer has the slightest wish to attune himself to the world, but rather insists that the world itself be changed. He is like a spoiled child, unheeding of others, unheeding of the plan by which the household is run. He thinks only of himself, sometimes even deluding himself that he is thinking of others, but he cannot see others at all. All things, all people, all events are only extensions of his ego, and as he is hurt, bitter, revengeful, joyful, victorious, or defeated so the world must change to meet his every mood. It is small wonder that he eventually is brought to his knees by force, by the laws of the universe, by disease, by misfortune, by fate. He has sealed his doom in his aloneness.

DEFINING THE EGO

For the purposes of definition it is perhaps best explained that throughout this text the term "ego" is used in the spiritual sense of the isolation of the individual self from the universal self, which is God. Under no circumstances is it to be interpreted solely in its popular sense as "conceit." Conceit, a sense of superiority, is only one face of ego. The other face is conceit's opposite, a sense of personal unworthiness, the all too prevalent "inferiority complex." The truly successful people in this world do not live in the ego. The successful person has subjected his ego to a greater power through a sense of personal devotion to a flame he does not always understand, whether he calls it God or not. It is the unsuccessful, the harried, the unloved who are bound by the ego, so turned in on themselves, so convinced in mind, body, and spirit that the world is a conspiracy directed against them that they subconsciously are manifesting every minute of every day those very conditions they fear and abhor. It is they who need the great vision of the vast Self underlying the egoistic self, of the power that is theirs to call upon once they have forsaken the ego and taken unto themselves their spiritual birthright. It is thus through a new awakening, a rebirth into spiritual oneness that all problems are conquered, never through attempting to dissolve the problem through an act of will.

LEARNING TO DECIDE

Virginia was thirty-eight years old when her asthma became unbearable. She had lived with it most of her life, but now finally it had reached the point where she scarcely was free of it for even a few moments of the day. Anything set her to wheezing, even the slightest emotional stress. She had taken pills, "shots," tried diets, moved from one corner of the country to the other, but still she continued to wheeze. At last she reached the point where she was both physically and mentally exhausted. She entered a sanitarium in an effort to regain her strength. There she settled into a state of complete apathy, refused to communicate with others, seemed decided not to disturb herself in any way. Her symptoms disappeared, of course, because they had been caused by emotional disturbance and Virginia now had suppressed her emotions completely. Eventually she was discharged and sent home, but her family was horrified at the change in her.

Her husband said, "Frankly, I'd a million times rather have her with asthma. At least she often was gay and charming and always a warm human being. Now she walks around like a zombie."

It was quite a problem to restore Virginia to life. By an act of will she had almost anesthetized herself completely. She not only had become incapable of feeling things emotionally, but physically she evidenced much the same anesthesia. She had an extremely high pain threshold, being insensitive to pinpricks over much of her body. She was completely involuted. The ego had turned in on itself by an act of will, and the rest of the world no longer existed for her. She had suffered, no doubt about it, but not enough for the ego to die. Rather it had magnified itself, grown inward in its isolation, until at last, in its little microcosm, it had become an entire universe.

Little by little Virginia was led back to life. One day she

was persuaded to umpire a ball game between the youngsters of the neighborhood. Much persuasion was necessary, but eventually Virginia took the field. Though she once had been an accomplished player herself, for the first two innings Virginia obviously was confused. Each time the pitcher threw the ball she stared at home plate with visible effort. She was being forced to make a decision! After what seemed minutes she would call a ball or strike. Her voice always ended on a questioning note. In the third inning the team that had been behind managed to get runners on all bases, and their leading hitter came to bat. He hit a sharp grounder to left field, and it rolled beyond the fielder. The three base runners scored, and the hitter decided to stretch his triple to a home run. Meantime the left fielder had retrieved the ball, and he threw it toward home plate. The ball and the runner arrived at the same time. Everyone was on his feet immediately. The runner was safe! He was out! It depended on which side you were on. It was up to Virginia to call the play.

Thirty faces stared at her, each in the grip of his own emotions, each daring her to call against him. She could not possibly satisfy more than half the people. She blanched, seemed to quaver for a moment. Then in the summer sun, with the dust yet floating on the warm air, she announced, "You're out!"

Shouts of approval and disapproval were equal. Those who stood to lose by Virginia's decision surrounded her in a moment, shouted at her, glared at her, seemed to hate her, demanded that she retract, tell the truth, not lie. Then something happened. A change seemed to come over Virginia. She straightened, seemed more poised, more resolute, possessed of greater powers. She did not answer. She turned and walked back to her position behind the pitcher's mound. Those watching her sensed immediately the finality of her decision. They retired to the sidelines.

It was only a small thing perhaps, a game between children that occupied two hours of a Saturday afternoon, but it changed Virginia's life. In those two hours she discovered herself, discovered she could decide, could refuse to retreat, and she learned that her decision could change the world. Today she is a happy, integrated, vital person, all because she learned the power of decision.

OUTGROWTH OF THE INDWELLING GOD

Oh, there is in us a thing invincible, a thing of such power that only the smallest fraction of it ever is unloosed through the greatest of men. What is going on in life is the outgrowth of the indwelling God, and each of us is a stage in the development of this drama. In deciding, in daring to take a stand no matter the hazards or obstacles, we are reaching upward, touching God. All the ages of evolution, up through the slime and mist of a newly formed earth, have prepared us for this moment, the moment we first decide and having decided remain firm; and all the future ages of evolution rest upon that moment of first decision, for it is then that we exercise God-power, the power of being, the power of creation; it is then that we know our divinity, our immortality, our mission here upon the earth.

> The past is but the beginning of a beginning,
> and all that is and has been is but the twilight
> of the dawn . . . A day will come when beings who
> are now latent in our thoughts and hidden in
> our loins shall stand upon this earth as one
> stands upon a footstool, and shall laugh and
> reach out their hands amid the stars.
> —Herbert George Wells

And so we must attune ourselves to Him Who created the universe and Whose hand is to be seen in all works. It is only by knowing God that we can in the end understand ourselves; it is only by knowing God that we can fathom the purpose of life, the nature of good and evil, sense the master plan whereby each of us fulfills himself as an individual and unites himself with the Divine.

THE SECRET IS BREAKING THROUGH

There is a secret, which when known and understood, has the power to set men free. It is not a thing that can be summed up in so many words, though it has been and will continue to be so stated, but is rather a thing of spiritual experience, a feeling, an outgoing of the soul, a breaking through the shell of individual identity, a flowing together with God. For this purpose does the endless drama of birth and death and individual manifestation progress on earth and throughout the universe. To this end does each individual live. According as he realizes his own nature and his relationship with God does he fulfill himself and life.

This secret is rapidly making itself known over the face of the earth. It has become the common meeting ground of all religions. Whether you are Christian, Moslem, Hindu, Buddhist, or Jew you stand with your fellows as one man the day you approach your Creator with single-mindedness and ask to know Him. He will not deny you. It is His purpose to enlighten you. Jesus said, "It is your Father's good pleasure to give you the kingdom of heaven."

You can develop your spiritual awareness by engaging in daily meditation periods. For that purpose a meditation is appended at the end of this chapter and each subsequent one. Some are designed to overcome specific problems, all strive for spiritual wholeness, each is a bridge between the individual and his Creator, each explores the nature of being.

◇◇

FIRST MEDITATION

I affirm that my true self is spirit, is not contained within the limits of my body, had no beginning, will never end. This thing that I am is a subtle thing, underlying my ego and my sense of personal self. It is of such dimensions that I constantly must strive to understand it. It is not my body, it is not my name, it is not the identity by which the world knows me. It simply exists, unchanged by the everchanging scenes of life, unaltered by any coloring that my ego may give it. This is my true Self, and I long to know it. I still the questions and imagined hurts, the vain goals of the ego. I slide deep within myself to a pool of consciousness that rests forever in absolute stillness. In a center as small as a pinpoint, I find infinity. I look inward, and there is God. All is contained in this center of consciousness. Smaller than the small is this pinpoint, yet vaster than the vast. Here I know myself. I center in God, become detached from my personal ego. From this vantage point I am able to look upon all things with love. I observe my ego as a person apart, with understanding but with control. I see that I never was what I thought I was, nor was I ever different than what I truly am. My consciousness is the consciousness of God. I declare my unity with Him. I exercise no will in the things and events of my life, but concentrate always on attunement with the purpose of God. Insofar as I succeed in this I cannot fail, for God's purposes surely will be realized. I subject my ego, I yield my will, I attune myself to the power that flows heavenward throughout the universe.

◇◇

2 THE SECRET OF SECRETS

Thou attaineth a deep and abiding bliss
When at last thou art able to see
That the hidden secret of life is this:
God wills, God acts, God lives in thee

ALL-PERVADING SPIRIT

Many people when they think of God conjure up the image of a giant-sized old man who dwells in the clouds, and this vision, or rather the lack of it, is a serious deterrent to their spiritual progress. In the first place it is especially difficult to unite with God if you envisage Him as having a separate existence from yourself, and this is doubly true if you visualize Him in an anthropomorphic sense, in the form of a man, for in so doing you cannot help but give Him human features and a human personality.

In contrast is the beautiful simplicity with which God sometimes is described to children by their parents. Nearly all children sooner or later inquire, "But if God is here, mommy, why can't I see Him?" And it is the wise mother who replies, "Because He is a spirit, dear."

God *is* a spirit. He is that very consciousness that is you, that is all creatures, and His form is not that of a giant-sized old man, but is all form, the countless, myriad, numberless forms of life.

We can know God two ways: By observing His forms and

works in the world; and by exploring His existence within us. The first method has been largely the province of the sciences—physics, chemistry, mathematics, electronics, etc. The second has been the province of the arts—literature, painting, music, and, more concretely, philosophy, religion, psychology. It is surely true that the more knowledge of life we have, the more we know of God, and it is extremely likely that we can learn as much about God from the discoveries of science as we can from the writings of philosophers. But the one place, the one irrevocable, indisputable place where all knowledge is contained, our own personal laboratory, carried around with us every minute of every day, is our own consciousness.

Here in the recesses of our awareness we can learn to meet God, expand the limits of our being, acquire knowledge, personal peace, increased power. As Mary Baker Eddy stated, "To live so as to keep human consciousness in constant relation with the divine, the spiritual, and the eternal, is to individualize infinite power."

THE INNER YOU

There once was a man, a sincere seeker after truth, who became so repelled by the workaday world and its apparent injustices that he retired to a remote region of the country and undertook the life of a hermit. "I am going to get back to nature and away from people," he said. In this way he hoped to find the God he had searched for so long and whose existence never had been revealed to him. He took only the crudest implements of living and disappeared into the western wilderness.

Eight months later a forest ranger chanced upon his camp. Our friend lay seriously ill. His once robust body had wasted away, and he was in a state of delirium. The ranger called assistance, and the sick man was taken to a hospital. For many days he lay near the edge of death, then he took a turn for the better. At last he opened his eyes. The doctor was bending over him at the time, watching him with care. A shout of joy gathered in the sick man's throat. He raised up in bed, reached out his hands. The doctor took them. The sick man wept, a smile of gratitude on his face.

Later, when he finally was able to speak of his experience, he said, "For eight months I had been alone in the forest. All that time I did not hear another human voice or look into eyes that mirrored human understanding. Always I searched for God, in the trees, the streams, the birds, the animals. I tried very hard, but the harder I tried the more the wall seemed to grow between me and That. Then I fell ill, eventually lost consciousness.

"When I awakened in the hospital, I found at once what I had searched for so long. I looked into the doctor's eyes, and there I saw God. I cannot tell you how I recognized Him. All I know is that I was possessed by such a feeling of warmth and lovingness as I have never known. I reached out my hand, my hand was taken. Now I see God in everyone I meet. Now I know God in myself."

It was a tremendous revelation for this man. He had been so blocked from love that he had been blinded. But in his weakened state, in his need, help was given him. He loved. When he loved, he saw God.

THE OUTER MASK

What is the nature of this infinite, eternal, omniscient, and omnipresent spirit that we give the name of God? If He is not a man, if He has no human characteristics, how is it then that He primarily is characterized by love, when love seems such a human thing?

He is one, infinite and eternal. He is all wisdom, all knowledge, all power. We know Him as He manifests in form, and as we see Him around us so we meet Him in ourselves. Love always will be the primary road to discovery of God, for That which is eternally one has divided, and the longing of the parts for reunion in the whole is love. Who loves God longs to meet God, sees Him in others, loves others as himself.

> Our souls sit close and silently within
> And their own web from their own entrails spin
> And when eyes meet far off, our sense is such
> That, spider-like, we feel the tenderest touch.
>   —John Dryden

The world is a stage on which God is working out through matter the infinite expressions of His own nature. Each individual, then, is one of the manifold expressions of God, yet each is altogether God, for God does not divide Himself but rather plays each separate role. Human personality, or ego, is only a disguise which God for a moment has pleased Himself to don, in which, for that moment, He actually has lost Himself, but which has no true existence, for what it seems to be is only the smallest indication of what it actually is.

WITHIN EVERY CREATURE

Reinhold Niebuhr said, "The self is not a particular self merely because it is in a particular body," and by so saying he summed up the entire religious question. Only one thing is at work here and throughout the universe. It has become all things and will continue to become all things. It does not separate Itself from Its many existences, but actually *is* them, complete and entire. It has not created man separate from Itself, nor does It expect man to change Its world. It does not stand in judgment on man, for why should It stand in judgment on Itself? It neither rewards nor punishes. It knows exactly where It is going. All created existences are illusions It has donned to work out Its many expressions. It refines each expression by conflict with other expressions, and the interplay of form against form, of form destroying form, is in itself an expression, as thinking might be, or building one thing from the ashes of another, but in actual truth nothing is destroyed, for only one presence ever truly exists, and why should It change or destroy or alter Itself, That which already is pure and complete, timeless and infinite?

> Who sees the Lord
> Within every creature
> Deathlessly dwelling
> Amidst the mortal
> That man sees truly
> —Bhagavad-Gita

DELUSION

Charles suffered a nervous breakdown and was committed to a sanitarium. He was a thin, sensitive man, well into middle age. He was an accomplished violinist, but his talent never had been sufficient to allow him to make a living in this manner. Before his breakdown, he had worked for a money-lending institution.

"I couldn't stand it," he said. "I used to take my job home with me at nights, the idea of people needing things and not having the money and having to borrow it and not being able to pay it back. All I could ask myself was why? Why do some people have to live off the misery of others? Why do we fight each other, beat each other, own things at the expense of others? Good God in heaven, we even have to kill living things to eat!"

Charles had an incomplete idea of heaven and hardly even a partial view of God's created universe. He separated all things into good and evil. The good things were those that benefited him or gave him pleasure or pleased his moral or ethical sense. The evil things were those that harmed him or threatened him or caused him discomfort or displeased his moral sense. So he divided the world in two. Bad things had been created by the devil, good things had been created by God. The obvious war that continually existed between these factors he mentally had chalked up to a war between God and the devil, and even his own self, his soul, he fancied enmeshed in the midst of this war, pulled two ways, now belonging to God, now to the devil, its eventual end uncertain as he faced the tides and forces of each day. No wonder he had suffered a mental breakdown.

Yet, in a manner, every one of us is a Charles, and every one of us, without the pure vision of a God Who is each of His creatures, suffers all of Charles's anguish. Separate from God we flounder through life, victims of each circumstance we meet. United with God we rise above circumstance, attract to ourselves those circumstances we truly desire, eventually seem to create circumstances. Our roots are in another world, and we stride through life with seven league boots, loving, being loved, emanating power.

Charles eventually was restored to an active and joyful life by an act of spiritual illumination that involved only himself and God. No one was with him when it happened, but many bear witness to the change in this man. Where before he seemed a straw in each wind, flying this way and that, torn always between conflicting desires and emotions, frail in both body and spirit, today he stands strong and steadfast, a rock to his family and friends. He is not bigger physically, but he seems bigger. There is sweep and dimension to his spirit. It stands in his face, looks out of his eyes.

He describes the change simply. "I had come to the end of my rope," he says, "and I knew I could go on no longer. I felt something die within me. There was bleakness, stillness, absolute coldness. Then God came. I knew it was He. Peace, joy, complete security possessed me. I have faith now, abiding trust, absolute unity with Him."

The lesson that Charles learned, the first spiritual lesson that each of us must learn, is that God is for us and never against us. When we know this truly, we begin to live up to God rather than living in fear of Him. We begin to live in His lovingness rather than in some fancied tyranny. And we begin to live as men, tall in the face of all evil. We learn not to fear, for God is in us.

> A creed is a rod
> And a crown is of night
> But this thing is God
> To be a man with thy might,
> To grow straight in the strength of thy spirit
> And to live out thy life as the light.
> —Algernon Charles Swinburne

SECRET OF SECRETS

This, then, is the secret of secrets: God dwells within each of us, He is our true self, we have no other. To understand this towering truth, not merely with the intellect but with the entire being, to feel it, to know it, is to change one's life. The world then appears different because the world then *is* different. The interplay of things and events takes on new significance. Where before all seemed the work of a machine, now all is seen as the work of God.

Wrote Sri Aurobindo, "The one secure and all-reconciling truth which is the very foundation of the universe is this, that life is the manifestation of an uncreated Self and Spirit, and the key to life's hidden secret is the true relation of this Spirit with its own created existences."

All spiritual experience recorded since man first became literate tells us the same thing: there is one God, one God only. Men have met Him on mountaintops, in abbey cells, in fields, in homes, in factories, yet always they testify to one God only, a loving God Whom they find within themselves. This is the Creator Who made the world of his own substance, Who dwells within the heart of each creature,

Who looks out upon the world through every pair of eyes. He is all things, good and evil, high and low, just and unjust, for in His creation all things progress through stress and strain, testing and trial, and all things are known and judged through His eyes only, not through the eyes of a particular ego or group of egos. There is no evil in the eyes of God, no injustice, no pain, no destruction. These are man-made valuations, have no place in eternal being, minimize themselves to the point of non-existence when a man has resolved his identity in God.

EVERYTHING HAS A PURPOSE

It is no small thing to give up one's judgment to God, to stand fast in the knowledge that everything has a purpose and nothing exists but what it plays an integral part in the divine scheme. So much of life seems unjust, unwarrantedly painful, without purpose. How often we are witness to the moral, just, and kindly person stricken with some misfortune, perhaps a financial reverse, perhaps illness, even death, and on all sides it is said of him, "Why did this awful thing happen to John? He was such a fine man. Just look at the town drunkard who goes merrily on his way. Nothing bad ever happens to him. Surely God must have his back turned."

Well, it just doesn't work that way, that's all there is to it. God doesn't go around rewarding some people for being moral and punishing others because they are not. Moral values are man-made as are all aspects of punishment and reward. A man is what he is and does what he does because of his nature and the things his nature has been exposed to. He didn't create his nature, and he didn't choose his environment; that far he is a creature of circumstance. The Godlike part of him is his ability to make a decision, to take a stand. Once he has taken stand with firm heart and unflagging resolve, his decision will turn into fact. Always, however, he must realize that good and evil exist side by side, different aspects only of the same basic truth, and that in the sight of God evil is non-existent.

> All nature is but art, unknown to thee;
> All chance, direction, which thou canst not see;
> All discord, harmony not understood;
> All partial evil, universal good;
> And spite of pride, in erring reason's spite,
> One truth is clear, whatever is, is right.
> —Alexander Pope

NOTHING IS LOST, NOTHING DESTROYED

It is spiritual growth in physical form, it is emergence of universal spirit from concealing substance, it is ever-greater refinement of form through conflict with form that is going on in life. Competition is as necessary as sunlight; in fact, it is life itself. The individual nature hones itself to an edge of self-realization by throwing itself full-bodied and without reservation into the maelstrom. In the end the individual is devoured, even as all individuals are devoured, but not before he has reached the limit of his capabilities, taken the flag a little farther, carried one step ahead the realization of God in man. Here, by development, by strife, by conflict, we see the emergent Godhead, even out of war and disaster, always triumphant, always moving surely toward His goal, striding across the human scene, into eternity.

So life exists at the level of competitiveness, and life feeds on life, and the question often is asked, "Isn't it pure hypocrisy to pretend to love your neighbor when you can see he is out to walk over you and you know that you are out to walk over him?"

No indeed. Such a belief is the furthest thing from hypocrisy, but instead is the deepest spiritual truth. When you have learned to love everyone, those you vanquish and those who vanquish you, then you have learned to live in accord with the deepest spiritual principle of life. The act that destroys another is the same act by which you, yourself, one day will be destroyed, and nothing will have been lost in either case, nothing actually destroyed.

GOD PRINCIPLE

While competitiveness may be life principle, creativeness is God principle. Much of the strife and headlong clash with others that exists in our daily affairs can be avoided simply by taking a creative rather than a competitive viewpoint of other things and other people.

Tony was a successful money-maker. While he disclaimed any spiritual guidance, he used the deepest spiritual principle to attain success. He confided, "Nothing bad ever happens to me. Sure, plenty of things happen that *seem* bad, sometimes so bad that I feel like bawling my eyes out, but I figured out long ago that right then, when things seem to be at their worst, is the time to pull out X-ray vision."

He laughed. "I call it X-ray vision, but all I really mean is that instead of looking at how bad the thing is, I try to look behind it, to see if something good might be growing back there, getting ready to come out after the bad thing is over. I've always found it. I know now that it's always there. I've decided that when things are tough it's just a test. If you hold on and don't whimper, pretty soon things get better, even better than they were before. Everything good that has ever happened to me has grown out of something bad."

Tony may disclaim any spiritual knowledge, but there can be little doubt but what he has learned one of life's great secrets!

There is no absolute good, no absolute evil. They are roots of one tree, entwined together and indistinguishable in the earth. Who is to say which root has reached the water? Only one viewpoint is valid in life and that is the viewpoint of God. He knows exactly where He is going. He is all serenity, all bliss, all knowledge. To Him each thing, each event has purpose; to him there is no evil. Evil appears only to the ego which is deluded into believing it is separate from God and thus has desire and sorrow.

> This is the supreme secret seen by the seers and sages: The one Godhead presiding over all action, master of past, present, and future, world-pervading witness, conscious knower and absolute, is concealed in the heart of each creature. The soul is engrossed in nature and is deluded and has sorrow because it is not the Lord, but when it sees its union with its greater self, then it becomes the Lord, then sorrow passes away.
>
> —Upanishads

GOD IN INFINITY

The nature of God is that He inhabits all of his creatures and manifests in each through progressive unfoldment. This unfoldment has reached a much greater degree in man than in the animals, but a far greater distance it still has to go. Yet, because we see and recognize more of God in man than in animals, we tend to feel that God is not in the animal at all. Because it is extremely difficult for most of us to feel that our sense of self is actually God's sense of self, we separate ourselves from Him. What degree of God-association we manage to perceive we ascribe to our being His "children."

We are not *children* of anything. We *are* that very thing that manifests throughout the earth and the heavens, that underlies and supports the universe. *We are God!* In this understanding is the liberation that sets us free of the ego, that releases our consciousness from its fleshy prison. Do we but don the mantle of God and our consciousness transcends space and time, we take on all understanding, all power, our lives are transfigured forthwith, and each day, each hour becomes a sacrament performed on the living altar of faith.

All roads of human inquiry lead to one goal—the discovery of God. Though science and religion often seem at sword's point, each has its tempering effect on the other. When religion has become stultified by myth, legend, and superstition, science has proved certain laws that have cleared the air. Now, in a day when religion perhaps has become too prosaic, science provides mysticism by stating that it finally is able to comprehend infinity and in infinity it sees God.

THE EXCITING SEARCH

Man is not on earth solely to build taller buildings, longer bridges, fly higher, dive deeper, and make explosions. Without doubt all human activity has its place in the scheme of things, but it is certain that all endeavor, all inquiry has only one end—the progressive emergence of God out of matter, of God out of man. To this end certain fields of inquiry into the nature of God and man have grown in the past decade. These are psychology, parapsychology, and mystical philosophy.

Mystical philosophy is as old as recorded history, perhaps older, but its modern interpretation and application are fairly recent. The wealth of writings left by the Taoists, the Essenes, the mystical Hindus, Buddhists, and Egyptians are now being found to contain spiritual and psychological truths as applicable to the modern state of man as they were many centuries ago. Mystical philosophy today most properly joins the old world and the new, provides a common meeting ground for modern science and ancient mysticism. It can be found in much of religion, is actually the basis of many of the "new thought" groups that have sprung up throughout the world.

Psychology is perhaps the second oldest of the more subtle fields of human inquiry. As a study of the mental and moral make-up of man, his impulses and motivations, psychology has provided invaluable insight into human behavior. But the study is overweighted with statistics, has concentrated too heavily on groups and masses, has lost touch with the individual and provides little insight into personal problems.

Its offshoot, psychiatry, is the individualization of psychology, but even here personal behavior too often is twisted to conform with theories evolved by two or three founding fathers, so that even though treatment is individualized it still is based on the individual falling into a category.

In parapsychology, however, there has arrived a new and exciting field, one that promises much, perhaps is even a gateway to man's discovery of his greater self and his vast invisible powers. Parapsychology concerns itself with the study of the unknown but suspected powers of the mind—extrasensory perception, thought transference, clairvoyance, precognition. Recent disclosures of a somewhat sensational nature tend to magnify the actual results achieved by this study, but the establishment of chairs of parapsychology at some of our leading universities is proof that the study has arrived as an art if not a science. Statistics compiled in endless experiments show that one man can read the mind of another, foretell events, see and hear events at a distance, generally surmount all limitations that would seem to be imposed upon him because his existence is confined within the fleshy limits of his body.

A DREAM

One night Joe had a strange dream. He dreamed that he awoke in a strange room. The lights were on, and seated in a chair was a small middle-aged man wearing thick glasses. The man said, "Open the window and walk along the ledge to the corner of the building. There you will find a drainpipe. Slide down it to the ground." Then he faded away. After a while the dream recurred. This went on all night. In the morning Joe was shaken and exhausted. For several weeks he couldn't get the dream out of his mind. As time passed, however, it became less vivid.

In the spring of the following year, Joe's firm sent him East for a tour of sales outlets, and in a small midwestern town he awoke one night in the same hotel room of his dream. He had not noticed the similarity when he went to bed, but when he awoke he knew at once it was the same room. He looked at the chair by his bedside, fully expecting to see the small gray-haired man who wore glasses, but nobody was there. Yet the feeling of repetition, of exact sameness, was strong and persisted. Joe arose and began to pace back and forth. Almost at once he felt heat and heard the shouts of terrified people. Running to the window, he saw flames licking out from the floors below him. He ran to the door. Smoke billowed in, fire blazed upward. For an instant he panicked, then he remembered the words of the man in his dream. He went to the window, opened it, found the ledge, walked along it to the corner. There was the drainpipe. He slid down it to the ground, blistering his hands in the process, but arriving safely. Dozens of people perished that night. Nobody escaped from the upper floor but Joe. There was considerable speculation over how he had managed.

An old-timer on one of the newspapers, a reporter, said to him, "You made it out just like old Alex."

Joe asked who Alex was. The reporter told him that there had been a similar fire at the hotel fifteen years before. Alex had been a traveling salesman, and he had escaped from the upper floor by sliding down the drainpipe. Joe wanted to know where Alex was now and was informed that Alex had died.

"What did he look like?" Joe asked.

"Little guy," said the reporter. "Gray hair, wore thick glasses."

BELOW CONSCIOUSNESS

There is in man, below the level of his consciousness, a vaster mind, a mind of enormous power and knowledge, a mind universal in scope, common to all men but exclusive to none. It is this mind that provides the study of parapsychology—Universal Mind. If one man can detect the thoughts of another it is obvious that there must be some kind of contact between minds. Many people have likened this contact to radio sending and receiving stations, as if thoughts were like radio waves, but an enormous bulk of evidence supports the premise that instead of individual minds contacting each other there is in each of us another different mind, a mind we seldom consciously use, one that exercises a vast influence, a mind in which there is no space, no time, and which contains all knowledge. This is the mind of God. It is the part of man that is indestructible, unchanging, fraught with all possibility, infinite potentiality. It is the mind in which each man fuses with his neighbor, becomes one with him and with God.

> Thou canst not prove that I, who speak with thee
> Am not thyself in converse with thyself
> For nothing worthy proving can be proven
> Nor yet disproven: wherefore then be wise,
> Cleave ever to the sunnier side of doubt,
> And cling to faith beyond the forms of faith.
>   —Alfred Lord Tennyson

FACING FACTS

So the nature of life is a universal intelligence underlying and maintaining all things, the growth out of universal mind of individual mind as the "I" of God becomes the "I" of the individual, and the gradual growth of individual mind to encompass or unite with universal mind. The end of life is the individual becoming God, consciously, even as he is in truth God subconsciously all the while. This is the destiny of man. How, then, may it be applied to the destiny of the individual man, your destiny, now, today?

Francis Bacon once wrote, "A little philosophy inclineth man's mind to atheism, but depth in philosophy bringeth men's minds about to religion," and there can be little doubt but what we are witnessing in the world today a great return to religion. Men have punctured the hard rind of knowledge, have learned enough to know how little they actually understand. Science has discovered God, and desire for spiritual security and peace of mind again once is filling our churches. To meet the need of changing times, modern Christianity is interpreting Christ's teachings in the light of contemporary psychology, parapsychology, and philosophy. The scriptures of the Buddhists, Taoists, and Hindus are being similarly treated. All holy writ is being applied to modern-day problems of individual men, and on all sides one constantly is assured that he can "think" his way out of any dilemma merely by adopting the attitude that the unpleasant aspects of the dilemma do not exist.

It seems obvious enough that an ostrich-like attitude is not going to make the problems of life more surmountable. The simple act of burying one's head in the sand does not automatically disintegrate an unpleasant reality. All problems, in fact, are only overcome by facing them, growing to understand them, and in so understanding them, overcoming them. The person who is sick, for example, and wishes to become well first needs to understand that his sickness is only a manifestation of the state of his alienation from God. By attunement, by a conscious spiritual and mental uniting with God, his body will regain its harmony. But it certainly will not do so simply by his ignoring the fact that he is sick.

LETTING GOD TAKE OVER

Alice had a case of migraine headache that had driven her to distraction. She was not yet thirty years old, but she was thin, haggard, listless, looked middle-aged. She ground her teeth in her sleep, fought most of the day with her two small children, nagged her husband, met each task with a tense burst of energy, only to lapse into exhaustion. She often wept and confessed she was completely frustrated, unable to summon the energy and strength for her job as a housewife.

"I can't even sleep at night from thinking about it," she said. "I have to feed the children, do the laundry, clean the house, cook the meals, do the shopping, I-I-I, nobody else. Everything depends on me, and there's so much to do. I just can't make it."

"Nothing depends on you," she was told. "Not really."

She snorted. "I'd like to know who'd take care of my house, my husband and my kids if I didn't."

"God."

She smiled. "You're kidding. God isn't going to do the housework."

"He will if you let Him."

"What do you mean by that?"

"God will do the housework if you let Him. Probably He will do it through you since you are prepared and on the scene, but He will undertake all responsibility for it, He will do it better and quicker, and you needn't ever worry about it or give it a thought. All you have to do is let Him."

She was puzzled now. "That sounds like some kind of trick. I still do the housework, but I hypnotize myself into believing that God is doing it."

"The opposite is true. You untrick yourself. It is delusion to believe that it is you, your little ego, that is responsible for doing the housework. You didn't make yourself or put yourself on earth; some other greater power did. That power is in you. All you have to do is recognize it, let it do the housework, let it do all your tasks, and your life will become easy and joyous."

It was a little hard for Alice to take, but she tried. She began to reach for God, to search for Him. Today her headaches are gone, and she has become an attractive young matron. Her tasks at home have been lightened to the point where she has time and energy for outside activities.

"It was really simple once I saw it," she said. "It was like finding a secret switch that turned on the power. All I had to learn was to let go and let God."

SPIRITUAL EQUALITY

Nearly all of mankind's ills, physical, mental, and spiritual, may be laid at the doorstep of the deluding ego, which has substituted a small self for the great Self, which has separated man from God. It is in the death of the ego that a man is set free; it is by identifying himself with God that a man attains to his vaster Self, discovers the depths of his nature and the enormity of his power. It is by searching for God and letting go of self that fear is vanquished, that the dimensions of eternity are perceived.

George Santayana wrote, "Let a man once overcome his selfish terror at his own finitude, and his finitude is, in one sense, overcome." And when we identify ourselves with God by living, acting, willing, and thinking in Him, we leave all fear and smallness; our natures soar until they touch the skies.

Some people, when told that the way to spiritual peace and power is to let go of ego and identify with God, answer, "That's a lot of rubbish. Instead of getting rid of ego all you do is take on a greater conceit. The greatest conceit in the world is to think that you are God."

That's not what happens. One doesn't set about thinking that he, alone, is God. What he sets about doing is understanding that God is all, everything in the universe, all objects, people, and things, and that the nature of God is that He becomes altogether each one. Thus when a man finally comes to the spiritual realization that he is that very intelligence and power that created the universe, he realizes at the same time that all others are that power also. Instead of taking on a magnified ego, he loses ego altogether. He identifies himself with God, but he also identifies himself with others. He is God, they are God, they are he. Thus he arrives at true humility. He is neither better nor worse than anything that is. His spiritual condition is one of complete equality to all things and all people.

ATTUNEMENT

It is this spiritual equality that is the mark of the mature person. He is content to be what he is, and he shows the same face to all. He seeks to improve himself, but not on the grounds of becoming better than or as good as somebody else—only to fulfill his own nature. He does everything easily, as if he had an especial talent for it, but the reason for his easiness is that he knows that another, greater part of himself is always the doer. He seldom is sad, never fearful, always stands foursquare to every problem. How else could he be? His assurance is deep and spiritual. He knows that God dwells in the depths of all beings, and he therefore is equal to every occasion.

How, then, can a person achieve spiritual equality and thus take the first step toward uniting with God? The answer is to cease living in the ego; and the way to set about undoing the ego is to curb egoistic desire. Desire always is the hallmark of the ego. It matters not if this desire masquerades as being altruistic, the cause and the outcome are the same. The cause is an attempt to impose ego-will on God's will, and the outcome is a heightened ego if the two for the moment happen to coincide or a frustrated and involuted personality if the two are opposed. Everyone has seen unbearable vanity and conceit, and everyone knows how a magnified ego always heralds coming disaster. Literature is full of cases of "pride goeth before a fall." Similarly, modern medicine and psychiatry are finding that much of physical illness and practically all of mental illness are caused by the emotional disturbance of an unhealthy ego. The plain fact of the matter is that unbridled desire can meet only frustration, and those who live solely by their desires are doomed to mental and physical suffering. The way to fall into juncture with life, to achieve peace and security, is to curb desire and attune to the will of God. In this manner the veil is lifted. This is the road to illumination, to transfiguration.

The secret waits for the insight
Of eyes unclouded by longing
Those who are bound by desire
See only the outer container.
—Lao Tzu

TOO MUCH ME

Martin was thirty-two years old when he finally accepted the fact that nobody liked him. Through most of his life he had been the fellow who always wanted to join the club but nobody wanted him. When they chose up sides for childhood baseball, everyone was chosen but Martin. In high school he applied for all the activities, but met only rejection. In later life he had difficulty finding a job, more difficulty holding one. At thirty-two he was unmarried and in the depths of great despondency.

"I can't understand it," he said. "I want people to like me. I try hard to make them like me. But they never do. Other fellows don't seem to care. They just go about with the attitude, 'like me or don't like me, it doesn't matter to me,' and they're the ones that have all the friends."

"Who are you?" he was asked.

He seemed surprised. "I'm Martin, of course."

"Who is Martin?"

He saw it was serious and tried, but he couldn't break through. "Martin is me."

"Are you different from those whom you want as friends?"

"Of course."

"What makes you think so?"

"I just am, that's all. Nobody has my problems, nobody really knows or understands how I feel."

"Martin," he was told, "everyone in the world is just exactly like you. Oh, they may look different, talk different, but inside, where it counts, they're just exactly the same. They all want to be loved, to be admired, to belong, and if these things don't come to them they grow afraid and tense and alone inside."

"That's hard to believe," he said. "They don't look it."

"They try hard not to show it, that's all."

"Suppose you're right. How's that going to help me?"

"It will help you this way. The other fellow has the same problems you do. Start thinking about him. Start thinking of how you can help him, put him at ease, make him feel more confident in himself. Show him you're his friend by letting him see that you have a sincere liking for him."

"How do I do that?"

"Just by starting to think it. When you think of his problems you put yourself in his place, identify yourself with him. Some part of you, however small, actually becomes him. In that way you become his equal, never greater, never less, but the same, just as you actually are in spiritual essence."

Martin nodded. "It sounds all right, but it might not be so easy to do. What about when you're dealing with someone you know darn well is superior to you?"

"Make an effort to understand that the consciousness that inhabits your body is the consciousness of God. Make an effort to understand that the same consciousness resides in the bodies of others. When the significance of this finally comes to you, you will understand the meaning of spiritual equality. No longer will the words 'superior' and 'inferior' have the same meaning, and you will become equal-souled to all things. Start out with a simple premise. Simply search for God in others."

Martin agreed to try.

The first week of his effort astounded him. He made two new friends, was invited to a social gathering by a person he had admired but who previously had ignored him. Within a year he belonged to a fine club, was active on its committees. It was easy to see he was headed for social success. His reaction was interesting.

"It's funny," he said. "Now that I find myself being liked it no longer seems so important. Much more important now is the peace I have found in myself. All the time that I was attempting to adjust to other people, what I really wanted was to adjust to myself and to God."

SPIRITUAL REALIZATION

When we throw off the fetters on our minds, open our souls to the universe, we automatically attune ourselves to the purposes of life. On all sides, wherever we look, we see life expanding, growing, struggling higher into the sun. These purposes must be taken for our own; in so doing we fulfill our natures. Each of our talents, all of our abilities are gifts which we are custodians of, which it is our duty to develop. By this development we carry life forward, add to the picture of the emerging God, bring one day closer the time when mankind shall exist as a race of spiritual giants.

When we identify ourselves with God we make of everyone our brother, we open a channel of communication with all people and all things. In a sense that cannot truly be fathomed we understand a tree for we have become the tree, we understand all nature for we have become all nature, and we understand our fellows for we have become our fellows. To know God is to see Him in all things as well as in ourselves; and to see the living God triumphant in all creatures, beyond birth and death and pain and disillusionment, is to become immortal. Who attains to this simple spiritual realization finds joy.

SEEK GOD, FIND YOURSELF

Will you lay aside ego and seek the will of God? In such submission you will find power such as you have never dreamed. It is not a case of whether you can *find* the will of God, for that question is always answered with the asking, that door is always opened to every knock. He is there, waiting to guide you. He will lead you in peace and serenity along life's strenuous paths. He will solve all problems. He will imbue your body and your affairs with power, peace, and perfect working. He will show you the reaches of eternity where you will find yourself. Make the decision today. Say, "God, I turn my life over to You. In all things I seek Your will. I recognize that it is You who thinks in me, You who wills in me, You who acts through me. I do not judge, I simply observe. I let Your power flow through."

As mankind grows to realize that there exists a greater power, a larger self that each may identify himself with and allow to govern his affairs, it becomes inevitable that men should grow into the image of this power. As God consciously is sought in human affairs, that much more rapidly must His emergence on earth approach. The day must come when all men correctly will appraise themselves as instruments only, will place their proper identification in a world of spiritual being. They will be what they are because they exist, but they always will know that their true existence is infinite, eternal, and changeless. Their consciousness will be that of Christ, and each man will have found within himself the source of all joy, the Kingdom of Heaven.

> Ring in the valiant man and free
> The larger heart, the kindlier hand!
> Ring out the darkness of the land,
> Ring in the Christ that is to be!
> —Alfred Lord Tennyson

SECOND MEDITATION

I search for the secret of life in depths of my soul. I retire inward, away from the noises and distractions of the world. In hidden depths of darkness and peace I find a core of my being that rests in absolute repose. There is no motion, no desire, nothing to be hoped for, nothing to lose. All roads, all paths meet and unite here. I am the center of the universe. Time and space are contracted to a moment on a pinpoint. Planets and stars, the universe itself, are contained in me. I sense all things to be myself, myself to be all things. That which lives within me, at the very core of my being, is that which lives in all others. Only one thing is at work throughout creation, only one thing lives in all creatures. This is God. I surrender my ego, give up my will, give over my life and its works to Him. I recognize that it is He who wills in me, thinks in me, acts through me. I shed my ego, divorce myself from any notion of an isolated self. I open wide the doors to the power that flows heavenward throughout the universe. I sense this power pouring through my being, molding, sustaining, lifting my life. I become an instrument for the work of the Lord. No more do I impose my will upon the world and its people. Always I seek the will of God and attune to it. By becoming one with the will of my Creator I attain to all power, for the purposes of God will not be denied. Each day of my life I seek the support of my vast Self. I discipline myself against the strident longings and desires of the ego. I seek no personal glory or profit, but perform all tasks for the Lord, knowing that He is the task, the performer, and the taskmaster. All solace, all profit, all glory, I find in Him.

3 THE TRUE PRINCIPLE OF ACTION

Action to thought is as light to the sun
And is only a visible link
Between the idea and the thing to be done
So listen to God when you think

FREEDOM AND DETERMINISM

The argument rages amongst all who delve into theology—does a man have free choice or are the events of his life predetermined? It is almost universally accepted that the two sides of this argument are incompatible. But they are not. It has become increasingly apparent that they are merely opposite sides of the same coin.

Those who contend that God knows the future have withdrawn free will from man on the premise that what is to happen *must* happen and allows for no choice. Thus man becomes a puppet, grappling with forces over which he has no control, the outcome preordained. Only lethargy can result from such a belief.

Those who contend that man has free will have adopted the concept of a fallible God, who not only is unsure of what is going to happen but exercises little control over it. Man may impose his will on this God and change the course of events. Such a conception of life is little better than atheism, is certain to aggrandize the ego, cause pain and suffering.

Yet the foregoing positions, each obviously incomplete in itself, embody truths that dovetail and stand together when the separateness of man from God is surrendered. It is only when one pictures man as isolated from God that he can think of man as a puppet or as imposing his will on God's. Let a man understand his identity with the Divine, his spiritual oneness, his complete fusion, and his will remains absolutely free while God's omniscience remains intact. They are the same, not different.

> Nothing in this world is single
> All things by a law divine
> In one spirit meet and mingle.
> —Percy Bysshe Shelley

ISOLATION AND UNITY

Since God is all, He knows only Himself in all, and not the individual egos by which we represent ourselves to ourselves. Since He is the only being, He does not consider things in the light of personalities, but only in the light of events. He knows exactly what is going to happen and He knows all things will occur in Him, that He will play each part, represent each force, resolve each action. He does not concern Himself about which of His myriad forms will be best suited to undertake a particular role in a particular event. He simply becomes many different forms and takes His delight from the play of form on form and the eventual resolving of the best form for the part. It is this restless movement on the part of the Divine that brings light, color, action, and personality into the world.

That the doctrines of free will and predestination are only partial truths is readily illustrated. Hinduism, for example, while based on some of the most beautiful theological tenets in recorded history, nevertheless has corrupted its disciples into lethargy through its efforts to annihilate human personality. In its doctrine of preordination, its establishment of the class system, in its complete surrender of personality in the nihilism of Nirvana, Hinduism has created throughout Asia a kind of people who surrender to circumstance, refuse to make effort, are resigned to the lowliest of fates. What many of the Hindu writings stress—union of God with man—modern Hinduism has interpreted as the dissolution of man in God. This, together with a doctrine of reincarnation, has made the average Hindu otherworldly, anxious to suffer through one life quickly so that he may get on with the next. Social, national, racial, and individual improvement are practically impossible under such a theological system.

At the other pole is the society based on ego-aggrandizement as best exemplified by the United States. In such a society competition is the keynote. Individuals are taught that the end of life lies in winning, in being better, in getting to the top. Here we see the growth of the cult of the "go-getter," highly stimulated people rushing about, taking on problems, seeking out competitors, always in the swim, always out to win. All who achieve success in their professions are fancied to be such persons, and this hero-image has been so firmly implanted in the subconscious of most Americans that they spend their lives vainly trying to live up to it. They exhaust themselves physically and mentally; tired heart muscles and ulcerated stomachs give way; frustration eats holes in self-esteem; nervous breakdowns are suffered. Tired little egos, sick and seeking surcease, turn to psychiatry, to religion, always seeking the security lost by separation from God.

TRUE FREEDOM

The way to true freedom is not by separation from God but by union with Him. Only one will is at work throughout the universe and that is the will of its Creator. If we oppose it, we are frustrated, eventually destroyed. If we attune to it, we are serene, all-powerful. By union with God His will becomes our will, and we are set free.

It is difficult for many to understand that by surrendering

one's will one can find freedom, that in living under the dominion of God, searching always for attunement, completely subjecting one's personality, actions, works, and thoughts to a higher and greater power, the qualities of aggressiveness, worldly interest, ambition, and zest can still remain. But remain they do, now heightened to a remarkable degree, so that a person attuned is as a power compounded upon himself, moving through life sedately yet accomplishing mountains of work with seemingly little effort.

> They that wait upon the Lord shall
> renew their strength; they shall
> mount up with wings as eagles;
> they shall run, and not be weary;
> and they shall walk, and not faint.
> —Isaiah

LIFE'S LAW

This discussion took place in the study of a large home. Jacob was a successful businessman, once had held the chair of philosophy at a leading university. He was being visited by his friend, Walter, who had undergone severe business reverses and was separated from his family. Walter was distraught. Jacob, knowing something of Walter's ordeal, had invited him for this talk. Walter had come reluctantly.

The study was cool and quiet. The two men had seated themselves and were smoking thoughtfully. The silence between them was not strained. They had known each other a long while.

At length Walter said, "I have been thinking of killing myself."

Jacob looked at him keenly. "Why do you consider such a drastic solution?"

"For peace. I am tired. The strain has been too much. There has been nothing but defeat."

"Suppose the strain could be eased? Suppose you could win? Would you then find life attractive again?"

"I doubt I have the resources to make such an effort. I am so tired. I imagine I have simply given up."

"Good," said Jacob.

Walter indicated his surprise.

"Has it never occurred to you," asked Jacob, "that there may be perfectly natural causes for the misfortunes that seem to have dogged you? Suppose you were to find out that there is a law of living, a perfectly just and valid law that you have been violating for years? Would it not cast your present predicament into an entirely different light? If that law were pointed out to you, and you saw that you need never suffer defeat and exhaustion again, how then would you feel about living?"

"That would be different, of course. Confusion has defeated me as much as anything. To know, to really know, would make all the difference."

"Here, then, is the law. *Lose yourself in God.*"

"Lose myself?" asked Walter.

"Completely. Immerse yourself. Feel yourself absorbed. Think of yourself in spirit as no longer being Walter, but as being God instead. Submit yourself, resign yourself, turn over your life, your every thought and action. You will lose all pain, all defeat, all sorrow."

"That sounds extremely difficult to do."

"No matter, do it. For forty years you have been running your life all by yourself, and now you have come to the verge of suicide. All right then, before you chuck this world altogether, try turning your life over to God. Cease imposing your will and desires on the great design of the universe, discover what a mighty change is wrought in your life when you turn it over to your Creator."

Walter agreed to try. Within a week he had recovered his spirits. Before the year was out he was once again established in business. His wife and family returned to him, and his life has been improving ever since. He is modest about it, however.

"For the first time," he says, "I truly understand what Jesus meant when he said, 'It is not I who doeth the works but the Father who dwelleth within me.'"

> By letting go, it all gets done
> The world is won by those who let it go!
> But when you try and try,
> The world is then beyond the winning.
> —Lao Tzu

THE POWER OF CHOICE

But if a man is God in finite form, and God's will for the events of life is ordained, established, and unchangeable, is it not futile for a man to believe that he can alter his life? By all means, no! A man is only changeless in spiritual essence; in physically manifested form he changes every minute of every day. You are not the same person today that you were yesterday, and you will be different tomorrow. Everything you learn, every experience you undergo, changes you still further. Always your life and abilities tend to grow into an image of your thoughts, so that you can, by making a decision, by taking a mental position and not retreating from it, grow into anything you are capable of visualizing.

It is this power, the power to determine the direction in which he will grow, that is the divine authorization to each man to change his life as he sees fit. This does not impose man's will on God's will. God's will is always in terms of events and never in terms of personalities. God sees the thing to be done and does it through one of His countless forms. He cares not which of His forms is the instrument. He simply acts through the instrument that is best suited, and that man who, by the power of decision, has best fitted himself, is chosen. Thus while the universe is run by God, a man may grow in the direction he chooses. This is his inner power, his God-given birthright. Few men exercise it, all men should.

THE PURPOSE OF ACTION

Much of pain and sorrow is the result of men wrongly identifying themselves with action. Reward-seeking action has only one eventual outcome—defeat. Even the world's greatest winners are winners only temporarily. Behind each champion is the already visible outline of his conqueror. While it is undoubtedly the duty of each man to do his best, to reach upward, grow taller, outdo himself, it is nevertheless equally true that to make such effort for the rewards alone—money, fame, self-love—is the way of pain and struggle. To make such effort in tune with the will of God is the way of joy and peace.

Action is always for the purpose of self-discovery and never for its apparent fruits. When we pursue an end for the end itself we are deluded into regarding action from the wrong standpoint. We fancy ourselves involved in an effort to mold circumstances to conform to our desires, when in fact it is our inner selves we should be changing. Any attempt of the ego or mind-force to project itself on the outer world is futile. In the first place, the outer world, or at least its coloration, is derived directly from the quality of the ego. In other words, each of us sees in the world those qualities that exist within himself. When he sees something that he does not like or wishes to change, he is wasting his time and frustrating his effort by attacking the problem in the outer world. Where it truly exists is within himself, and when he has changed himself he will see the problem disappear from his world.

It is because the ego is a finite and imperfect thing that our abandoning it and centering our consciousness in the perfect repose of God-self leads to such a vast improvement in our health and affairs. When our consciousness is cen-

tered in the ego, all things are colored for us by the limitations of the ego. But when we center our consciousness in
God, the world begins to appear as it actually is. We begin
to see the limitless possibilities of all situations, and we
allow God's will to work through us without obstruction and
consequent pain.

Sri Aurobindo wrote, "Always indeed it is the higher power
that acts. Our sense of personal effort and aspiration comes
from the attempt of the egoistic mind to identify itself in a
wrong and imperfect way with the workings of the divine
force."

THE EGO AT WORK

Harold was a perfect example of a man who had cut himself off from the wellsprings of his true nature. A brilliant
research physicist, he had graduated *cum laude* from one of
the nation's finest universities. He went directly to work in
the laboratories of a large company, and in twelve short
years rose to head the research department. Harold had a
mind for detail, and his energies were always at the flood. He
drove himself and his associates unsparingly. There was
never time enough in the day to accomplish all he wanted
done, and his constant displeasure at this fact eventually
began to alienate his subordinates. At last feeling against him
grew so strong that the company was forced to consider replac-
ing him. This they were loath to do, finally suggesting to
him as diplomatically as possible that he undertake visits
to a personal relations counsellor.

Harold was enraged. He quit his job. He took such personal affront that he antagonized his employers. When he
sought employment elsewhere they not only refused to recommend him but made a complete disclosure of his problem.
As a consequence he could not find a job.

He searched for two years. His resources became exhausted.
He was distraught with shame and bitterness, did not know
which way to turn. One evening he disappeared from his

home and a few hours later was fished out of the icy waters of the bay by a passerby who just did manage to save him from drowning. The examining physician suggested psychiatric treatment and recommended that Harold be institutionalized. With some reluctance his family agreed.

Harold would sit for hours staring into space. He seldom spoke, then only in monosyllables. His personality was completely disjointed, out of touch with reality. His over-developed ego had shut itself off from the world rather than face the fact of its own inadequacy. Treatment took the form of gradually leading him back to an interest in life. He always had been skillful with his hands, so he was given a woodworking bench and encouraged to follow his own ideas. Shortly, he was making useful pieces of furniture. There came a day when he smiled with pride at a particularly successful table. After that his restoration was rapid and in a few more weeks he was discharged. He was far from being cured, however. His ego was wandering and unsure, its security in its omnipotence gone. He needed an anchor, a secure mooring against life's buffetings. He found it in religion.

It matters not the church or creed that Harold found. What is important is that he found God, and he found God on his knees. At the end of his rope, incapable of finding a job, supporting his family, being a useful member of society, Harold asked for help. He bared his soul, opened his heart, confessed his inadequacy. He turned his life, his mind, his soul over to God. His prayer was simple. "I can't do it, God," he prayed. "I've tried hard, but I just can't do it. You'll have to take over now. Do with me as you wish."

Today Harold has transcended any success he may have won previously. His discoveries in research physics have contributed immeasurably to advances made in the field. More than that, he has become a friend to associates and subordinates, a loving father and husband, a man with a place and a stake in the community. His whole attitude has changed. He radiates poise and serenity, never seems to hurry.

"I'm just letting Somebody Else do the driving," he says with a smile. "Good thing, too. He's a perfect driver."

BEGINNINGS OF MASTERY

When a man learns to undertake each action with perfect equanimity to victory or defeat, when he learns to place his personal desires to one side and allow God-force, working through him, to achieve whatever end it will, he has arrived at the beginnings of mastery. He cannot be defeated for he has taken the viewpoint of God, who is never defeated. He cannot be carried away by victory for he knows that God's ends were being served and that victory could not have been avoided. He lets go of all, and by the very act of letting go, attains to all. No matter how lowly his tasks, he performs them with sacramental care. He knows that in some manner the whole world hinges on what he does. He asks not to be shown the final end or does he even ask for a reason. He realizes that, in God's good scheme, all things, great and small, are equally important.

> Knows he who tills this lonely field
> To reap its scanty corn
> What mystic fruits his acres yield
> At midnight and at morn?
> —Ralph Waldo Emerson

Subordinating the ego to God-self is the way to desireless action, and desireless action leads to mastery and power. It may seem a contradiction that a man attains to mastery by letting mastery go, to power by letting power go, but such is the nature of existence. All things are done from the viewpoint of God, nothing is done from the viewpoint of the ego. By letting go of the desires of the small self one arrives at identification with a vast Universal Self, whose will is supreme and whose actions are omnipotent.

GROWING INTO GOD-SELF

Cervantes said, "Make it thy business to know thyself, which is the most difficult business in the world." Indeed, little else seems to be going on under the sun than self-discovery. Such self-discovery has nothing to do with a man becoming acquainted with his surface mind and personality, but is concerned altogether with the study of the unplumbed depths of mind and consciousness. When a man looks inward, undreamed of worlds open themselves for his appraisal. Instead of the vital animal whose image has been revealed to him in the mirror, he now discovers selves on selves, personalities on personalities, ranging onward, downward, outward for as long as he has time to contemplate them. He sees that instead of being any one of these selves, each of which is a momentary thing, he is all of them and more. For behind all these momentary selves is a vaster Self, a Self without beginning or end, timeless and changeless, infinite and eternal. He senses this Self as the very core of his being. He is in It. It is in him. By losing himself in this greater Thing, he becomes It. He is God.

> I am the owner of the sphere
> Of the seven stars and the solar year,
> Of Caesar's hand, and Plato's brain
> Of Lord Christ's heart, and Shakespeare's strain.
> —Ralph Waldo Emerson

GOOD AND EVIL

If only one thing, God, is at work in the world and knows exactly where It is going, then every single event, object, and person plays an absolutely necessary part in the accomplishing of Its goals. Therefore everything that exists, exists for a reason, and all things from the Viewpoint of God must be good. Evil is only another-face quality of good, drawn by the individual man or groups of men about something that appears harmful. Evil is an illusion drawn by man to account for that which he does not understand, cannot control, and consequently fears. He who arrives at a complete understanding of God sees there is no evil, that all things have their purpose, that this purpose is, in the eyes of God, always good.

The man who guides his actions solely by what is considered good and what is considered evil is guided by his ego only, for he seeks to satisfy a compulsion that will aggrandize his sense of self. He may delude himself that he is doing the work of God when he chooses always the path that is sanctioned by society as good, but this is not necessarily so. He actually cannot exercise any judgement over the thing to be done, for only God sees that. The individual man, following the precepts of good and evil, right and wrong, pain and pleasure, is as often apt to be wrong as right as far as the will of God is concerned, and if he is wrong, he can only suffer.

Moral and ethical values are like good and evil. What is moral in one society often is immoral in another, ethical in one society, often unethical in another. For a man always to guide his actions solely by moral or ethical values means that in some hidden manner he is attempting to appease his neighbors, sway their opinions, seek approbation, build his ego. He who would turn his life over to the Divine must turn over his values also. He must come to God in absolute trust, in complete subordination, with consummate faith. He must not seek to guide his actions along any path but must resign all with faith that God in his wisdom knows the thing to be done and will do it.

PAIN AND PLEASURE

Epictetus said, "Two rules we should always have ready— that there is nothing good or evil save in the will; and that we are not to lead events, but to follow them."

All individuals are guided in their actions by the pain-pleasure principle of existence, drawn to that which produces pleasure, repelled by that which produces pain. Such a sensual basis for living is perfectly all right for the lower animals, but when used by the human being with his complicated mental, emotional, psychological, and spiritual make-up, it is small wonder that he often is drawn in many directions at the same time with consequent frustration and confusion. It tastes good to eat, but if we eat everything we want we will become fat. Sexual intercourse is pleasurable, but indiscriminate sexual intercourse leads to broken lives. It is pleasant to lie around, be lazy, but too much lying around may reduce us to poverty and a condition of want. Always the excess of pleasure produces pain, and the mature individual, conscious of this, seeks outside the pain-pleasure principle for guidance in his actions.

Thomas Henry Huxley wrote, "Perhaps the most valuable result of all education is the ability to make yourself do the thing you have to do, when it ought to be done, whether you like it or not." In all things, of course, we will weigh pain and pleasure, but a course toward each goal should be chosen with full knowledge that sacrifices must be made.

A young man named George, happily married for three years, was offered a promotion by the company for which he worked. One condition was necessary, however, that he transfer to an eastern office. George had no serious objection to this, but when he told his wife, she was against it. Under no condition, she said, would she move East. Her home always had been on the west coast, and she was determined to stay. If George decided to take the promotion, he could just go East without her.

George was torn by the problem. Much as he wanted the promotion he could not bring himself to insist that his wife go with him. In the end he gave in, told the company that he could not accept and stayed on the west coast. During the next few years, he saw several men, all his juniors, raised above him. He became bitter about this, blamed his wife. If it had not been for her, everything would have been fine. If she hadn't insisted on staying on the coast, he could have taken the promotion when it was offered. By now he would have been a vice-president, at least.

When George finally got around to taking stock of himself, he not only was earmarked for failure in business, but his marriage was on the rocks as well. He had developed a habit of placing blame elsewhere for every misfortune that befell him, had become psychologically incapable of facing an unpleasant fact. "It's all because of her," he said. "My wife absolutely refuses to think of me at all. If she's happy, she thinks everybody else should be happy. If she's unhappy, she can't understand why everyone else isn't unhappy too."

He was told, "Maybe you are only transferring your own attitudes to her."

"What makes you think so?"

"Because most of us are incapable of understanding anything that does not already exist within ourselves. We live in our egos and see all things as extensions of those egos. If you blame your wife for being selfish, chances are it is you who are selfish instead. Try looking at her without the coloration of your own problems. Try to see her as an individual, as a unique embodiment of God. And for goodness' sake, stop feeling sorry for yourself."

"I don't feel sorry for myself," George said.

"Of course you do. If you didn't feel sorry for yourself you'd have the courage to take the blame for your mistakes and not keep transferring it to others. If not accepting the eastern job was a mistake, then make up your mind that it was yours and yours alone. You could have taken the job if you had been prepared to sacrifice a little. All you had to do was endure the discomfort of forcing the issue with your wife. She would have given in. In your heart you know she would have. What you really wanted was an out, an excuse for failure, and you found it."

"Suppose you're right? What do I do now?"

"Profit by your mistake. Realize that nothing in life can be gained without giving up something else. A sensitive scale is evident throughout the universe, and the balance is always maintained. You can't hold things. Grasp them loosely. Be prepared to let them go. And whatever you do, face each issue foresquare. Arrange all your actions so there is no one but yourself to blame in case of failure."

Through the ensuring months George gradually managed to accumulate some humility. He began to see other people in their true light. He found a longing in himself for a religious belief, and he began to search about for a church to satisfy his needs. Eventually he found one, and it made all the difference. Today, George is still with the same company. He is a director and a vice-president as he always wanted to be. And, most interesting of all, he is in charge of an eastern office.

SPIRITUAL INSIGHT

What most of us fail to realize is that we gain nothing through self-seeking and everything through God-seeking. When we analyze people and events in terms of our egos we give them a color they do not truly have. We are prevented from really seeing them, and consequently we live in a make-believe world. Things never seem to work out the way we anticipate because we do not truly see things in the first place. But when we search for the Divine and put our faith and trust in Him, recognizing His will as the supreme working, identifying all our thoughts and actions with His, then we arrive at insight and spiritual illumination.

"I say the whole earth and all the stars in the sky are for religion's sake," wrote Walt Whitman. He had pierced the veil, the rough outer shell of things, and he saw within the one spirit, always the same, never different, working out its infinite manifestations according to a finite, momentary form. He saw all things were God.

Some people think that if they are going to live in constant spiritual communion with God they must take an entirely different attitude toward nature. They think they no longer can be aggressive, competitive, combative in life-principle. They believe they no longer can destroy, eat flesh, take life.

Nothing exists under the sun that is not an integral part of the scheme of life and that was not created by the central spirit that pervades all. Each thing is God-made, made from God, is God Himself, whether beautiful or ugly, vicious or kind, lovable or hateful, evil or good. The nature of life and existence is duality, the play of force upon force to some momentary resolution, but always constant play, everlasting flux, high and low, near and far, hot and cold, and always God. His is all extremes and middles and opposites and identities.

GOD'S GRACE

We will come a long way toward understanding life and the universe and ourselves when we finally realize that God is not alone the beautiful, the pure, and the benevolent but is also the ugly, the corrupt, and the predatory. For all these are human values, simply names given to situations or qualities that attract or repel individuals, but which could not possibly have any qualitative connotation in the supreme scheme. All things exist by grace of God and are therefore good and necessary whatever their human or social valuations are deemed to be.

> Nothing useless is, or low:
> Each thing in its place is best;
> And what seems but idle show
> Strengthens and supports the rest.
> —Henry Wadsworth Longfellow

A man will act according to his nature whatever his spiritual enlightenment be. If he is a warrior, he will fight. If he is a writer, he will write. If he is a builder, he will build. If he is a destroyer, he will destroy. Think not that the destroyer is Godless. His place, too, is necessary in the scheme.

All forms wither and fade, are replaced by new forms. The very act of building is a destruction, for nothing is built except that it replaces something else. In the eyes of society there may be a difference between the wrecking crew that tears down the slum dwellings and the building crew that erects modern structures in their stead, but they both are necessary, absolutely essential to progress.

So a man will act according to his nature, according to his form, according to the framework of his knowledge, education, social and family environment, but if his nature is limited by identification with a personal, isolated sense of self, he then acts in the ego and all his actions are limited and without scope. But let a man shed the ego and identify himself with a universal Self, and his actions and thoughts will take on the scope of that Self. He becomes bigger because he is bigger. He reflects in the body of mankind the ever growing image of God.

TRANSFIGURATION

Emily Dickinson wrote, "Reverse cannot befall that fine prosperity whose sources are interior." If all our actions are predicated on the knowledge that God is in us and supports us, we shall have such strength and security as the very world is built on. We may enter into the maelstrom of events, engage in aggressive strenuous action, become involved in situations the outcomes of which appear always in doubt, but some part of us, an inner core, remains absolutely still. It witnesses but does not become involved. By its very detachment in the heat of all action it guides the action, controls the outcome. This is God in repose within us. This is our strength, our infinite, eternal Self.

> Resolve to find thyself; and know that he
> Who finds himself loses his misery.
> —Matthew Arnold

When we learn to develop God-power, to cease struggling and striving and let the universal Self guide our lives, then we will live in tune with the cosmos. See the universe, it does not struggle. The planets revolve about the sun, solar systems around solar systems, all sedately, with rhythm, following law and order. Should we as human beings be any less guided? Yet we are so sure that all things depend on our little selves that we always are rushing around, hurrying with this, fretting about that. We develop ulcers from tension, faulty hearts from strain. We eat too much, sleep too little, work and play too hard. We are busy, oh, so busy, frantically running around in circles, never looking inward, never discovering ourselves, seldom venturing into the mystic realms of mind and spirit. We must lift up our eyes to the sky. Too long have we allowed ourselves to be little. Now the greater Self is coming forth. Our image soon is to be transfigured.

SPIRITUAL EXILE

When the doctor told Ralph he would have to retire from his business and lead a quiet and sedentary life, Ralph felt that the world had come to an end. He was still relatively young, just into his fifties and at the height of his mental powers, and he had taken his business from a humble beginning to the high place it now occupied. Ralph loved his business. It was all he knew and all he ever had done. Each day he looked forward to going to the office. At night before going to sleep he would go over business problems in his mind, lovingly, savoring each factor, always deliciously certain he had the answer. In the business world itself, Ralph was regarded as a titan, more machine than man. He was respected, but (and he was neither aware of nor concerned about this) he was not loved. Even his family did not love him. He lived in an ivory tower, completely cut off from human ties. His entire world revolved around facts such as mathematics, things that were cut and dried. He would say to associates, "Give me the pieces of the problem. They can be round, square, oblong, whatever shape, I'll find the proper places for them. But spare me people. You can't predict them. Leave them out of all calculations."

Ralph left them out, indeed. When he retired to the beach because the doctor said he wouldn't live six months if he didn't, he couldn't find a blessed thing to do. He wrote long letters to the factory. He telephoned. He became agitated. Finally the doctor forbade both phone calls and letters. Ralph's banishment was complete. He was in exile, cut off from the one thing he knew.

One day as he walked along the beach, morosely looking out at the sea, Ralph came upon an old man sitting upon a rock. The old man tended a fishing pole and smoked a pipe. He had a white beard, and his blue eyes sparkled. Ralph was drawn to talk to him.

"Catch anything?" he asked.

The old man smiled and nodded.

"What have you caught?" asked Ralph.

The old man touched his head, then he touched his chest.

"I don't understand," Ralph said.

"Sit down," said the old man.

Ralph sat down. Something about the old man was compelling. Ralph's interest stirred.

"I've been watching you," the old man said. "You walk along the beach every day, but you never see it. You don't want to be here, you want to be some place else, but you can't be, and you refuse to accept it. Now I'll tell you what I catch when I come here to fish. I catch the knowledge that God is running the universe. I get that with my head, just by looking at the sea and sky. Then I catch the feeling that God is running me. I get that with my heart, just by sitting still and listening. All there is to catch in life can be caught right here, that's how good the fishing is. Why not try it?"

Ralph did. He fished from the rock with the old man for many months, and he felt his joy and vigor increase. Within a year his physician pronounced him healed. Today he is back at his job, just as successful as ever, but successful now with people too. He works only four days a week, and nearly every weekend he can be found at the beach, fishing. Most people never understand why. He seldom brings home any fish.

THE SERENE MOVER

George Bernard Shaw wrote, "All this struggling and striving to make the world better is a great mistake; not because it isn't a good thing to improve the world, but because struggling and striving is the worst way you could set about doing anything." When we perform each action for the sake of God, with the implicit understanding that God Himself is performing the action, with the unshakable security that He sees the thing to be done and the perfect way to do it, why should we struggle or strive? To the outside world we may appear to struggle, certainly to make effort, to meet circumstances with a surge of energy, aggressively, with a will to an end; but inside, where it really counts, we exist in stillness, in absolute serenity. We are both the doer and the thing to be done, and because of this unity we have infallible power.

> Be still while you work
> And keep full control over all.
> —Lao Tzu

The flame of human aspiration never burns brighter than when a man searches the world and himself for his Creator. Surely the greatest mystery of all is the mystery of life, of human existence. No avenue of investigation offers such rewards as that promised by the study of self. To all of us at some time comes a momentary flash in which for one sparkling instant we intuitively know our relationship to the universe and to God. We may be walking along the street, involved in the hubbub of a busy world. We may be closeted in the seclusion of library or study. We may be in the midst of friends, amongst the lonely grandeur of nature, in the mountains, on the desert, at sea. But when the flash comes we know it immediately, for in that instant the whole world is transformed. We see beyond the veil, truly see. Time and eternity are in us. Everything dwells within. We try to focus on this feeling, to penetrate it, to understand it, but it disappears, and all our concentration, all our fervent desire will not bring it back again. It comes only in its own time.

THE HUMAN DRAMA

No one is ever the same again after having had this experience. His life is changed forever, and all his moments are consecrated to establishing once again that rapport, that ecstasy, that all-knowledge and complete unity between him and That. He loves God because he knows God, and he sees God in all things, all events, all people, wherever he goes. No longer does he desire to inflict his small, egoistic personality upon the majestic flow of events, but now he sees that all things, all happenings are the working of that larger Power, that greater Self which he longs to behold permanently, to unite with eternally. In all things he seeks the will of this greater Self. He turns over his life, his actions, his very being to that which he knows as his Creator. And just because he casts off his egoistic identity, he takes on a greater mantle. He becomes universal in the sense that he allows himself to be God, and in such manner his power is tinged with infinity, his life with eternity, and all his works with truth.

Now he sees with Marcus Aurelius, "One universe made up of all that is; and one God in it, and one principle of Being, and one Law, the Reason, shared by all thinking creatures, and one Truth."

Playing out upon this sphere is a drama the outcome of which lies beyond the power of any man to predict. Glimmerings of the end we can perceive by analyzing the past, and when we look into the beginnings of life we see it rising from out of the ooze and slime of a newly formed and fetid earth, in single cells, in amoebic clusters, green of plants, finniness of underwater forms, reaching ever upward, ever outward, always adapting, always seeking, always aspiring, always exhibiting a central intelligence, a purpose, a will to be, a will to improve. Multitudes of forms come and go. The path of human progress has been peopled by billions of lives, each a little world in itself, existing for a day, waxing bright, waning, subsiding again into the unknown, but always this Thing, That, a Creator, a giant Self, God, existing within each creature.

THE DESTINY OF MAN

Where are we going? Upon what final end should all our actions be predicated? It is early yet to tell. Man is so newly arrived upon the earth that he scarcely has had time to get his breath. In the words of Richard Carrington, "Let us imagine that, by some magic, the whole earth's history could be compressed into a single year. On this scale, the first eight months would be completely without life. The following two would be devoted to the most primitive of creatures. No mammals would appear until the second week in December. Man, as we know him, would strut onto the stage at approximately 11:45 P.M. on December 31. The age of written history would occupy little more than the last sixty seconds on the clock!" That recently has man begun to think.

Yet what giant strides he has made. He has traversed the earth, climbed its highest mountains, explored the depths of its oceans, harnessed electricity, discovered the secrets of the atom, transmitted pictures and sound from continent to continent, healed with a pill, destroyed with an invisible beam, fired his projectiles into outer space, and now, having nearly conquered his own, is preparing to explore other worlds.

Even as his investigation of the outer world has produced such startling results, man now is turning the powers of his mind to an investigation of himself, his own nature, the wellsprings of his being, the secrets of life and death. Who can say that he has not arrived at the millennium, that the veil being rent will not now be torn wide? For all things exist in order to be understood, and the destiny of man must be that he will understand all.

> Here the free spirit of mankind, at length,
> Throws its last fetters off; and who shall place
> A limit on the giant's unchained strength,
> Or curb his swiftness in the forward race?
> —William Cullen Bryant

THIRD MEDITATION

All about me I see the infinite, eternal movement of God. In the surge of the sea, the flux of the tides, the precise patterns of the heavens, I see the purpose and presence of the Creator. He knows where He is going. All things, past, present, and future are apparent to Him. In His infinite wisdom He sees immediately the thing to be done and the perfect method of doing it. Therefore I turn over all my actions to Him. No longer will I be guided in my daily tasks by the wilful promptings of the ego, but instead I turn inward to the very center of my being and listen for the will of God. He is the master and the mover of my works. He is all that is, and I am being of His being, power of His power, conscious only of Him. No more shall I hunger after the fruits of my labor. They belong to God, and I renounce all desire for them. I know that God never blunders, that He never is indifferent, and when it appears that I have failed in some immediate aim, I know it is only to prepare myself in the end for some rarer joy, some truer delight. I open myself to universal power and joy. I declare there is no limitation, no lack, no malfunction in my life. A perfect power is governing all my affairs, pervading my very body. I identify myself with that which is all-powerful, all-perfect. I throw off the limitations, hurts, and frustrations of the finite ego. In the depths of my being I am no longer a name, a past, a place. I am pure spirit, infinite, eternal, all-encompassing. That which I truly am I can never cease to be. I cast aside ego, become one with my Creator, live in the light and the love of the Lord.

4 A METHOD FOR MASTERY

The ego is only a fakir
Through whose fingers the sands of time sift
'Tis from finding within thee thy Maker
That thou gainest life's most precious gift

DIVINE WILL

"It has been my observation," wrote a young student of philosophy, "that those people who set out to take what they want get what they want, while those who wait around for somebody to give it to them, usually get nothing. How can you possibly expect to achieve mastery over events unless you attack those events?"

At the time, this young man had not been bruised sufficiently by attacking life to have respect for its irresistible force. Later, well battered, he was to heed the advice given him. "You mistake attunement for aggression," he was told. "An energized man performing in accord with his nature and the will of God naturally gives the appearance of dominant aggressiveness. He appears to mold the event because he is part of the event, and since he moves with the will of God, his success often is attributed to his own will or energy when in truth it is only the will and energy of the Divine that have been apparent. Coming events are a steam roller. A man can walk down the broad path behind them and thus arrive at his destination, or he can attempt to swerve the machine from its path, and be crushed."

Life is largely a matter of deciding in one's own mind whether one believes in a Supreme Being. If there is a God, life must be ordered, proceeding toward an end, the outcome sure. To know this, to accept it both spiritually and mentally, is to perceive in all things a purpose and a grandeur. People and events no longer are seen as things to be molded and coerced to one's will, but now it is seen that each contains a hidden meaning, a barely recognized and mystical purpose that must be realized and will brook no interference. Seeing this, the God-knowing man adjusts to life rather than demanding that life adjust to him. To do this he turns himself over to the Divine. It is as if he separates himself into a kind of duality, part of himself remaining ego, part of himself becoming God. The ego he places in a subordinate position. It becomes passive. When it moves it does so only in response to divine instigation; it thinks only in response to divine inspiration; and it does not will at all, but seeks the will of God and follows it.

A man attains to mastery by seeking spiritual union with God, forsaking his egoistic sense of identity, and centering his being in universal consciousness. By surrendering himself he truly finds himself, and by the death of his ego he finds rebirth into a new spiritual awareness. Wrote Thomas à Kempis, "Forsake thyself, resign thyself and thou shalt enjoy much inward peace. Give all for all; seek nothing and ask back nothing; abide purely and with firm confidence in me; thou shalt be free in heart, and darkness shall not overwhelm thee."

CONSECRATION

Therefore the first step toward mastery over life is made by a man's consecrating himself to God. In this whole and utter giving of himself to the Lord and Master of Creation, a man forsakes forever all physical and mental goals and centers himself foresquare in the search for the Supreme. Nothing exists for him except that it reveals the face of the

Divine. All things he sees as manifestations of that one power from which he, himself, has descended, and he longs for complete and final union with the One. All his works, actions, thoughts and desires are motivated by love of God and a longing to unite with God, and he turns over his life, his every moment, his every thought and desire to the Divine. He does this because he knows the love of God; in the stillness of his soul the call has come to him, he is encompassed round with the warmth and security of that love, and like an impassioned lover he seeks to know more of his Beloved. To this he dedicates his existence.

Jesus Christ was such a one, as was Guatama Buddha, as was Saint Paul, Moses, Mohammed, all the great religious leaders, each knew the love of God and sought to live in this love and return it. From such a dedication, from such purposefulness of existence have come all the great spiritual values of our day. That many more still are to come is evident; that man has barely penetrated the mystic realms of spiritual truth is made obvious by the fact that as yet he does not even know himself. He longs to know, to discover the road to spiritual and mental security, and in the love of God lies his salvation.

> I know not where His islands lift
> Their fronded palms in air;
> I only know I cannot drift
> Beyond His love and care.
> —John Greenleaf Whittier

THE UNLOVED

Sally was an alcoholic. She had been married and divorced and had lost the custody of her two children. She would have been the first to admit that liquor was the cause of her downfall, but in truth it wasn't liquor at all, it was her sense of being unloved.

When she first had been married, her husband willingly

had displayed the attentions she needed for her insecure ego—flowers each day, a new dress each week, statements of affection morning, noon, and night—but as time went on and the marriage began to settle down, Sally grew frantic. She was sure her husband didn't love her. She became jealous of his business, his associations, his hobbies, his interests. Each seemed to belittle her somehow, to draw love away. When the children came, she sought at first to find in their childish dependency the affection she needed, but here too she was disappointed. She began drinking in the afternoons, soon discovered that alcohol stilled the gnawing ache of loneliness and insecurity. Shortly she was drinking in the mornings also; before long she scarcely was drawing a sober breath. Four years after marriage, Sally's husband was forced to commit her to an alcoholic sanitarium.

Gradually liquor was withdrawn from her. There came a day when she no longer felt such an urgent craving. Then the long work of psychological rehabilitation was begun. Sally's subconscious feelings of being unloved were clearly understood, but it was difficult to touch her in this area, to uncover, as it were, those forgotten experiences that had forced her into such feelings. At last it was decided to give religion a try. In the whole of her adult life, Sally never once had set foot inside a church. When the idea of attending one was suggested to her, she laughed.

"I may be a nut," Sally said, "but I'm not feeble-minded. What makes you think I'd ever swallow the junk they hand you in churches?"

"What makes you think it is junk?" she was asked.

She waved her hand. "All those stories, people raised from the dead, walking on water, they're nothing but fairy tales for kids."

"Many adults believe in them."

"They're only kidding themselves. What's it all about, anyway? Somebody dreams up these stories and starts a church that gets rich by taking money away from the poor. There's your answer."

"There's another answer, Sally."

"And what's that?"

"The love of God for man."

"You talk about the love of God, and you can't even prove there is a God."

"I think I can."

"Prove it then."

"All right. I want you to spend the night thinking about who you are. You're not to think of yourself as being Sally, as being born of certain parents, as having had certain experiences, friends, a particular kind of education. Think of yourself only as existing, just being aware. Think about the scenery of life—the earth, sky, trees, flowers, rivers, the movement and drama of people. Then think about not existing and see if you don't feel, in some intuitive way, that the scenery of life would not exist either. Dwell upon this. If you are lucky, you will get a flash of mystical insight. Then you will know who you are. Then you will know that there is a God, and you will also know His love."

Sally listened with skepticism, but she agreed to do it. She said it was only because she was willing to try anything, but there was about her attitude a slight sense of alertness, as if deep inside she had been startled to attention. Three days later she was missing from the institution.

Her trail was followed to a large city; there it was lost. Her husband made public appeals for her return, all to no avail. Six months passed, then he had a letter from her, posted from across the country. She said that she was all right, that she would be home soon. Several weeks later she walked in the front door, radiant, brimming with health and vitality. She threw herself into her husband's arms. Such demonstrativeness he had not known in all their married life.

When everyone had calmed down, she told about it.

"I finally found out who I am," she said. "I had reached the end of my rope, the very depths of degradation, then I was told to meditate on who I actually was. I can't tell you my astonishment, my absolute ecstasy when I discovered that my own animating spirit was one with God, that He and I, in a spiritual sense, were actually one. I knew the call had come to me. I left the institution because I had to be alone, to make this total discovery by myself. Now I've come back because the discovery is complete. I'm whole now, one with God, finally able to love."

> We never know how high we are,
> Till we are called to rise,
> And then, if we are true to plan,
> Our statures touch the skies.
> —Emily Dickinson

OPENING THE SOUL

It is by loving God, then, that we first get outside our egos. It is by our attempt to know the ineffable, our longing for union with our greater Self, that we first are drawn to cast aside the trappings of desire and vanity and to center ourselves in the serene consciousness of universal mind. As we love the Divine, we come to know the Divine, and as we come to know Him, the time rapidly approaches when we completely surrender our lives to Him. That day marks the beginning of our spiritual resurrection, our enlightenment, our transfiguration.

Self-surrender, ego-surrender, is a good deal more difficult than it sounds. It takes but a little honest appraisal to realize that each of our days is spent in self-seeking, in ego-aggrandizement, in attempts to be better, look better, have more, get it faster, not because we feel that we are in any way fulfilling our natures, but because we entertain in our ego-minds either the idea that we are better than others or the fear that we are not as good. Consequently, all our actions are based upon the desire to prove ourselves. Such motivation is false, of course. If we have glimpsed the outlines of a vaster picture, a greater meaning, then we must be willing to put aside all our goals and vanities and hurts and give ourselves entirely and completely to That which seeks to express Itself through us. Once we have made this decision, taken this stand irrevocably, the veil at once begins to lift.

THE WAY AND THE WAYFARER

This consecration, this giving of one's life, one's very self to the Divine is much more than just a mental movement, an intellectual seeking toward something higher and greater. It is an entire opening of the soul to the penetrating powers of the Supreme. It is an emotional, loving, joyful self-giving, one made as much with the heart as with the mind and will. No one can enter into the light and power of the Lord with half a decision. All his being, every last iota of it, must be given. Let him give his heart to God, all else must follow.

The demands of the ego at first will continue to be strong. There may even be a short reaction when the individual throws himself into material pursuits with greater intensity than ever. He may seek to surfeit himself with sensual activities, goals of pure pleasure, of egoistic satisfaction. He may go from this stage into a period of utter bleakness, when nothing seems worthwhile, when joy seems to have been drained from everything. If he fancies that it is he who engages in this frenetic activity, who suffers the bleakness and the withdrawal of joy, he is wrong. It is only the ego as it senses its diminishment, its eventual subordination, and its struggles have caused the reaction. No matter, the end is certain. No one is led along the path to self-discovery without traveling all the way. Once the soul is called to this deep and vast change in being, eventual transfiguration is assured. Sooner or later all of life will be cast in divine colors, and the multi-possibilities of the simplest thing or event will become apparent. Everywhere the enlightened soul sees the emerging Godhead. To this emergence, in himself and others, he dedicates his life.

Not of the sunlight,
Not of the moonlight,
Not of the starlight,
O young Mariner,
Down to the haven,
Call your companions,
Launch your vessel
And crowd your canvas,
And, ere it vanishes
Over the margin,
After it, follow it,
Follow the gleam.
—Alfred Lord Tennyson

INFINITE ORDER

Out of first consecration to our vaster Self comes an almost immediate and disconcerting discovery. We see ourselves scattered, diffused along a lengthy row of multiple personalities which are all ours but not one of which contains the truth of our being. We find that every part of us, will, desire, nervous system, intellect, sense, mind, heart, each seems possessed of its own small self, its own personality, which we now discern was seldom in agreement with the other components of our whole nature. We see that what we actually have been is a sort of battleground for our many personalities, and what has happened to us in the past has been largely the result of one personality, then another, achieving temporary supremacy. We now perceive that there is to be introduced into this chaos a guiding principle, a divine order, a centralizing and organizing identification that will achieve in us a unity of being. Out of such perception comes a deep and abiding sense of peace, a restful sense of security, a knowledge of peace and power that stem from the ends of the universe. We intuitively possess the knowledge that our conscious mind is overtopped and surrounded by other vaster planes of consciousness, that these planes of consciousness, when perceived, will open new worlds, that action and life here on earth are from there sustained, nurtured, and fed, and that when we finally break through the veil we shall see at once that the truth of our existence lies not here but there.

From consecrating one's life to God, then, comes a spiritual awakening that casts the entire world in a new light, that gives new meaning to each event, every person, every single thing. One wonders how one could have been so blinded as not to have seen it before. The truth is that the hand of the Supreme has been laid on the brow of the chosen one; God has selected a human vessel for the light, and the many depths and planes of existence soon are to be made apparent. First comes the consecration, the centering of one's life, the living by, through, and for God, then the end is certain.

SURRENDER

Sri Aurobindo wrote, "It is not possible to enter utterly into the spiritual truth of the Eternal and Infinite if we have not the faith and courage to trust ourselves into the hands of the Lord of all things and the Friend of all creatures and leave utterly behind us our mental limits and measures." And the second step toward mastery is a complete surrender of ourselves to the Divine, a surrender that means far more than giving up a few pleasures on certain days of the year or performing certain prayers at certain times, a surrender that means an utter and complete forsaking of all of our hopes, pleasures, joys, and goals, an absolute giving over of all of them to God. This second step is perhaps the most decisive step of all, for it is the turning of the ego to something greater than itself, an utter self-giving, a complete surrender. Here, in subordination, the ego as a primary mover ceases to be. It becomes agent only, instrument or vessel only, and the enlightened man attaches no significance to it except as an instrument for the Divine. The identification of the individual shifts from his egoistic center into a new and vast consciousness. In this shift, which is never painless, the individual emerges as though through a rebirth. He literally shucks off values and accumulations of limiting mental and spiritual "prompters" and takes up his tasks with new force and purpose. He begins to understand that it has been for this meaningful development that the Godhead descended into matter, and he sees that the purpose of life itself is to subordinate the limited and outward-looking ego and install the Divine in its place as the ruling and inhabiting Presence.

TRANSFIGURATION

There now is accepted a complete surrender of one's capacities to the Divine, so that the sense of the individual as the doer and worker begins to disappear. The enlightened man perceives that it is God himself who is the doer, who is also the task to be done. He allows himself to be used by the Divine; he joyfully surrenders himself over to each task, understanding all the while that he is the instrument of a greater power. He neither attempts to ferret out the thing to be done nor lets egoistic desire sway his feelings about the result. He is equal-minded to all results. He understands that God knows the thing to be done, its real purpose, its ultimate truth.

Surrender of the ego to its Lord and Master effects a complete transformation of the limited mental and spiritual life into a large outpouring of energy, will, and purpose which descends into the individual from Universal Mind. Such outpouring might easily change the entire pattern of a person's life, as witness the ministry of Jesus, but the transformation of each man, in the end, will be according to his nature. He need not take up a spiritual mission at all. Whatever he does will take on significance to all about him. He will, in fact, be a living example of the descended Godhead, whether his worldly position be high or low, material or spiritual, mental or physical. His works will be done with the harmony, the serenity, the perfection of the Supreme.

Surrender to the Divine, however, often brings with it a burst of religious fervor. A young man giving up his life to God might easily decide to take monastic vows, a young woman to enter a nunnery. But this first flush of emotional outpouring usually passes and leaves the individual in the same profession as before, infinitely more capable, however. As in the case of Arjuna of the Bhagavad-Gita, the enlightened man pursues a life dictated by his nature, but that life takes on a new and highly charged significance.

CRISIS AND SOLUTION

David was a gunner's mate on board a United States destroyer during wartime. His ship was part of a task group escorting a landing force. As dawn broke the day of the landing, enemy planes appeared out of the east and began crashing into American ships. This was one of the first wholesale suicide-plane attacks of modern warfare. From atop his gun mount, David viewed the approaching planes and felt his first real fear. While most of the attack was focused against the transports, a number of planes veered off toward the escort vessels. David's gun was ordered to begin firing. Hugging the water as they came in toward David's ship, the planes kept themselves in line with the transport vessels. To fire at them, American ships had to risk hitting each other. The captain of David's ship dared not fire his big guns. Only machine guns (David's was one) engaged the approaching planes.

"When they were about a mile off, I knew we were going to be hit," David said later. "We were putting up a stream of fire, but they came right through it, just as though they were charmed. Then, when the first plane was maybe two hundred feet from the ship, it veered and headed directly for my gun. It bore in. Orange dots flashed along the leading edge of the wing as machine guns fired. It loomed across the sea, blotted out the sun. I prayed. I screamed at the top of my lungs for God to take my soul. Then the world exploded."

David recovered consciousness nearly two weeks later. During much of that time no hope was held for his life, but some tiny spark, some invisible thread kept him breathing, kept his shattered body fighting off the fingers of death. A leg was amputated, an eye removed, broken bones were set, a steel plate was emplaced in his smashed skull. When finally David recovered consciousness, the amazed doctors knew that he would live.

Psychiatrists were called in to help restore David's personality, to help him to adjust to his crippled body. These men were even more astounded than the physicians. David needed no help. He was cheerful, serene, self-possessed. He set his mind at once to the problem of learning to walk with an artificial leg. He enjoyed things—people, sports, current events. He showed no signs of depression, no symptoms of feeling sorry for himself. The psychologists at first were fearful that David was covering up some deep psychological wound, but as time passed they became convinced that David had discovered some terrific spiritual secret, some anchor to windward that made him in his crisis amazingly tough and resilient. They decided to probe for it, but shortly learned there was no need. David talked about it cheerfully.

"There's no secret," he said. "When that plane was bearing down on me there came a second that seemed like a week, and during that time I prayed. I knew there was absolutely nothing I could do. I was trapped, and I was going to be killed. I didn't ask God to spare me. I just gave myself to Him. I gave myself completely, entirely, for all time. I gave Him my life, my body, my soul, whatever I am. Now that I find myself still alive, I am completely sure that it is His will, that there is work for me to do, that He will show me, guide me to it, perform it through me. I am happy because I am close to Him and He is using me. Whatever I do henceforth in life will be God working through me."

Today David is head of a flourishing manufacturing company. Much of his time is devoted to boys' work, to his community, his industry. He is loved and respected.

> Yet spake yon purple mountain
> Yet said yon ancient wood
> That Night or Day, that Love or Crime
> Leads all souls to the Good.
> —Ralph Waldo Emerson

THE PATH TAKEN

The one free will in the world is the Divine will, and the true import of this fact is understood only by one who has surrendered his life to God. In this surrender, in this absolute giving of himself, a man is made one with the will of the Eternal and arrives at true freedom. He discovers that the divine will is not something foreign to himself, but rather that he is a part of it, is in a deep and mysterious sense actually all of it. This divine will he understands as being different from his conscious mental will, but inasmuch as he surrenders his mental will to That, That becomes his mental will and imbues him with security and power. Surrender also brings with it a knowledge of spiritual goals—to live and act in God and not in the ego, to be perfectly equal to all events and to all persons, and to allow all action to develop under the impulsion of the divine will and not from any eogistic desire. He who takes the initial steps to mastery —consecration and surrender—has placed his feet irrevocably on the path to spiritual knowledge, and it shall not be denied him.

SACRIFICE

The third step to mastery lies in a law that imbues the universe; this is the law of sacrifice. "For with sacrifice as their companion," says the Bhagavad-Gita, "the All-Father created these peoples." The intrinsic nature of being is that each separate existence is compelled to give, to contribute. A toll is exacted from each of us as we cross over the causeway of life, whether we like it or not, whether we give it willingly or not. If we fight against this toll, if we protest and harangue the heavens over the injustice of it, we do not alter it one jot. We only destroy our emotional balance and warp our vision of the truth. Sacrifice is imposed by the Divine as a seed of redemption, of illumination, for by it we place the ego in proper relationship to its Creator and the truth of things begins to emerge. Acceptance of the law of sacrifice is practical recognition by the individual of a Supreme Being, a greater power, a divine plan. It is the final step by which the ego liberates itself from the delusion of its separate existence, of its independent being. It is the door by which the individual enters into the knowledge of the hidden unity and secret oneness of all life. By acceptance of the law of sacrifice we grow into understanding of true love, we perceive the growing outline of the emergent Godhead.

The law of sacrifice is this: Give; give joyfully and freely; give your labors and their fruits; give your love, your hopes, your dreams; give all to God. Ask back nothing, expect nothing. Lay your entire life on the altar of your worship of the Divine. Thus you will find joy, serenity, benign power.

JOYFUL GIVING

Spiritual sacrifice is not to be misconstrued as self-punishment or self-effacement. Such a conception of sacrifice is both archaic and vulgar, necessary perhaps at a certain stage of man's evolution in his endeavor to exceed a naturally violent and obstinate ego, but no more. Sacrifice is not self-mortification; it is self-fulfillment. Its object, far from being mutilation and torture, is transformation into a greater life, into divine perception, into an all-encompassing serenity and power. Sometimes it is painful, true, especially in the beginning, as the ego is first being brought under subjugation. But in the end, sacrifice is pure joy, complete and unadulterated. It is the soul's giving of itself to God, a reunion, a fusion, an ecstasy of wholeness and unity that gives hidden meaning to every act. And the soul does not give itself to God in vain. Claiming nothing, it yet receives all.

While the recipient of the sacrifice is always God, it may easily and justifiably be offered to any one of His countless forms, to another person, to an institution, to a friend, an enemy, to life itself. It matters not if a human being or human agency rejects this sacrifice or ignores it. The Supreme always accepts. In His veiled works and hidden meanings He always accepts and by His acceptance we are purified, transformed, prepared for enlightenment and union. Yet the one true sacrifice is always oneself, offered directly to the Divine. In such surrender, in such utter self-giving made face to face with Him, in knowledge and love, joyfully and without reserve, is the individual at last brought to illumination. Only one who offers himself completely finally finds God. Only one who utterly renounces the ego and its desires ultimately attains to the Supreme. Only one who musters resolve to make of his entire life a sacrifice stands at last in the light and love of the Divine.

SUBLIMATION

So it is that each thing we do, every action, every thought, every feeling and desire must be turned into conscious sacrifice. Our inner consciousness must live in dedication to a greater power, an imbuing presence to which we give all and which we accept as our guide and ruler. Even the commonest of our everyday actions must be so offered, no matter how grossly material—our eating, drinking, physical gratifications —all must be tempered by this sublimation and offered as sacrifices to the Divine. Such an idea, begun in devotion, grows in devotion, until the individual inevitably merges with the object of his worship, becomes a living example of the emergent Godhead. He sees the Divine emerging all about him. He sees all dwelling in God, God dwelling in all, that all are God and there is nothing else under the sun. This is the core of his knowledge and his faith, the seed of his coming power.

As we practice sacrifice in our lives we soon come to know that which is true sacrifice and that which pays lip-service to the idea while all the time remaining a tool of the resurgent ego. When we truly have performed sacrifice it is a completely selfless thing. It is not directed in any way toward ourselves as a separate existence, not done for others because of their relationship to us, not done for institutions or governments because of their relationship with us, not, in fact, connected in any way with the preferences, likes, or hopes of the ego. Always it is performed in response to a hidden light, a diffused but apparent illumination that spotlights the thing to be done and the method of doing it, in the full knowledge that it is an act and a method of the Divine. In true sacrifice we always recognize that we are possessed by and used by God. All other sacrifice is false, though not futile, for it is a step by which we proceed to true sacrifice. In true sacrifice it is the Divine who officiates. By it we are united with Him.

DISPLACED EGO

When Arthur was twelve years old he already knew that he wanted to be a priest. In the eyes of his parents as well as the priesthood, he had the "calling." He was a gifted boy, excelling in his studies and possessing a highly inquisitive, speculative turn of mind. Eventually he was apprenticed and chose one of the most rigorous sects for his time as a novice. He was perfect. He was humble and reverent, devout and industrious, looked on with favor by all who knew him. Then, unaccountably, he suffered a nervous breakdown, was found in his cell in a state of psychic withdrawal. He recognized no one, seemed unable to recall his own name. Efforts were made to restore him to normal, but they were futile. Finally, with deep regret, the monastery returned Arthur to his home. There, he gradually returned to an interest in things, began reading, puttering in the garden, finally resumed his studies. Eventually, he was well enough to be able to obtain and hold a job. One day he was led to speak of what had happened.

"It was strange," he said. "I was wound up inside like a spring. More than anything else I wanted to achieve a place for myself in my chosen religion. I knew I was gifted; I had won enough honors to realize that. I felt I could go high, clear to the top. In a manner I cannot quite account for, I felt there was no stopping me. I thought I was destined for success. Now I see I merely had a severe case of swelled head."

"What happened to change your mind?" he was asked.

"I don't really know," he said. "I kept thinking of all the things I had to do, of how good I had to be. I kept thinking of all the people who had made it before me, of all those who had tried, all those who were trying at that moment. Without my quite realizing it, a feeling of futility began to come over me. Such a feeling I never had experienced before. It was like a cold vacuum, devoid of warmth and energy. I felt frozen. I could move, but did not care to, talk, but was disinterested. I realized what was going on around me, but I was completely untouched by it."

"How did this feeling happen to leave you?"

"It wasn't exactly that it left me but more as if it was forced out by the entrance of something else. This something I can only describe as God, a warm, living, joyous presence that came and settled in me, a presence far greater than I, greater than all."

"You think that you are possessed by God?"

"Yes. I think I truly have found myself in Him. My being *is* in Him, even as I know He is in me."

"What about the bleakness, the coldness that you knew before?"

"That, I believe, was brought about by the death of my selfish self, a kind of false identity that wanted to take everything and give nothing, that wanted fame, honor, and position to add to its vanity. Since it refused to give, refused to sacrifice something of itself to the Almighty, the Almighty simply made a compulsory sacrifice of all of it. When it disappeared, a void was left. Into this void, God came. He has regenerated my life."

> Not in entire forgetfulness
> And not in utter nakedness,
> But trailing clouds of glory do we come
> From God, who is our home.
> —William Wordsworth

LOVE

The fourth step to mastery is the principal one. In it are encompassed the other three, and he who achieves it is led the whole way on the path to enlightenment, whether or not he is able to achieve the others. The fourth step is love of God.

The axiomatic spiritual truth is this: He who loves God is made one with God. Love is a desire for fusion, a yearning to join with another to establish a kind of whole, a mingling, a mixing, a supporting, a joining, in which something greater than the original aspirant is established. Love is the secret wellspring of the heart reaching out in subconscious knowledge toward the perfect, the ideal, the uttermost. Over all human failings, errors, and disappointments love leaps like a gazelle, spans the universe, flies in a twinkling through the reaches of time, joins together those who aspire to the same goals and are possessed by the same visions.

Divine love is a star of wisdom, casting its rays on those

who mirror the emergent Godhead. It is the bubbling up through vast subterranean depths of a warmth and a tenderness for all spiritual creations tendered by the Supreme to His manifest forms. That soul who returns this love, who abandons self and takes complete refuge in his longing for his Master, attains to the image of the Master, finds his home in infinity. Wrote Thomas à Kempis, "Nought is sweeter than love, nought stronger, nought higher, nought wider; there is no more joyous, fuller, better thing in heaven or earth. For love is born of God, and cannot rest save in God, above all created things."

All works, all knowledge, without the guidance and tempering influence of love are, in the words of St. Paul, "become as sounding brass or a tinkling cymbal . . . profiteth nothing." And the truth of love is not the love of man for God but the love of God for man, and in the love of God for man lies the secret of man's love for God. Therefore whoever would take up proper works with knowledge and power also will take up those works with love. Love will unite him with the Divine, and the Divine then will do the work, provide the knowledge. Serenity, poise, and power will pervade the enlightened man's life, for through love and union he acknowledges that God is the doer. "It is not I who doeth the works," said Jesus, "but the Father who dwelleth within me."

> And as he succeeds he takes no credit
> And just because he does not take it,
> Credit never leaves him.
> —Lao Tzu

THE PERFECT TEMPERER

It is a deep, pure, and constant love of the universal Divine that must be the rule of our lives if we are to attain to mastery. This does not exclude individual forms of love, for family, friends, organizations, but rather is a basis for all of these, transcends them, is greater than each, yet supports and nourishes every one. The enlightened man sees the emerging God in all creatures and, loving God, loves all creatures, not for their creaturehood but for their inherent Godhood. He loves the Divine inhabitant that he perceives in all, and his love is an adoration, a spiritual force that molds and tempers the world about him. Where he walks, his presence is felt, not in any egoistic, individual sense, but in a universal sense, a divine sense. An aura of warmth, of peace, of perfection, accompanies him. Who is to say, in such a one, where the man ends and God begins?

All consecration, all surrender, all sacrifice is made perfect through love, indeed is only perfectly effective when done through love. He who takes up the path to spiritual knowledge with love in his heart will not be denied. Consecration, surrender, and sacrifice will naturally follow, enlightenment will come, spiritual peace and perfection, power and mastery over life. Within the enlightened man awakens a psychic being, growing out of union with the Divine as mind and will and thought cease being anything but instruments for the Supreme. Ego-will disappears and is replaced by the true Spiritual Person. Consciousness becomes deep, wide, potent, the vital nature tranquil, strong, luminous, many-energied, always obedient to the Divine will.

STEPS TO MASTERY

These then are the steps in the method for mastery over life. 1) Consecration—a complete focusing of one's self inward and upward, an absolute concentration of the individual on his God, on his rationship with the Divine. 2) Surrender—a complete and utter giving of one's self, works, thought, and will to God, an absolute yielding and submission to the will of the Divine. 3) Sacrifice—an offering to God of one's every act, every thought, every desire, in constant reminder of the relationship that the Divine holds with each created existence. 4) Love—abandonment of self in a longing for union with the Divine, an all-pervading and governing attraction to God in all His forms, works, and ways, a fusion, a oneness, a wholeness with the Supreme.

This method applied to all works, all knowledge, all human relationships will carry the individual higher and higher in a divine self-exceeding, lead him to perform far above his normal human capabilities, develop depths of intuition and divination. The psychic being then will slowly emerge. In this psychic being will be seen the unveiled Divine in the impress of human personality. All those vast fields of consciousness hitherto hidden from us—the subconscient, the superconscient, numberless planes of mind and being—will become apparent to the enlightened one. He will touch that secret place where the original determinant of things exists. He will understand how to call down to earth those powers and influences, and he will know that they, if called down in their entirety, could alter completely the whole of the universe and all of life.

THE PSYCHIC BEING

The psychic man's consciousness will not be confined to his body. It may go out to other worlds or areas of this world; it may act there, bring back its experience. The body itself will be but a small part of this new consciousness, which, far from being contained by anything, actually grows toward containing all. The man becomes universal in scope and purpose, begins to know and to understand inwardly that which he once only grasped at externally. Now the movement and play of divine forces are sensed as existing at the core of his being, and a power of decision is known, one that may operate at will upon these forces, accept their action and results, modify, change, reject, and thus influence the material world. The truth about thought becomes apparent, and it no longer is attributed to the ego, but is seen as the working of Universal Mind projected through the modifying mask of personality. The power of decision may then be applied to thought itself, and its field and scope enlarged, its purpose channeled, focused, directed, as the enlightened one becomes master of his own action and mind and capable of shaping the movement of the Divine in the world about him.

He detects the origin of all things, of himself and all others, of matter and energy and form, and he perceives that the flow and surge of such forces through him constantly are urging him to rise to ever greater planes of perception, higher regions of consciousness. He discerns the truth at the heart of matter, that it is not simply form or potential energy but rather involved and restricted consciousness, and the possibility of the liberation of this consciousness is perceived. Thus the infinite potentiality of each thing is fully understood at last.

SPIRITUAL DESTINY

Such is the end of transfiguration, complete enlightenment, spiritual mastery. All depends on the psychic awakening of each of us, the completeness of our response to the Divine, our growing surrender. This path has been trod before, is, in fact, well worn. Preceding us have been the great avatars of history—Jesus, Buddha, Confucius, Mohammed, Moses, Lao Tzu, and many quiet ones whose works and power in the world have been equally important. Theirs has been the torch to bear. Many of their teachings have been misconstrued, sometimes deliberately warped, yet their message rings clearly down the centuries: Man has within him the power of his own liberation, a divine consciousness, a universal mind. Such is his destiny that one day there will appear upon the earth a race of superbeings, mental and spiritual giants possessed of undreamed of psychic powers. A divine force is at work and has chosen the moment for this superbeing to appear. Such men already have been upon the earth, are making their appearance today. Each of us is this latent superbeing, each of us can become the avatar in fact. To that end, live and act in the Divine and follow the four steps to mastery—consecration, surrender, sacrifice, and love.

◇◇

FOURTH MEDITATION

I acknowledge the existence of the Divine, and I dedicate my life to Him. I focus my mind on God each waking moment, seeking His presence, longing to know Him. All that I am, my work, my thoughts, my very being, I consecrate to the Divine. In Him I have my existence. I see His hand in every flower, bush, tree, created thing; the warmth of His presence is everywhere. Into whatever dangers I go, by whatever roads I travel, He is there. He is my comforter and guide. I surrender my life to Him, forsake myself, take refuge in the Supreme. No longer will I struggle with the events and forces of the world. I accept them, see them as the divine will working out the thing that needs to be done. I join forces with God by surrendering to Him my human hopes and aspirations. I attain ascendancy over my mental and material mind, over my individual ego, by making a sacrifice of all my works, my goals, my thoughts and dreams. I see that all of life is a sacrifice to the Divine. Through all the confusion and struggle of ego against ego, He works serenely toward His ultimate purpose. Nothing is lost, nothing destroyed, for in reality there is nothing but God. Upon the altar of His presence I lay my action, my thoughts, my emotions, my will. By consecration, surrender, by sacrifice of personal will and vanity, I enter into a state of pure adoration for That which is true and eternal. Love grows in me as the ruling passion of my life, for it is my longing to be reunited with my Universal Self. I know all things by my oneness with them. They are me; I am they. We are fused, united, bound together by divine love.

◇◇

5 PEACE OF MIND

At the heart of each storm is a center of calm
Find thy own heart and cease from all fear
No matter the tempest thy strengthening psalm
Ring out, "Peace and be still, God is here."

THE ROOT OF INSECURITY

The greatest toll of our modern civilization is exacted by nervous and emotional strain. The stresses of heightened competition make of our daily lives rounds of struggle from which even sleep does not give surcease. We become tense inside to the breaking point, grow nervous and irritable, unable to stand the slightest pressure without venting steam like a danger signal. We look about and do not know where to cast anchor. We long to be able to say, "This is unchanging, this I cling to." Fluctuating tides mold the shape of our shores, each day differently, and we are seized with vertigo, unable to feel solid substance. Our insecurity grows, sometimes into fits of depression. The whole world exists in a dim and bleak light, purposeless, chaotic. We are so isolated from our spiritual selves that we not only do not know who we are, we do not even believe in God.

Fear is the root of all insecurity, of all nervousness, tension, and anxiety. Fear is an immobilizing, paralyzing knife that severs a man's reason from his action, casts him adrift in a dark world of blind impulse and primitive reaction. Fear

109

is the shadow that lies like a pall between man, the animal, and man, the god. Fear is the crippler, the turncoat, the scurrying run for survival, the detractor, defacer, blemisher. Reason is the enemy of fear, but reason does not always defeat fear. Reason needs an ally, an indispensable and always present ally—faith. For fear springs from spiritual insecurity, and spiritual insecurity springs from the chilling failure to have found one's self in relation to God. Only when a man ceases to war against himself and life is he free from fear. Only when he finds purpose and plan to the universe and rests secure in his faith in God does he face material uncertainties with inward peace and security.

GET OUTSIDE YOURSELF

George had the face and manner of a frightened mouse. Lines of anxiety creased his face, and he forever seemed balanced in an attitude of apprehension, as if he had not quite made up his mind whether to run or hide. He worked in a bank as a teller, behind a barred window, and all day long he collected and handed out money, and all day long he was in constant apprehension that his accounts might be short. If ever they were, he was certain that he would be suspected of stealing. He often found Osborne, the assistant manager, watching him suspiciously. Osborne, George was sure, could hardly wait to catch him. He hated Osborne passionately.

For five years this situation persisted, then one evening George actually was short. He was not short just a few dollars, but well over three thousand. He was questioned of course, but failed to account for the shortage, and his manner was so strange that he was asked to submit to a search. The money was found on his person.

Everyone was aghast. Of all people, good old faithful George, how could he possibly have attempted such a theft? Osborne understood, though. For years he had recognized fear in George, perceived it growing inside like a cancer, filling, squeezing out everything else, even reason. Osborne talked to the manager. They did not call the police. They talked to George instead, urged him to submit to psychiatric treatment. In the face of their concerted pressure, he agreed. He was given a leave of absence.

Five months later, George returned to his job. Gone was his old manner of anxiety and indecisiveness. He was a different man. The psychiatrist said of him, "George had a classic example of fear neurosis. He actually stole the money because he was afraid that someday he might do just that. His fear became so enormous that he had to justify it. All this was done subconsciously, of course, and George had no recollection of it. His mind was such a hodge-podge of repressions that it would have been a life-long job to get at all of them through psychiatric techniques. What I ordered for him was religion. First he was sent to a monastery for two months. There, in retreat, he attempted to commune with God. When he finally wrote that he'd had a religious awakening, he was brought back to the city and asked to join a church of his own choice. Today he is active in that church. By dedicating his life to God he seems to have gotten outside himself. He has spoken of this, saying, 'I know now that God is inside me, that He is not afraid.' "

Abandon all laws of conduct and take refuge in me alone;
I will deliver you from all sin and evil; do not grieve.
　　　　　　　　　　　　　　　　　—Bhagavad-Gita

REASON VERSUS FEAR

Fear, some people maintain, is an essential reaction, necessary as an instinct for man's self-preservation. Without fear, they contend, a man might walk off a cliff, wrestle a tiger. What they fail to take into account is reason. Reason allows a man to walk off a cliff if he finds water under it and knows he can dive from that height. Reason allows a man to wrestle a tiger, if he knows that the tiger is trained to obey him. Men aspire and dare and challenge and overcome, in spite of fear, in spite of instinctive reactions to the contrary, because reason assures them that the thing they attempt is possible, because faith in God and human aspiration allows them to attempt what never has been done before. What in the name of heaven is good about fear? Who in the world does not find it easier to run away than to face a danger? Let a man decide to face his problem, then the peace and power of God flow through him. Faith and reason reduce every problem to its proper size.

Yet there is nothing abnormal about fear; this is a dangerous world. All around us is the constant threat of bodily injury and physical pain. We must eat to live, so there is subconscious fear that we may starve. Invisible organisms assault the body, cause disease and physical disintegration. Animals walk the earth to whom we are potential meals. Man wars upon man, so that we often are prey to each other. All these threats, these potential bringers of destruction are natural inspirers of fear. To be alive is to know fear, but to really live is to conquer fear. When man fears he may starve, he makes his granaries bulge. When he fears disease, he discovers cures and preventions. He faces animals and tames them. He forms world-wide unions and establishes laws to prevent one human from preying on another. All this he does in response to fear, but before he can do it he first *overcomes* fear. He calls upon some hidden reserve, some unseen power that raises him above his petty self and reduces the enemy to ashes. This reserve of power he instinctively recognizes as being divine. All who go into combat, who scale the unscaled heights, probe at the hidden secrets of the universe, listen with the artist's ear or look upon form with an inner eye, all these know what it is to call upon a greater power for the vision and strength needed for the task. It is God Himself who overcomes all fear, for God is love, and love knows no fear.

ETERNAL REFUGE

We love too little, we who live today, and fear rules more of our lives than we care to admit. All about us we see fear break its bonds and run amuck—in the murderer, the depraved, the lustful, the thief. Fear takes over the entire nature; and in blind desperation the individual lashes back at that which threatens him. Such people are our psychotics. They are more to be pitied than censured, but they cannot be allowed at large. More to the point are the millions of us who go about daily tasks with reasonable capability while all the while fear gnaws at our hearts and souls like a cancer. Unnamed anxieties plague us. We suffer from depression, loneliness, feelings of inferiority, guilt, hostility. Yet we present the world with a reasonably serene demeanor. We smile, we nod, we talk affably. We have contained the enemy, fear, but the enemy is wreaking havoc inside. We delude ourselves that by containing fear we defeat fear. How wrong we are.

We think that we can get over being lonely by having lots of friends, but we learn to our sorrow that we are lonelier than ever in the midst of many. We think we can overcome depression by being around laughter, but the laughter rings in our ears like mockery, and we are more deeply engrossed in our sadness. We think we can get rid of inferior feelings by defeating others, and our aggressiveness alienates them and we feel more inferior than ever. We think we can allay our feelings of guilt by serving others, but we wear our servitude as a harness and grow bitter at life. We think we can overcome our insecurity by amassing possessions, but we become deathly afraid of losing those possessions, more insecure than ever in the knowledge that they will rust, corrode, disintegrate.

Guilt, loneliness, insecurity, sadness are only symptoms of a major spiritual disorder—man's alienation from God. To treat such symptoms is a great delusion, for after treatment the basic problem still exists—death and destruction, mortality and fallibility—which never can be solved by dealing with it directly, but only by dealing with one's relationship with God.

> God is our refuge and strength,
> A very present help in trouble.
> Therefore will not we fear,
> Though the earth be removed
> And though the mountains be carried
> Into the midst of the sea
>   —Psalm 46

SPIRITUAL ELEVATION

Peace of mind and inward serenity come from an absolute faith in the presence of love of God. From such faith comes union of the individual with the Divine, an end to all isolation and inferiority, a changed viewpoint from whence all things are seen as proceeding according to an infallible plan in which nothing is wasted, no one suffers, and each in his inmost soul is God Himself. To know this, to feel it in one's heart is to arrive at a peak of security and lovingness that alters the entire world. We begin to see that those things that caused anxiety simply were being perceived wrongly, that now, when seen in their entirety, they take on a different aspect, no longer threatening but useful, immensely significant in the scheme of things, embodying the Divine as we ourselves embody the Divine. Fear leaves us. That which we were afraid of we now see as an extension of ourselves. We begin to feel our union with it, so that it is no longer a separate thing in our awareness, but rather another aspect of our own being which, when we delve under the layers of consciousness, we can alter at will.

Mary Baker Eddy wrote, "Being is holiness, harmony, immortality. It is already proved that a knowldege of this, even in a small degree, will uplift the physical and moral standard of mortals, increase longevity, will purify and elevate character. Thus progress will finally destroy all error and bring immortality to light." He who attunes himself with his Creator and attains a spiritual elevation where he sees his kinship with all things automatically receives the gifts of infinite repose and unshakable security. Left behind with his struggling ego are all his anxieties, fears, guilts, and hostilities. He embraces everything he sees, and everything he sees showers him with abundance in a natural return of his lovingness.

It is not so easy as it sounds, it is true. We awake in the morning with a troubled heart, full of unnamed fears and vague anxieties at a barely remembered dream. It lies heavy on our hearts so that we have difficulty stirring ourselves from a desolate lethargy. We look into the faces of our loved ones and see nothing. Those very personalities we love now stir us to revulsion for we find in them a fickleness, an almost assumed happiness that grates harshly. In their opinion we are "out of sorts," but in our heart of hearts we know we have lost sight of some hidden truth; we have isolated ourselves from the wellsprings of our being.

EVERLASTING LOVE

Such a spiritual impasse always results from the growing ego squeezing out all truth, blowing itself up until, at the first setback, it is shattered, desolated. We may, for example, be riding high after some material conquest. Perhaps things have been going well in business, and we have been appointed to a coveted post. We are elated, filled with our own importance, convinced of our great and earth-shattering talents. Then suddenly we are leveled. Something, a small thing perhaps, proves our dispensability, our insignificance in the larger scheme, and we are deeply wounded. That which we puffed up so high now deflates so low, and if we have not God in our lives, we must sink into the nethermost depths of depression. That which we have anchored ourselves to, the ego, has shown its fallibility, is crushed, defeated. We have nowhere else to turn.

The way to inner peace is opened by abandonment of the ego. When a man sloughs off vain strivings and desires and gives over everything to the Supreme he is able at last to admit peace and surety into his life. By enfolding his being in the Divine he commits himself irrevocably as an instrument of the Divine, and in all things he rests secure in the knowledge that the thing that he does is the thing that must be done. Through identifying himself with the Supreme he takes on the foreknowledge of the Supreme, and this intuition becomes manifest as skill in works, confidence in the future, faith in things to come. The ends of life no longer are sought in the outer world but in the inner. There, in the depths of his soul, a man meets himself and his Maker, abandons his ego, finds himself born anew. All those things that he once gave importance to, those threatening things that inspired fear and desire, cease to be, drift away, and he finds himself cloistered in encompassing warmth and everlasting love.

> The world that time and sense have known
> Falls off and leaves us God alone.
> —Elizabeth Barrett Browning

INNER TURMOIL

Sidney was a hard-driving executive. He was president of a large corporation, and he worked unremittingly to make it the biggest and best company of its kind. He was a strong man, heavily muscled and energetic, and even into middle age he still looked like an athlete. Each day he took his setting-up exercises. He watched his diet carefully. He did not drink or smoke and was meticulous in getting the required amount of sleep each night. Yet before he was fifty years of age he was forced to retire by a recurrent duodenal ulcer.

At first he was flabbergasted, then enraged, finally bitter. "All my life I've taken care of myself," he complained. "I watched my weight, ate the right foods, never drank or smoked. Look at me. Don't I look fit? Then along comes something like this, knocks the props right out from under me, and there's not a darned thing I can do about it."

"I believe there is," he was told.

At first he looked hopeful, then his eyes dulled. "Sure. The doctor says rest, complete relaxation and no business. Well, that's just fine. All I have to do is lie around and the ulcer goes away. I think I'd rather have the ulcer."

"Perhaps that's not the only answer. Perhaps you can work and cure the ulcer, too."

"How?"

"By getting rid of your inner turmoil. By making peace with yourself."

He looked up sharply. "What makes you think I've got any inner turmoil?"

"Sometimes, Sidney," he was told, "physical ailments like an ulcer are only symptoms of an emotional disturbance. Perhaps that fits your case. If you have to fight hard to contain fear and uncertainty, they may be finding a way out of your armor through the ulcer."

"Psychosomatic, you mean? I've read about it."

"Exactly. And if that's the case, what we have to do is get rid of the inner conflict that's causing the ulcer. If we are successful, you will be able to return to work."

"You really mean it?"

"Nothing is certain. But it's worth a try, don't you think?"

"You bet! When can we start?"

"Right now," Sidney was told. "We can start by your telling what's bothering you."

His face froze immediately. "I don't know."

"I think you do, Sidney."

His eyes were narrow now. He was careful. It was a secret he had guarded well. "Maybe it has nothing to do with anything."

"You know it has."

"I'll think about it. I'll let you know."

"Right now, Sidney."

He stood up. He paced a bit, turned back. "I can't," he said.

"Of course you can. You have the power to make any decision you want to make. You want to be well, don't you? You want to return to your job, to a useful life? Then make the decision right now that you will leave no stone unturned to accomplish that end. Tell me what's bothering you. Tension will leave you. You will find peace."

His heart had come into his eyes. His lips moved nervously. He mustered his courage. "I'm afraid of failure," he said.

For Sidney the cure was rapid. Once he had admitted to someone else the gnawing fear that had plagued his business career, his demon was at last out in the open where he could get a perspective. Now he was able to see that his apprehension was ridiculous, that he subconsciously had been making a mountain out of a molehill. His successful career he placed alongside his spectre, and fear disappeared entirely. He let down, he relaxed, he lost the appearance of being driven. Before many months passed he returned to his job, where he served ably and without a recurrence of the ulcer. His associates noticed a change in him. He no longer drove himself so hard but seemed more steadfast in time of trouble. They asked him about it.

"I've got a little motto," he said. "It's from the Bible, Romans, chapter 8, verse 31. It says, 'If God be for us, who can be against us?' "

DESTRUCTIVE TENSION

Tension is the bugaboo of all successful endeavor. Whatever we strain and strive at invariably is doomed to failure, first because we are going about it the wrong way if we find it so difficult, second because the mere attitude we take from straining and striving makes the task nearly insurmountable in our minds. We must learn to do things easily, to find in our hearts and souls unshakable patience and faith. Thus we insulate ourselves against discouragement, against depression, against defeat. When we live in the knowledge that it is the Divine who acts and thinks in us, we no longer strive and strain. Always we perform our tasks in the full bloom of the knowledge that it is God who works through us, and He understands the full import of the thing to be done. In such a manner we find ourselves equal-souled to success and failure, victory and defeat. There is no failure in the eyes of God, and inasmuch as we identify ourselves with Him there is no failure in our lives.

> God moves in a mysterious way
> His wonders to perform:
> He plants his footsteps in the sea
> And rides upon the storm.
> —William Cowper

Athletes are prime examples of the manner in which tension can play havoc with performance. There once was an outstanding young golfer whose mechanics of play were acclaimed as being the finest ever brought to the game. In practice rounds with his friends he invariably would execute a series of remarkable shots, shoot far below par, and thoroughly astound everyone. But when he entered a tournament it was a different matter. He played like a duffer. He scarcely managed to qualify, let alone win. People said of him that he simply wasn't made of stern enough stuff for competitive golf. It was a harsh judgment, but probably true. This young man's nervous system simply filled him with such tension in competition that he could not perform. Had he been able to get outside himself, had he found release in religion, for example, he might have been able to play. As it was, he eventually dropped out of tournament golf entirely.

YOU ARE NEVER ALONE

We simply cannot do our best when we have nothing holding us up but ourselves. If we enter into life with the feeling that we are alone, that everything depends upon us, we are bound to choke with tension and apprehension, and why should we not? Are there not millions of the same animals as we upon the earth? Alone among them what can we possibly amount to? We need a foundation, a basis, a bulwark for our insecure ego. So it is that all men are led to seek a greater Self within, a guide, an immortal Presence. Riches and acclaim do not make a man at peace with himself or give him insight into the nature of existence. Search, scramble, fight, struggle as he may, he is led to peace only through the simple act of surrender, and until he finds it all things turn to ashes in his hands.

Joshua Liebman recounts how, as a young man, he made a list of all the things in life that were most desirable—health, love, beauty, power, riches, talent, fame. This list he showed to a friend, proclaiming it to be the sum total of all things to be coveted. "An excellent list," his friend said, "but it leaves out the most important item of all, that which makes possession of the others worthwhile, lack of which makes their possession a torment. That is peace of mind."

We are never alone. The Lord is always with us. It is this knowledge that liberates a man, that allows his spirit to soar in rounds of ever-increasing activity and consciousness. "Yea, though I walk through the valley of the shadow of death, Thou art with me." From such surety comes courage, steadfastness, the ability to dare and do. They who stand alone shiver in the corners of life, have not found themselves and are afraid. But those who have admitted the Supreme into their souls make works in the world that are for the progress and enlightenment of all. Wrote Epictetus, "When you have shut your doors, and darkened your room, remember never to say that you are alone, for you are not alone;

but God is within, and your genius is within—and what need
have they of light to see what you are doing?"

GIVE YOUR PROBLEMS TO GOD

So it is that from the four steps to mastery a man is led
directly into inner peace. He finds it early in his quest, at
his first act of surrender. By this giving up of his life and his
work to God the soul is relieved of its inner turmoil, gives
up its struggle, finds serenity. Surrender is the key to inner
peace, but it is extremely difficult for most adults. We have
been conditioned so competitively, so imbued with ideals
of courage and stick-to-itiveness that we instinctively feel
like cowards if we make any surrender at all. The fact that
such surrender is to our acknowledged superior seems to
have little to do with it. It is amazing the number of grown
men who cannot bring themselves to get down on their
knees to pray. This sign of humility simply seems too much
for them. They stand and tremble and contain their fear
and know not their own power because they resist union
with That which is all power.

Do things ever get too tough for you? Do they sometimes
grow took difficult to bear? Then give up. When you do, God
will take over. He will provide you the strength you need,
the will you need, the plans you need. Do not fear. Rest
secure in the knowledge that He will work through you and
the thing will be done. Just give up and get yourself out
of the way so He can take over.

Never carry your problems around with you. When you
think about a thing, examine all factors and try for a solution.
If the solution is not apparent, do not fret or worry. Put
the problem out of your mind. It will be solved. You simply
have given it over to a power greater than you are, and one
morning while you are eating breakfast or reading the paper
or walking down the street the solution will come to you,
in a flash, complete and whole and so obviously true that you
will be unable to understand why you did not see it before.

Above all, never carry problems to bed with you. "Sleep," wrote Shakespeare, "knits up the ravelled sleave of care." If you lie abed and worry you may as well get up, you'll be happier for it. When you go to bed, surrender all problems, all fears, guilts, and worries. Give them to God. Drift off to sleep on any pleasant fantasy you choose, but do not think about your problems. Offer them to the Divine in complete surrender, and sleep will be both solver and restorer.

> Of all the thoughts of God that are
> Borne inward into souls afar,
> Along the Psalmists music deep,
> Now tell me if that any is,
> For gift or grace, surpassing this:
> "He giveth his beloved—sleep?"
> —Elizabeth Barrett Browning

THE STIRRING GIANT

Vanity is the great destroyer of serenity. When we harbor inflated ideas of our own worth, when we secretly long to prove ourselves better than those we meet, we cannot find peace within ourselves for we have nothing to hinge our values to but the ever-changing ego. Today we win a victory and everything in the world is wonderful; we are sure of ourselves and our personal prowess; we are winners, and our whole future seems cast in a rosy aura. Then tomorrow we lose, and now we see nothing but bleakness; all others are better than we; we dare not even try for fear of losing; we scarcely can show our faces, the shame is so great in us. The ego is frightened, humiliated, with nowhere to turn. The soul cringes, its God-quality long forgotten, tool now of the frightened ego, one with it instead of God.

Always it is the ego that suffers, that struggles, that mirrors the ever-changing tides of human fate. That man who places his soul in the hands of the ego literally is torn to shreds by the buffetings of life, clinging now to despair, now to hope, now to sorrow, now to gladness. Such living in the emotions makes for much of the drama of existence, but as a refuge for the human soul it is a battlefield indeed. Yet there is a haven of utmost serenity, a harbor where the waters always are calm. It exists at the core of each of us, in the very depths of our being. Can we but find it we become as gods, but isolated from it we are victims of every circumstance. The business of living is that each man discover this place. To that end all his days, all his life, his acts and thoughts, whether he knows it or not, are dedicated. Within him a Giant stirs and would make Himself known, and the Giant will out.

HUMILITY

For a man to discover his vast Self, for him to perceive within the indwelling God requires great humility. Those to whom this revelation has come often have undergone the greatest suffering and privation before the recalcitrant ego has been brought to its knees. No man perceives the kingdom of heaven unless his eyes are open to the infinite oneness about him. Until he sees his kinship with each living thing, he cannot avow his own divinity in complete selflessness. Many there are who have proclaimed themselves supermen, by virtue of certain talents, certain intelligence, certain acquisitiveness or ruthlessness. But always their reign has been short-lived. Life's law is to bring to his knees the man who lives in an aggrandized ego. Find such a man and observe the fearful burden he carries. He always must be proving to himself that he is great, accomplished, superior, while in his heart he knows that failure and defeat await him. This terrible spectre often drives such men to suicide, to other less obvious forms of self-destruction. Yet they might turn from their false god anytime they choose. They have only to accept the Divine into their lives, to reject all notions of themselves as particular and superior, to be humble in the face of their Maker and in all things identify themselves with Him. Then peace comes, true power.

It is not just a queer quirk of fate that many rich men have given away all they possessed. They simply have sought to get rid of vanity by getting rid of possessions and thus to admit God into their lives. The Hindu fakir sits all day staring at the sun, maintaining a single position for days, even weeks, against terrible pain and fatigue, for only one thing—humility. For when a man dispossesses vanity, God is free to enter into his soul, to possess it, to freely use it. All strain, all tension, all struggle, all anxiety and fear then disappear. When a man achieves humility, he places his life in the hands of the Supreme, attains to peace and serenity.

GIVINGNESS

Humility dispossesses fear, and givingness is the road to humility. A man lives in the ego when his standards are based upon what he accomplishes, how much he accumulates, how much applause is accorded him. In the Life Plan held by the Master a thing is judged not by itself but by what it contributes, and the worth of a human being is always a measure of his givingness. Vanity predisposes the individual to taking; humility predisposes him to giving. A man who is at oneness with the Divine and perceives the Divine in others, loves all humanity as he loves God, and his life is dedicated to giving all he can, all that he is to others. He seeks nothing, strives for nothing, fears nothing. That which he is and aspires to be is in the hands of the Supreme. To this he dedicates his life in complete surety that his steps are guided, his path marked, his way chosen. By this giving of himself to God and to his fellows a man arrives at true humility and peace of mind.

Each of us at one time or another has been witness to the rise of the acquisitive man or the power-hungry man or the vanity-seeking man. We have seen him in the arts, the sciences, business, politics. Often he is talented and his drive that of a fiery rocket, but like the rocket he soon sputters out and his false motivations leave him stranded on the shoals of his own aspirations. Such a one was Albert.

He was barely twenty-five years old when he acquired his first million dollars. This he had done by the highly illegal device of buying Italian lira in Egypt at a deflated rate and reselling them in Italy where the mony was standardized. To accomplish this end he masqueraded as a merchant seaman on a variety of vessels, always using borrowed capital. Six years of this enterprise made him a million. Then he bought several ships. By the time he was in his early thirties he was sole owner of a flourishing steamship line. He installed himself in a villa on the Riviera. There, one day, he was discovered unconscious in his bedroom. He had taken an overdose of sleeping tablets in an attempt to commit suicide. He recovered, but was in the depths of despondency, seeming to hate those who had saved his life. Eventually he was allowed the freedom of his villa, but a male nurse was kept in constant attendance.

One day the pastor of the local church came to visit Albert. He was gray-haired but erect. He insisted on an audience, would not be turned aside. When finally he stood before Albert, he said, "If you would lift the sadness from your soul, I have the solution for you. Give what you have to the poor. Give all and ask back nothing. God will show you what to do then. Your heart will be light, and you will find peace." Then he left before Albert could answer.

But the ego in Albert was strong. He sneered at the advice of the pastor, just as he refused to heed the voice of his tortured conscience. He continued to live at the villa in complete isolation, and a pall of loneliness settled upon his soul. He lived out his life in a prison of his own making, only half alive, surrendering all hope because he refused to surrender his vanity.

That man may last, but never lives,
Who much receives, but nothing gives;
Whom none can love, whom none can thank,
Creation's blot, creation's blank.

—Thomas Gibbons

MERCY

So fear is dispossessed by humility, and givingness opens the way, and givingness is made possible by tolerance, by kindness and mercy. All things that exist are part of the divine plan, are created from God-stuff, are imbued with the divine spark. To wholly understand this fact is to possess a complete oneness with all of God's creatures, with all of His created things. Good and evil, right and wrong, fit and unfit are necessary standards in society, for the preservation of the group, for its advancement, for its security. But a thing in essence is never good or evil, right or wrong, fit or unfit; it is of God, created by God, holding inherent in itself the divine spark. Though it be exorcised from society, nothing of God is destroyed. But for destruction to be performed in hate, vengeance, fear, or envy is to act in the ego and to aggravate one's own insecurity. Mercy and tolerance we all need in order to live without fear.

Tolerance is always the hallmark of the mature person. It is fear and insecurity that cause people to seek advantages over other races and groups, over other religions. That man who is unduly prejudiced in favor of his group, his race, his religion, even his country, has built walls of containment for his ego so that he may, by identification, consider himself better or worthier than others. But that man who truly knows God sees in all persons the Divine. He finds in all persons the image of his Beloved, and his heart sweeps out to all mankind. He has no prejudice or intolerance because he knows that the Supreme is concealed in each creature, that there is purpose to everything under the sun. Therefore he joins forces with life. He accepts all as the working of a divinely omniscient Intelligence. He adjusts himself to what he finds around him. He seeks for tasks within the already ordered movement of life, tasks to which he is especially adapted and to which the Divine calls him. The enlightened man roots his hopes in no material things, no persons, no groups, no institutions. All these he knows must change, wither, fade away. His faith and hope rest always in the Supreme, in the immutable presence of God within him.

To accept all, to love all, to treat all things with mercy and kindness is to dispell fear and anxiety. Who can be afraid of that which he loves and feels mercy for? The mere act of helping a stranger increases one's knowledge and understanding of that stranger. In the bond created by an act of kindness there is felt the common knowledge of God. Your new friend may have a different colored skin than yours, worship God through different rituals, speak a different lanuguage, live under a different government, but in just one act of kindness all these obstacles to understanding are swept aside, and each man, by the light in the other's eyes, perceives his common sonship of God.

Give. Give of yourself, your knowledge, your understanding, your warmth, your love. Be not harsh to opponents, but embrace them. The combat itself is only a play of the Divine. Let your kindness and love go out to all those about you, not in shrinking from competitiveness, but in participating with joy, with faith. You will find your kindness returned a thousandfold. The act of giving will open doors in your inner self that you hitherto had not perceived. You will find depths of feeling and perception that will increase the worth of life beyond all previous considerations. Open the doors of your inner self. Freely allow life to pass through. All fear will leave you.

> The quality of mercy is not strain'd
> It droppeth as the gentle rain from heaven
> Upon the earth beneath. It is twice blessed:
> It blesses him that gives and him that takes.
> —William Shakespeare

ATTUNEMENT

Humility, tolerance, givingness, each is a road whereby fear may be met and overcome, each is a path to peace of mind. Yet the one road that encompasses all other paths, that never fails to lead the aspirant into complete spiritual security and peace, is the road of attunement, of identification of the individual self with the great Self that pervades the universe. To attune means to listen, to get quiet and let the frequencies of thought play about the spectrum of mind until at last the voice of the Supreme speaks within the soul. Jesus said, "Everyone that asketh receiveth, and he that seeketh findeth," and he that seeks God finds Him within his own consciousness. Attunement with the Divine is the great leavening agent that makes of life a single unit, gives to everything, however apparently small and insignificant, a great purpose and necessary place. From Ecclesiastes, "To everything there is a season, and a time to every purpose under heaven." Each season is God's, each purpose His. Who understands this achieves attunement, dispossesses fear, moves through the events of life with serenity.

Attunement may take the form of daily meditation or prayer, not self-seeking prayer, but prayer that is bent upon the end of bringing the Divine into consciousness, holding Him there, and knowing Him there. Attunement may make itself known through works. Much art, all creative work is a manifestation of God. That man who cloisters himself with the creative spark brings forth a child of the union of himself with the Divine. All artists, all creators do their greatest work when they abandon self and let their "talent" take over. Their talent is God. Attunement may make itself known as a great religious urge. Many men so taken have joined the clergy, finding increased attunement in monastic living, in seclusion, oftentimes by dispensing the word of the Divine through speaking and writing. In any case it is the proper business of life that each of us should discover his true self, his relationship to the universe, his relationship to God. The man who becomes so absorbed in created things that he forgets about his Maker is due to suffer sorrow and disillusionment, for that which is created must pass away, but the Creator never passes away; in this knowledge lies the key to peace. The enlightened man builds no attachment to created things. He holds them with loose hands, prepared to let them go. His faith, his trust, his attachment are to God. In God he finds his repose, the meaning of existence.

LEARN TO LISTEN

The inner ear attuned to God hears extraordinary things. There are spiritual voices that whisper in the soul, and they are not discernible to the outer ear or to beings who are focused in the workaday world. He who hears them moves through life with an intuition that surpasses earthly knowledge. His is the indefinable knack of being in the right place at the right time, of effortless achievement, of joyful and harmonious relationships. He unfailingly moves in the right direction just because he does not will it, but resigns his will, lets God run his life.

In the world of the soul there is no time, no space, no separateness. Everything is complete unity where everything is God; everything is timeless where there is eternity. All the time that ever was is just one time in the soul and that time is now. Therefore the soul knows no sorrow, for sorrow is caused by separateness, by the passage of time. When a man no longer is separate but has become one with that absolute unity that is infinite and eternal, what sorrow or sadness can he know? To realize that the animating spirit within you is the Divine Himself, is not that bolster enough to ride out life's most resounding storms? You cannot be destroyed, damaged, or hurt. That which is you is pure spirit, is infinite and eternal, formless and changeless, one with all things, greater than all things. It is the Divine in you that is great, and it is by discovering the Divine within you that your life can be molded to your inner vision. Each of us sees in the outer world that which he sees within. We cannot see anything else.

Seek God. Seek Him with all your heart and soul and mind. Seek Him in the high places and the low, in your fellow men, in all creatures, all events. Most of all, seek Him within yourself. You will not be denied, and the discovery will change your life. You will banish all fear, attain to power, peace of mind, serenity of soul. In quiet and steadfast faith make this seeking the main aim of your life. All other things will come to you.

> Give me my scallop-shell of quiet
> My staff of faith to walk upon
> My scrip of joy, immortal diet
> My bottle of salvation
> My gown of glory, hope's true gauge
> And thus I'll take my pilgrimage.
>
> —Sir Walter Raleigh

FIFTH MEDITATION

No matter the chaos in the outer world there is within me a place of utter quiet and absolute repose. Here, in the center of my consciousness, my soul meets and unites with God. Here I know my true self, a spiritual being that is infinite and eternal and untouched by the harassments of the world. In time of trouble and trial I turn within, and my heart and mind and energies are restored. In the quietness of my room, in my study, during a solitary walk I let my consciousness drift to that place of pure being, to that eternal "I" that dwells in all bodies. No time and space are there, no separateness, no isolation. All is unity, infinite and eternal. There is perfect love, perfect wisdom, perfect serenity, perfect peace. There is no struggle, no pain, no sorrow; these cannot exist where separateness and time are not. I see my kinship with all things, with all people, with all creatures. Envy and hate, vanity and greed are but errors of the ego which I banish from my life. I live in the consciousness of God. I am equal-souled to all things, for I am neither better nor worse than any person who lives. I kiss the feet of beggars, shake the hand of kings, and it is always the feet of God I kiss, the hand of God I shake. I banish intolerance, for how can I be intolerant of that which is made by my Father and in which my Father dwells? I view all creatures, all beings with love, for in them I perceive the Divine. I motivate my life with givingness, with tolerance and humility, with love. I banish fear, and peace of mind is mine.

6 HEALTH AND WELL-BEING

Think upon this as a hidden key
To the vault where all secrets lie sealed
Pray for thy neighbor and thou wilt soon see
That the healer when healing is healed

THE ASTRAL BODY

Most of us become so absorbed in the world, in created things, in ourselves in relation to others, that we seldon stop to consider what we really are, what essential stuff we are made of. Biology teaches that our bodies are made primarily of a substance called protoplasm, and that this substance, in its functioning state, assimilates, excretes, and pulsates and otherwise exhibits what is called a condition of being alive. We are able to observe protoplasm in a state of not being alive. It appears much different than before. It no longer functions, gives off heat, has the power of movement, of choice, or exhibits awareness. The more we contrast the state of being alive with the state of not being alive, the more it appears that aliveness is not an inherent quality of protoplasm itself, but rather of some inhabiting presence, an "engineer" so to speak, who has taken over the protoplasmic machine and is operating it. We observe that when protoplasm ceases to live this engineer departs, or perhaps the correct order is that the engineer departs and then the protoplasm ceases to live, but in any case a personality, a complicated, knowledgeable, aware force suddenly has ceased to be present in the protoplasm and we do not see where it has gone. All the things known about a body, all the things attracted to it, all its triumphs, tragedies, loves and hopes are not the result of the body itself, but of the inhabiting presence within it. Each life, then, is an image of something invisible. The body that represents it is only a symbol.

Behind each life is an astral body, an invisible spiritual body that makes itself known through a material body and material things. This spiritual body, essentially the Supreme, nevertheless is warped away from the perfection of the Supreme by having assumed a finite state, by having become a specific thing. In its self-seeking, it manifests upon the physical plane those doubts and fears and hopes and aspirations that are part of its quest for its true self, that are, in absolute fact, physical counterparts of man's mental and spiritual search for God. Each astral body occupies a physical body that is a manifestation of its knowledge of itself, and that body is as strong and vigorous and healthy as the image of the Divine held within the subconscious of the individual.

NEGATIVE PROMPTERS

If you would be strong and healthy, sound of body and mind, let your thoughts dwell always on the perfection and power of the Supreme, upon the wondrous fact that it is He who is the dweller in your body. Once you have gotten thoroughly outside the limiting idea that your ego is that dweller, you have made the great stride of liberating your body from the bond the ego has imposed upon it. All egos, without exception, are sick. They are sick because they are not whole. They say, "I don't feel well," "People don't like me," "I'm not very smart," "I'm ugly," "I'm tired," "I'm lonely," "I'm poor." In every subconscious that is ruled by the ego there exists a thousand negative prompters that not only clog the aspirations of the individual in his daily affairs, but literally restrict and harm the body through the attraction of disease and injury.

The great and all-reconciling truth is this. There is a Mind, a Spirit, infinite, eternal, omniscient and omnipotent, and the world as we know it is a field of manifestation for this Spirit. Each thing in the world, each event, each shade of meaning represents movement within that Spirit, movement that is creative, that is joyful, that is expressive of that Spirit's totality. Each thing in essence is perfect, for it represents a perfect expression of That which is perfect itself. Where it is apparently warped away from perfection it is because a blurred perception has obscured its real nature. Mary Baker Eddy wrote, "The basis of all health, sinlessness, and immortality is the great fact that God is the only Mind; and this Mind must not merely be believed, but it must be understood." He who believes in the ego as the dweller in the body is doomed to suffer pain and limitation, but he who perceives the indwelling God achieves perfect health and immortality.

THE MIRRORED IMAGE

So it is that the outer world is only a mirrored image of the inner, and a vigorous body is the result of a free and vigorous spirit; and where illness and disease are manifest the cause always can be found on the spiritual plane. To cure the spirit is to cure the body, but to cure the body and not the spirit is to cure a symptom only, for the cause then remains unchanged and the illness must recur. There is an inner being whose total existence is unknown to us, but glimmerings of whose power we can perceive through the workings of the subconscious mind. This being seeks outlet in the material world through a material body, and is warped away from its perfection by the limiting action of that body. Where such limiting action also includes negative attitudes of mind and spirit, the perfection is so stultified that it may go into periods of decay and disintegration. Beneath the surface of the apparently unruffled conscious mind lie buried guilts, fears, hates, and rages that eventually must erupt into physical ailments—cancers, ulcers, heart disease, paralysis.

The origin of disease is in the spirit, just as all the things of this world essentially are spiritual, and if we would be possessed of healthy and vigorous bodies we first must look to our spiritual well-being. Once this is properly seen to, health will follow. Such health cannot be won by a sick person "willing" himself to be well. This spiritual opposition—the subconscious calling the disease into existence and the conscious mind willing it to be gone—simply sets up a conflict in the whole nature of the individual with the result that, instead of the illness being cured, it is almost certain to become aggravated, even chronic.

FIGHT AGAINST PHANTOMS

When Wallace finally was reduced to visiting the doctor it was only because the pain and discomfort of his situation had grown too much for him to bear. His back had bothered him for a very long time. It had begun with a dull ache in the region of the sacroiliac and had grown to encompass the entire lower region of his spine. Then his headaches had begun. They started in the morning with the onset of sharp pains on one side of the head, by afternoon they were agony. His digestion and elimination often were faulty also. He suspected he had an ulcer. He didn't drink; he watched his diet; he got plenty of rest. He had to.

Wallace was well into middle age, but he looked younger. When he stood naked before the doctor that good man was impressed by his patient's youthful appearance. Wallace carried no extra weight, and his muscles were taut and well-conditioned beneath his skin. He had all his hair, most of his teeth, and his eyes were clear. The doctor began his examination already half convinced that he was dealing with a hypochondriac. He took a blood test, a urinalysis, X-rays, a fluoroscope, brain waves, basal metabolism, blood pressure.

When at last he sat across the desk from Wallace he couldn't quite bring himself to be as brusque as his findings warranted.

"The tests were negative," he said finally. "Physically, you seem to be all right."

Wallace was defensive immediately. "So you think my trouble is all in my mind?"

"Perhaps," said the doctor. "Does that distress you?"

"You're darned right it does! That's the same story I keep getting from my wife and friends, and I'm getting sick and tired of it! Let me tell you, nobody tries any harder than I do to keep from feeling lousy. I concentrate on it all the time. Seems to me that's all I do, always telling myself I feel great when all the time I hurt. Other people are unconcerned because they never ache. Well, I do, and no matter how much I tell myself I don't, I still keep right on hurting."

"Then you have been trying to get rid of your trouble by force of will?"

"You bet I have. And I've tried hard."

The doctor leaned across his desk. "Wallace," he said, "do you believe me when I tell you that there is nothing physically wrong with you?"

"I'm the only one who knows whether I've got pain or not, and I've got pain."

"Try to forget about the pain for a moment. Examination shows you to be physically sound, in fact, to be in remarkably good condition. Can you accept that?"

"Maybe."

"I mean really accept it. Completely. With your whole heart and mind."

"I guess so."

"Then think of yourself as being perfect, as functioning perfectly, as being perfectly adapted. Cease thinking of yourself as being in pain, as having something wrong with you. And above all cease using your will against this pain. By such willing you acknowledge the pain and call it into existence rather than get rid of it."

"You mean I should give up trying to fight?"

"Exactly. Give up trying to fight. Do not acknowledge the pain at all. Think instead of your physical perfection and well-being. Think also of your mental perfection. Be at peace with yourself. Stop struggling. Do you believe in God?"

"Of course."

"Then think of yourself as being in the sure hands of God. Leave everything up to Him."

Wallace left the doctor's office with a lot to think about. In the first place the doctor had sounded more like a friendly philosopher than a doctor. In the second place, he had not scolded about being a baby over fancied pain, but had acknowledged that the pain was real. Wallace determined to follow the doctor's advice.

He took it upon himself to engage in regular periods of prayer and meditation, morning and night. He started attending church regularly, and he began studying philosophy, psychology, religion. In a short time his new interest had opened another world for him. He was fascinated. When his spiritual awakening had proceeded to the point that his physical pain had left him, he made up his mind to turn his whole life over to the service of God. He enrolled in theological school and in a few years became an ordained minister. Today he occupies a responsible pulpit, and his church is an inspiration to his community. By allowing God to enter his life, this middle-aged man overcame pain and altered the entire pattern of his existence.

SONSHIP WITH JESUS CHRIST

Aldous Huxley wrote, "There's only one corner of the universe you can be certain of improving, and that's your own self." And even here the first requisite is courage, the willingness to take a stand, make a decision. For the ego is strong in each of us. It cajoles us into believing we are wronged, wounded, unloved, when in truth it has blinded us to our kinship with all others, with all life, with God. If we will open our hearts and minds and let the power of Universal Being pervade us, we will be rid of all illness and disease, all suffering and pain, all lack and limitation. It is this divine aspect of our being, the fact that we can call upon the indwelling God to free us of evil, that is mute testimony to our common sonship with Jesus Christ.

Being is spirit, and matter is only a manifestation of spirit, and that which is manifested is never the entire truth of that which supports it, but only one aspect, a side, a perspective; and the spirit is always greater than matter, animates it, gives it form, supports it. Thus when the body falls prey to disease, to illness, to malfunction and weakness, it invariably is because the spirit has fallen prey to conflict, repression, or compulsion. For whatever is present in spirit must become present in matter; this is the nature of existence itself. All disease has its origin in the invisible world of spirit, and all illness may be cured by spiritual treatment. Scoffers of such treatment, those rooted in the world of material effects, state that if all disease is spiritual why is it that spiritual treatment often fails to cure. And such an observation is much like being startled that everybody doesn't discover a new continent who sails across an uncharted sea. Spiritual treatment *always* works when it is administered correctly. Medical science itself is coming to use it more and more. Under the guise of psychiatry spiritual treatment is given to thousands of sufferers when the pills and scalpels of the physician have failed. One of the founders of psychiatry itself, Carl Jung, stated that he never had witnessed a psychiatric cure without a religious awakening.

THE INFINITE RESERVOIR

Visualize an immense reservoir of power extending in all directions throughout the universe. Envisage this reservoir as infinite, with a tiny outlet into your heart. You have now the proper proportion between what you seem to be and that which sustains you. And in the tiny connection between you and It is the bottleneck so easily clogged, so liable to human tampering, that, once clogged, it withdraws the power of the infinite, warps and distorts it, brings illness and disease to a being that otherwise might be perfect.

In order to use the power of the infinite you must allow the power of the infinite to move through you. You must open the doors of your being, remove all obstacles between you and That, so that It may fully possess you, sustain you, nourish you, transform you. In spirit is perfection, and he whose inner image is perfect lives in perfect health. But he whose inner self is in torment because it is ruled by the ego is liable to all the frailties of the flesh. Since he evaluates all things materially, he does not see spiritual causes, alienates himself from his Creator, from the true roots of his being, and by his spiritual and mental conflict brings down upon his body infirmities and pain. In isolation from others lies his bitterness. In failure to see God lies his rage. In reliance upon ego lies his guilt. In dependence upon flesh lies his fear. Bound to these by lack of inner vision they play havoc with his health, condemn him to bodily misery even as he knows spiritual misery, and there is no way out of his dilemma, no solution for his problem except that he take a stand, make a decision for God. Once he makes the shift of spiritual viewpoint, once he perceives within the animating Self, he is cured. No longer can he suffer from that which is inconsequential, or be defeated by that which is bound to obey him. Once he makes a spiritual identification with the Divine, illness and disease are banished from his experience and he lives in joy and utility. His limbs and his organs are perfectly ordered by a divine working that pervades his being, that keeps him in utter fitness for the task at hand, for the role to be performed.

ALLOWING THE POWER TO WORK

Spiritual healing is not a willing; it is an allowing. One does not impose his will against the disease or illness in an attempt to exorcise it. Instead he recognizes that the illness is not physical in origin, but mental, that it is only a material symptom of a spiritual malfunction. He recognizes that the diseased creature has been deprived of the source of its power and perfection through a wrong-seeing, a subconscious aloneness, an egoistic centering. To cure the disease he first cures this impression, in his own mind, then in the mind of the one to be healed. He envisages this person as a manifestation of the power and perfection of the Divine. He sees that the One who created the universe and every living and inanimate thing dwells also in the one to be healed. He recognizes this hidden Dweller, states that it is He who inhabits the body, sees His perfection, expects that perfection to become apparent, states that the ego no longer will obstruct or intrude, warp and distort the perfection of spirit from manifesting. As he sees perfect spirit so he sees also a perfect body. It is this correct and truthful perception of the indwelling God that is the basis of all spiritual healing, that was the root of Jesus's ministrations to the sick. "Dost thou believe?" he asked. "Yea, Master, I believe." "Then take up thy bed and walk!"

Believe you are well, and you are. Believe you are vigorous and you are. But by willing yourself to be well, you simply involve yourself in greater difficulties than ever. It is the natural state of being to be energetic, forceful, dynamic. To be anything less, to manifest the negative qualities of illness, disease, lethargy is to have diffused the divine power, to have dissipated it, to have obstructed it, to have used it the wrong way. You need not *do* anything to heal yourself or a loved one. Simply clear your mind of doubts and fears and defeatism and have faith. Know that the Inhabitant within is the Divine, that His presence is perfect. Trust Him.

> Talk happiness. Talk faith. Talk health.
> You cannot charm or interest or please
> By harping on that minor chord, disease.

Say you are well, or all is well with you,
And God will hear your words and make them true.
                                        —Ella Wheeler Wilcox

To know God, to be aware of the Divine in all creatures, to live in this awareness, is to be a spiritual healer. Such a one need not try for that end; he cannot avoid it. There is only one mind in all creation, one spirit, one presence, one being, which is God. Who perceives God perceives his perfection, perceives Him inhabiting all creatures, and calls forth that perfection to manifest in the world, through all bodies, through whatever obstacles. The essence of spiritual healing is thus spiritual awakening. No amount of willing, ranting, praying, or commanding will rid the unenlightened of disease or effect a spiritual cure in those upon whom they practice. But the lame and the halt were cured simply by touching the robe of Jesus. Such was his spiritual oneness with the Divine that he called God forth in all upon whom he focused His attention. Purity of vision, absoluteness of union, surety of being, complete faith in the omnipotence of the Supreme, all these are qualities of the spiritual healer. He heals himself by being himself, and others by being one with them.

THE MAGNIFICENT MACHINE

Physical health and vigor are such integral parts of living that they usually are taken for granted until they leave; then the loss is earth-shaking. Pain and discomfort and restricted activities bring a lessened light to the world. Everything is dark and mauve and somber, and life no longer seems much worth the living. Small wonder that health tops the list of all material desirables. He whose physical energies are at the flood meets life with joy and anticipation, joins in, participates, learns and contributes. While one whose energies are dissipated, warped, diffused, is overwhelmed constantly.

Yet the answer to any physical problem is spiritual, just as the answer to everything is spiritual, just as cause always exists on the invisible plane of mind and what we perceive in the physical world is simply a series of effects. But we know far too little about our bodies, about their proper functioning, and we treat them so shabbily, give them so little care, it is small wonder they often run down early or wear out too soon or suffer breakdowns of important parts. It often has been noted that most people take better care of their automobiles than they do of their bodies, seemingly cognizant of the complicated machinery in their cars but relatively unaware that they, themselves, reside in the most marvellous machine of all. Mental and spiritual identification with the Supreme is the greatest step toward spiritual health, but understanding the functions and care of the body certainly are essential in our modern civilization.

The threefold nature of the living organism is that it 1) assimilates food and converts it into energy, 2) circulates this energy through the cells of the organism, 3) eliminates waste matter. If any of these three major functions is impaired, the organism breaks down, illness and disease result. Disease is a symptom, not a cause, and so is the breakdown of any major physical function. Cause lies in mind, in spirit, and until that is set right, symptoms may be cured again and again, but they always will return. Yet where spiritual understanding is lacking, it is necessary to treat symptoms directly, physically, medicinally. It is foolish to attempt spiritual treatment of disease unless one already has strong indication that his understanding will produce results. Far better to treat the disease in the material world of symptoms, for here at least are solids that one may touch and taste and feel and see, and when we take a pill we are absolutely sure that something has been done, but when we appeal to God we doubt. Oh, we are of little faith and less understanding, but the veil gradually is being rent, light slowly is penetrating through, so that the greatest healings continue to come to us as miracles, while the world of science labors to trap and treat each separate disease, one by one.

SENSIBLE DIET

Jonathan Swift wrote, "The best doctors in the world are Doctor Diet, Doctor Quiet, and Doctor Merryman." If we eat right, get plenty of rest, and maintain a sense of humor, our bodies seem to fall in tune with life, to function effortlessly. Diet, of course, is perhaps the greatest material factor in attaining health, for we become what we eat and in many cases are walking testimonials to our eating habits. Obesity, except in extremely rare instances, is the direct result of gluttony. It is next to impossible to become too fat without eating too much. Anyone who ever has seen a person suffering from starvation will realize how true this is. One youngster, used to diet conversation and never before having seen or heard of starvation, stumbled across the picture of a man who had died of malnutrition. "What a diet he must have been on," the child exclaimed. "Boy, is he thin!"

We not only eat too much, we often eat too many of the wrong foods—pastry, starches, sweets, synthetics, soda pop, and liquor. While modern regulations and scientific methods are putting more and more vitamins and minerals in our foodstuffs, it is wise for all of us to concentrate on eating a balanced diet—plenty of proteins, meat, fish, eggs—plenty of carbohydrates, carrots, peas, spinach—plenty of vitamins, fruits, vegetables, milk. The truth is that to all in America these foods are at hand and available. We need only exercise our common sense and a little self-discipline in eating them in the proper amounts and proportions. If we do this simple thing we have taken a great step toward good health, and we are enabled to take this step by putting our faith and trust in the Divine. We then stop using food as a substitute for love, and use it as it should be used, for the simple gratification of a bodily need. It has been said, and rightly so, that Americans often dig their graves with their teeth.

Gluttony, perhaps more than any other single thing, brings about the breakdown of the body. Clog any functioning system and that system eventually will stop working. So it is with overeating. Heart disease, hardening of the arteries, high blood pressure, nephritis are usually the result of gross dietary habits clogging the digestive tract, overloading the circulatory system, throwing the endocrine glands out of balance. We eat too much because it tastes good, because spiritually we are out of sorts with life, and we use food as a compensation, as a solace, and we eat ourselves into ill health, into our graves. If we will make our peace with the Supreme, find faith and inner serenity, the act of pushing our chairs away from the table will become as simple and as habitual as it should be.

> To take all you want
> Is never as good
> As to stop when you should.
> —Lao Tzu

GLUTTONY

When Katherine reached her thirty-fifth birthday she weighed nearly three hundred pounds. This enormous bulk she gradually had accumulated over a period of twenty years. She ate constantly. When she wasn't eating, she was drinking. She also smoked cigarettes and always seemed to have something in her mouth. Though she eternally was chewing, puffing, or swallowing she just couldn't understand why she kept growing fatter. She insisted that other people ate a great deal more than she. She was certain there was something wrong with her organs. Eventually, there was too. By her thirty-fifth birthday she had an enlarged heart, high blood pressure, an extremely high cholesterol count, and her digestive and circulatory systems had slowed to a walk. Her examining physician grew alarmed. He had tried everything to get Katherine to lose weight. Now he told her seriously that if she didn't take off a hundred pounds she wouldn't live five more years.

By this time Katherine was having difficulty climbing stairs. One morning she broke into a run to catch a bus, then collapsed on the sidewalk in a faint. When she revived, she became deeply frightened. She looked up into the faces of the strangers who surrounded her and suddenly saw herself through their eyes—a great shapeless hulk unable to support or sustain itself, placed in this miserable condition through an uncontrolled gluttony. She broke into tears. When the ambulance came, the attendants had difficulty lifting her, and many in the crowd laughed aloud at the sight of this great, crying, fat woman whom two grown men could not move. Katherine never forgot.

At the hospital Katherine refused all food, would not talk to anyone. Her face was stony and set, her eyes unseeing. Eventually the hospital began feeding her intravenously, but they could not make her eat. She was moved to the psychiatric ward. In a month's time she lost forty pounds. Now her health was as imperiled from eating too little as it once had been from eating too much. There came a day when she hovered on the brink of death. From a huge bulk of nearly three hundred pounds she had wasted away to under a hundred. She looked like a death's head. Her doctors had not been able to touch the traumatic shock that had caused her refusal to take food, and she still had to be fed intravenously. She did nothing but lie abed all day, staring at the ceiling. Little hope was held for her recovery; she obviously was waiting to die. Then one day it was Easter Sunday. Bells rang in the church steeples, and their notes drifted through the windows of the psychiatric ward. That afternoon a young minister came by to talk.

He was a different kind of preacher, this young man. He was not at all impressed by the sobriety of his job. He always laughed a lot and told jokes, and when he occasionally was chastened by the elders of his church, he would say that he just couldn't help it, he figured life was supposed to be joyful. He usually won the argument because his elders wound up laughing with him, and this infectious humor, this joyful interpretation of life, was why the hospital asked him to address their wards on Easter Sunday. He was glad to. It was the kind of thing he did so well that he knew God wanted him to do it. He talked to the psychiatric ward that afternoon, and he told some stories, and pretty soon Katherine began to smile, after a while to laugh. Her eyes brightened, and she listened to everything the young minister said. Afterwards, she talked to the nurse for the first time in months. She asked for a Bible.

Three months later Katherine was discharged. Her recovery was regarded as miraculous. She weighed one hundred and thirty pounds, looked trim, healthy, energetic. Those who had given her up were astounded. They scarcely recognized her, could hardly wait to learn her secret. How had she lost the weight, and how had she regained her health?

"I suppose I always ate too much because I subconsciously thought that nobody loved me," Katherine said. "When I finally became consciously convinced of it also, I refused to eat at all, as if in that way I could get back at people, make them suffer. Then it was shown me that life is not made of such serious stuff. Suddenly I saw that if I would be willing to laugh a little, take things with a touch of humor, people would respond to me, perhaps even like me, and I might even get to like myself. I tried it, and it worked. I just can't tell you what a change a smile can make. It helped me find myself. It helped me find God."

ANGRY CHURNINGS

In the vast reservoir of mind and energy that exists below the level of consciousness there lies in each of us innumerable buried pain memories, so unpleasant that our conscious minds refuse to recollect them. These buried pain remembrances act as prompters of certain emotions, triggering us into fear, hate, rage, etc., when we are faced with situations that remind the subconscious of the original. For example, when David is eight years old, he sneaks matches from the kitchen and plays with them in the back yard. Inadvertently, he sets fire to some dry rubbish, and in the ensuing conflagration the dog house catches fire and his puppy is burned to death. The howls of the dying animal drive little David into hysteria. Years later, as a grown man, he remembers nothing of this. He only knows he is deathly afraid of fire and cannot stand suffering in any animal. These two phobias, the result of the triggering prompters in his subconscious, set up constant conflict in David's life, in the end may affect his health. He might undertake psychotherapy in an attempt to clear out his subconscious, and indeed, much success is often achieved by such therapy, but it is not necessary to treat each of the prompters in the subconscious in order to be master of one's own mind and life. There is a panacea that smooths the stormy subconscious, that makes of its angry churnings an unruffled flow of power. This is the recognition that the mind and the being of the Supreme is within you. Once the human heart takes unto itself the knowledge that God, Himself, is the Presence within the body, no storm, no defeat, no pain, no sorrow can penetrate that insuperable knowledge and joy. The emergent Godhead then takes over the whole life, and the entire being is sustained by the radiant energy of the Divine.

The care and feeding of the human body is indeed an adjunct of the care and feeding of the human soul, and it is surely a recognition of this principle that prompted Confucius to advise his contemporaries to keep both their minds and their bowels open. There is a school of thought that holds that improper elimination is the principal cause of disease, that retention in the lower bowel of waste matter results in the poisoning of the blood stream and the eventual attacking of the tissues by those toxins. Whether this is true or not, there absolutely can be no quarrel with the fact the improperly functioning bowels and kidneys eventually will result in the breakdown of the body mechanism.

We must see that the elimination systems of the body are cared for properly and not misused. We may care for them by not putting undue strain on them as might result from a diet high in starches, fats, or sugars, and we especially can be careful to submit to periodic examinations by our doctor. We also can exercise care in drinking liquor.

ALCOHOLISM

Alcoholic beverage, taken to excess, is bound to put undue strain on the kidneys and liver. If we must drink, we should drink sparingly. Liquor, in moderation, can have a beneficial effect on the entire organism by helping to shake off the effects of fatigue. As a tonic before mealtime, a single drink can be an aid to digestion, help to relax taut muscles, dispel nervous tension. But overindulgence in any good thing makes of that thing a poison, and this especially is true of liquor. Our hospitals and institutions are full of people who have poisoned their bodies with it, who have drunk themselves into the shadows where there is no hope. Their alcoholism is only a symptom of a deep psychological frustration. They drink to escape some haunting picture buried in the subconscious, be it guilt, loneliness, a feeling of being unloved. The simple withdrawal of liquor certainly is not the whole answer for these people, though without doubt better than allowing them to immerse themselves in their misery. When alcoholism is cured by simple abstinence, psychological frustrations often crop up in new areas—overeating, hypochondria, phobias, compulsions—for only the symptom has been obliterated, the basic cause remains.

The cure for alcoholism, just as the cure for any psychological disorder, is the reorientation of the spiritual self of the individual to where he no longer is focused in his own narrow likes and dislikes, hates, hopes, ambitions, and desires, but takes on a larger spiritual identity, a sense of self that is deeper, wider, all-encompassing, a new sense of being that sees the old self as a thing apart, almost as another person, is touched with compassion for it and anxious to aid it in its struggles. This psychological resurgence, this spiritual rebirth washes away all sin and guilt, washes them clean and in such a manner that they never can return. For the Divine has entered into the soul and possessed it, made it an instrument of His Presence, Power, and Perfection, and no finite thing may touch it, no sorrow, no pain, no defeat. The man who achieves spiritual union with his Creator has made for himself a haven where there is eternal joy, where the buffetings of life do not penetrate; and no matter the state of flux about him, no matter the strife he is involved in, a part of him remains always in a state of absolute repose and utter calm. This is the cure for alcoholism, for all human disorders.

THE INVISIBLE PART

The third major function of the body, after assimilation and elimination, is circulation; and circulatory diseases have become a major concern of our society as more and more people in the prime of life fall prey to them. It generally is assumed that the tensions of modern living, a kind of fierce and abstract competitiveness, lie at the roots of this trouble. Another school of thought blames it on diet, holding that those who eat too many fats wind up with too much cholesterol in the blood stream and that this cholesterol thickens the walls of the arteries, places too great a load on the heart, gives rise to arterial occlusion and coronary failure. No doubt both tension and diet have a great deal to do with circulatory diseases, but a great deal of research will have to be done to determine why it is that some people may indulge in high fat diets, lead rigorous lives full of all kinds of dangers, yet maintain excellent circulatory systems into advanced old age. If we grant the premise that there exists behind creation an order, an intelligence, a force of energy that gives form and purpose to all created things, then we are bound to realize that original cause, first impetus, the divine stuff, is invisible. We cannot see it, touch it, feel it, hear it. We see only its effects, its forms, its partial manifestations. That which animates and sustains a man is spirit, and that spirit, when free and unfettered and uncluttered with false notions of its separateness and aloneness, makes itself known by the perfect functioning of the organism it inhabits. Thus perfect health of body is the result of perfect health of spirit, and he who would replace lethargy and pain by energy and joy need only turn his entire self over to the great Self that underlies the universe. In this self-giving, in this consecration, in this final identification, God will take up the perfect coordination of all the functions of the body and imbue them with the energy and joy of His Presence. We must learn to rely on our inner, invisible Part. Once we learn and master that, we attain to perfection, both physical and spiritual.

> Thirty spokes will converge
> In the hub of a wheel
> But the use of the cart
> Will depend on the part
> Of the hub that is void.
>   —Lao Tzu

STRENGTH THROUGH COURAGE

Strength is the bulwark of physical health, and strength springs not from physical causes but from spiritual ones. "Ah, but no," say the materialists. "Some people are born strong and some are born weak. One man can lift huge weights while another has not a fraction of such strength." Muscular strength is not true strength. True strength is spiritual, the power to dare, to make a decision, to remain steadfast, to be true, to take a stand. Muscular strength is incidental, for man is not a physical animal but a spiritual being. Dozens of animals are his superiors in physical strength, but not one is his spiritual equal. Man has developed the power of awareness, an awareness that leads him to investigate the world around him, himself, his relationship to the universe. Thus he is led to God, eventually must uncover his own divinity, unveil his own power. In the interval, while he still is blinded to his true relationship with God, he is out of spiritual sorts with the universe. In his isolation and separateness he no longer instinctively relies upon the sustaining, healing, and nurturing power that gave him life, but rather seeks to assert his domination over that which is greater than his separate self. In his failure, he falls spiritually ill, and this spiritual out-of-jointness manifests itself in his bodily health and in the affairs of his life as restriction, inability, suffering, and pain. He cannot possibly heal himself by elevating his ego, but only by achieving proper humility, by perceiving the Divine in all as well as himself and by surrendering his life and works to the Supreme.

Joy, laughter, optimism, and inner peace provide the spiritual strength upon which physical health is truly based. All these come to the man who is able to see his true relationship with the Divine. He does not struggle, for he understands that he is being led through the work that the Supreme within him must do, and he does not suffer pain or defeat, for he sees that in the end there are only victory and joy for his true self. He does not rail or cry out in bitterness or distress, but suffers all gladly, knowing it is the will of God and that enlightenment will be his, knowing that good grows from apparent evil and that the ends of all actions and events are perceptible only to the Divine. Thus he remains steadfast in all storms, unthreatened in all danger, untouched by all pain, equal to victory and defeat. God dwells within him, and he is unafraid. "Be not afraid of life," wrote William James. "Believe that life is worth living, and your belief will help create the fact."

Yet always there are those who run, those, who, by immersing themselves in constant activity, seek to fly from the gnawing doubts and fears that plague them. If they stand still for a moment, they become aware of the limitless chasms of infinite space and time, and that which sustains them, the ego, is dwarfed into nothingness; then they are overcome with a sense of dizzying vertigo, and they are afraid. Hate wells up in them, bitterness at the fate that has cast them down as a tiny speck on a tiny speck in immeasurable space. Furiously they attack the problems and events of life, as if by such activity they can forget, but always their fears gnaw at them. They run faster and faster, but they never escape.

YOU CAN'T RUN AWAY FROM YOURSELF

When Darrel was only a little lad he couldn't stand to be beaten. His parents used to play games with him, but if ever they won, Darrel went into a rage. He lay down on the floor, beat and kicked at it with all his strength. His parents soon learned to let him win. It was just a quirk, they thought. Otherwise he was a bright, alert, courteous boy, constantly on the move, seeming to overflow with nervous energy. He received excellent marks in school, excelled in sports, was class president, seemed popular with his schoolmates. Occasionally, however, he would go into a blue funk, would take to his bed, stay there for several days. During such times he would be overcome by lethargy. He would sleep twenty-four hours at a stretch, lose track of time, all events. Attending physicians labeled such attacks as nervous exhaustion, said that rest would take care of it. Rest always did.

Darrel graduated from business school at a leading college, then entered the employ of an industrial firm. His energy and devotion soon brought him to the attention of his superiors. Before he was thirty he was a supervisor, by the time he was forty, a vice-president. But these years of furious activity took their toll. Darrel looked fifty, had difficulty sleeping, was troubled by an incipient ulcer, high blood pressure, an enlarged heart. The day following his appointment to the board of directors he collapsed in the factory and was taken to the hospital, unconscious. His physician diagnosed a mild heart attack brought on by the shock of a perforating ulcer. An operation was performed.

Gradually, Darrel recuperated. As his strength returned, so did his nervousness. He hardly could wait to be up and around, to return to his job. The hours in his hospital room palled on him, seemed to drive him to distraction. He wanted to be doing something. He said he just couldn't stand idleness. What he truthfully couldn't stand was being forced to look at himself, but there was no escaping it. Darrel had to look inside Darrel.

What he saw appalled and frightened him. He saw how small he was, how he had been running, and now that a final curtain of darkness almost had managed to settle over him, he knew his own mortality. Why had he been doing it? he asked himself. Why had he always been so infernally anxious to be successful, to be better, richer, more secure than the other fellow? Suddenly he saw that it was because he always had been afraid. He always had been so concerned with himself, so unaware of the existence of others, so driven to prove himself, to become secure, to somehow hew out from the physical world an immortality he utterly had failed to perceive. Now he strove anew to see it. He reached out his hand for God's.

Evenually Darrel was back at work with his old company. No mountains to climb now, though, no driven urges to get all possible things done within the shortest length of time; Darrel had found peace, a kind of inner surety that he was performing each task the best possible way when he went about it without hurry or anxiety. Today, he is nearly seventy years old, still active in the company, admired and loved by many, and strong enough to play eighteen holes of golf three times a week, to fish for trout, and tramp the wilds of Wyoming for elk. "I really found myself," he says, "when I stopped running away."

He pays too high a price
For knowledge and for fame
Who sells his sinews to be wise
His teeth and bones to buy a name
And crawls through life a paralytic
To earn the praise of bard or critic
    —Ralph Waldo Emerson

THE MOLDING MASK

Oh, we fight many demons, we who inhabit the earth, and our heritage of God will not be proven until we have purged from our souls those conflicts, repressions, and compulsions that so often make our behavior irrational. Our vanity is so dear to us that we hide our wounds, tend them in the festering darkness of blind ego, foster hate, bitterness, and fear as our constant companions. Yet as we live in the ego, how else can we act but in the ego? According to how we suffer by comparison with others, we assume limitations and predicate our opinions, thoughts, and actions on the poor thing we fancy ourselves to be. More often than not we live in constant fear, rail at fate, cry out at injustice because we are not some greater ego, some aggrandized small self, and we have not the courage or heart to abandon the ego altogether, find refuge in a new and greater identity, and with that one towering spiritual decision remake our world and our very selves.

We are spirit, pure and simple, and the extension of ourselves that we discern in the physical world is only a physical counterpart of that spirit. According to how straight the stream flows through the molding mask of our humanity, we approximate to God, become like Him in presence, power, peace, immortality. It is always the molding mask of ego that limits, distorts, that maladjusts, brings pain, remorse, guilt, that engenders hate, bitterness, and fear. Rejections of the ego live in the subconscious of each of us, and it is they that bring forth within our bodies symptoms of our mental and spiritual maladjustment in the form of disease and illness. When we have learned to completely surrender ourselves to the Divine, when we have learned to live and act in the consciousness of God, then we will purge ourselves of all pain, all repression, all compulsion, all limitation. Then will our lives truly become an exemplification of the workings of the Supreme, and illness and disease no longer will touch us.

PHYSICAL AND SPIRITUAL UNITY

The argument is sometimes made that if all disease and illness are spiritual, why not treat them in a purely spiritual manner instead of often treating them on the physical plane by consulting doctors of medicine and receiving their ministrations. The miracles of this world are achieved through perfectly natural means, and if the treatment of a disease requires the employment of physical means, then spiritual causes will move the sufferer to a doctor and the subsequent treatment will cure him. Those who divide life in half, into the physical and the spiritual, never can hope to approach its truth, for each is only a different aspect of the other and the truth lies in their unity. The physical is an extension of the spiritual, and the spiritual is the sustainer of the physical, but to believe that the physical is false or an unimportant side-effect of the spiritual is to deny the importance of life and its great and secret goal. Spiritual treatment for ill health, just as spiritual treatment for any negative condition of life, never is properly undertaken with the end in mind of effecting some supernatural solution. The Divine always works through His instruments, and where some supernatural solution occasionally appears to have resolved a problem it is only because we are ignorant of divine law and divine manifestation. One who treats himself for abundance with the idea in mind that it may start raining money is not likely to achieve much success for he is closing his mind to the natural means for gaining abundance—the rendering of service to his fellows. Similarly, that man who treats himself for health with the mental image of suddenly throwing down his cane and walking is closing his mind to the natural means of regaining the full use of his legs—the gradual and faithful exercising of the muscles until they rebuild their normal strength.

SPIRITUAL TREATMENT

What is always primarily important in spiritual treatment is the recognition that first cause is spiritual and that all physical manifestations have a spiritual basis. Thus, if we suffer ill health or disease, we can approach treatment with the sure knowledge that some erroneous impression, some warping of essential divine power, some restriction, has, via the molding mask of ego, entered the human soul and is making itself known through the malfunction of the body. When we treat this spiritual negation we properly do so not by refusing to recognize that the body is diseased, but by the absolute awareness that the spirit is perfect. We visualize our unity with all things, with all life, and we envisage our absolute identity with God. We see that there is only one mind, one life, one sense of self at work in the universe, and that this mind, this life, is within us, sustains us, *is* us. We know it is perfect because it is perfectly adaptable. We know it is all-powerful because it is infinite. We simply turn ourselves over to it in complete surrender, with consummate faith that its perfection will become apparent in our affairs and in the function of our bodies. The degree of surrender, the completeness of the "turning over" of all of one's self to the Divine, determines both the speed and the quality of the healing, for insofar as God pervades our being He pervades our physical body and our affairs and His perfection is made manifest.

Each spiritual ailment has its counterpart in the world of physical ailments. If it were possible to index all the various kinds of fear, for example, we quite possibly could affix to each the physical malfunction or disease likely to result. Such a refinement has not yet been done, but meantime it is feasible to list the most common physical ailments of mankind together with principal spiritual causes and most effective methods of spiritual treatment.

COMMON AILMENTS AND SPIRITUAL CAUSES

Colds, influenzas, and other congestive diseases. Frustration and consequent futility cause a dimming of spiritual perception, a kind of bleak night of the soul in which those things that would express themselves cannot get through, are hung up, and this congestion of spirit makes itself apparent as congestion in the body, in the form of the common cold, influenza, pneumonia, sinus trouble, etc. Treat yourself spiritually for freedom of spirit and freedom of expression. Treat yourself to see that there is no restriction, no limitation in the spirit of the Divine and that this spirit is within you, able to expand infinitely, only waiting for your recognition.

Insomnia, nervousness, and tension. Some baseless fear that proceeds out of the subconscious, that has resulted from a basic notion of separateness, that exists because of failure to perceive unity with God, gnaws at the consciousness day and night, causing irrational action. This fear must be stilled or there will be no peace, no capability, no success. Surrender, give up, cease struggling. God will take your cares and woes and transmit them into instruments for your enlightenment and redemption. Give your life and your cares to Him. He will free you from all pain. You will find peace, strength of mind, joy.

Circulatory diseases and paralysis. When we visualize life as constant competition, we constantly gird ourselves for imagined battles and exhaust ourselves against fancied foes. Life is a battle, yes, competition, yes, but until we see that one being, one mind, underlies all struggle, only seeking to refine its manifold expression by becoming in any particular instance the best there is, we have failed to recognize our own embodiment of the Divine. If we struggle alone, we eventually see hovering on the horizon the spectre of our defeat, and as in the dream of the child pursued by the monster we cannot run because we are paralyzed by fright. Such subconscious delusion manifests itself in restriction of body movement, in paralysis, in the breakdown of the circulatory system. Treat to be rid of fear. Treat to be rid of pessimism. God is within you. It is He who animates your body, and He is perfect. Be courageous. God is with you every minute of every day. There is complete freedom in the universe, for each of us is an expression of That which may be expressed countless ways and yet remains more than all.

Obesity. This is the ailment of the unloved, who may not actually be unloved, but always fancy they are. If you are overweight it is because you have sought solace in food for the frustration you have found in love. He whose feeling of being loved must come from the admiration and assurance of affection that he receives from others is doomed to eventual loneliness and bitterness. The basis of all true love is the spiritual unity of each man with his neighbor. There is only one spirit animate in creation, and that spirit is in everyone. Treat yourself to recognize the indwelling God in each man. See your kinship with others. When you do, the subconscious feeling of being unloved will evaporate into a feeling of joy. Eating of itself will become a pleasurable necessity to be practiced with restraint. There will be so much work for you to perform, so many areas of feeling to explore that you scarcely will have time for eating. You will become slim because to be slim is to be utilitarian, and you will be utilitarian for you will be an instrument of God.

Indigestion, ulcers, constipation. Those who fancy a hostile universe around them, who distort all events and all people into threatening symbols of destruction are held in the constant throes of apprehension. They believe they must hold tight to everything or it will be taken away, and they think they must wrest what they want from the grasp of others. Their curse is the blindness of isolated ego. They cannot expand, they cannot soar or aspire because they are so concerned with holding on. They must let go, relax, cease worrying. They must place their hope and faith and trust in God, and treat for absolute assurance of identity with Him. Then limitation will go, restriction, and the necessity of holding on to fading things. Everything in God's world is available to each of us. We need only open our minds and our hearts so the power of the Divine can flow through.

Cancers, tumors, and other hidden growths. The person who buries in the subconscious some event or deed that he cannot stand to examine still remembers this deed in unthinking motivation and with unbridled emotion, and his guilt lies heavy on his soul and he cannot contain it and it grows within his body as an unwanted thing. Treat for the guiltlessness and sinlessness that is God's. All experience, all action, all thought is part of the process of growing and merits neither censure nor praise on the part of the Creator. All experience is for learning, is a step on the path to knowledge, and the greatest error of all is the assumption of guilt as a result of error or wrong thinking. God is all things. He is the saint, the sinner, the victorious, and the defeated; and in the limitless and final scheme of things, you are He, no less, and cannot be censured despite the abasement of the ego. Take unto yourself identity with the Divine. Guilt will leave you, all pain; no longer will you grieve.

Arthritis, lameness, bursitis. An inner hostility, a rage, a bitterness, a deep pessimism over disappointments in life, all contained and never shown, often will crop out in bodily restrictions such as lameness of the limbs, arthritis, bursitis, and various muscular incapacities. The containing of rage causes the restriction, for where rage and hostility are freely vented such bodily affliction seldom is present. However, it is not the containing that is the cause in the end, but the emotional content of the frustrated and unenlightened nature. Rage and hostility are only possible to the little ego, and until it is subordinated to the larger Self, the nature of the individual must perforce fall heir to all manner of malfunction. Treat for largeness, for compassion, for peace, for a sure knowledge of the nature of the Divine. Treat for the presence of God within you.

Alcoholism. Alcoholics are those who would run away and whose legs and energies do not provide sufficient speed. They seek escape through the forgetful narcosis of alcohol, and once immersed in it, they fear to return to reality. Therefore they drink constantly, often turning to drug addiction to make the escape more convincing. The solution for each is simple—the facing of reality. But this act of decision and courage becomes increasingly difficult each day it is put off. The alcoholic's power of decision finally becomes so low that he must undergo supervision in any simple task, lest it become too great for him and he seek refuge in alcohol. Alcoholics Anonymous, recognizing this, places its initiates under constant surveillance until the first period of abstinence is over. But, since the alcoholic drinks to escape, the only true solution to his dilemma is not to escape, to have the courage to face reality. Once he has mustered this courage it never will desert him.

TAKE GOD UNTO YOUR HEART

Health is a matter of spirit, and spirit is a matter of faith and courage, and if we take God unto our hearts, reach out with our souls to encompass His nature and power, we will find changed lives and joyful and vigorous bodies. We will not do this thing by continually focusing our attention on the negative, the evil, and the restrictive, but rather by seeing our identity with the positive, the good, and the powerful. The Divine dwells within each of us. Let us exercise our good sense and get our limiting egos out of the way so that His power and perfection may become manifest in our bodies and our affairs.

◇◇

SIXTH MEDITATION

I accept my body as a manifestation of spirit. Spirit
created it, spirit moves it, spirit sustains it. I know this
spirit to be greater than myself, to be an all-encompassing, divine Presence that inhabits all creatures,
that pervades the universe. My heart beats, my tissue
lives in response to some perfect order, some supreme
harmony, some absolute power. I need not command
the organs of my body to function. Health is mine,
perfect function is mine by the simple surrender of
my will to the Divine. Yet I recognize that the power
of decision remains with me, that I may take a stand,
choose a way, and that universal spiritual power will
then lead me on the path that I have chosen. I therefore
assert that I retain no hidden memories of pain in my
subconscious. I bring up from the dimly remembered
depths of mind all those memories that prompt in
my consciousness feelings of hate, bitterness, anger, and
fear. These negative emotions I cast out of my life
forever. By aligning myself with God, by identifying
my being with His, by becoming one-souled with all
things and all beings, I depose all negative emotions
and enshrine reason in their stead. Reason and attunement lead me down life's most hazardous paths with
perfect composure and absolute surety. Because of attunement my body functions in harmony with all
nature. There is perfect assimilation for there is perfect integration. There is perfect circulation for there
is complete freedom. There is perfect elimination for
there is absolute utility. I follow the path of joy, for
that is the road to attunement. I seek laughter, for in
laughter all bonds disappear. I believe in the great and
good ends of life and of man, and this optimism rules
my existence, leading me into inner peace, perfect attunement, strength, health, and vigor.

◇◇

7 LOVING AND BEING LOVED

A candle burns in the depths of the night
And illumines the path and the goal
With the promise of God to redeem with His light
The lost and the fallen through love of each soul

THE POLARITY OF LOVE

Most people when they think of love think of *being* loved and seldom of the spiritual act of loving. As a consequence their idea of love is unreal, one-sided, impossible of attainment, for being loved is only one pole in the magnetic field of love, the other is loving; without both there can be no love at all. Probably we have grown into this anachronistic state through over-concern with applause. Modern society sets great store by the winner, the entertainer, the performer, and undoubtedly we have grown to measure our social acceptance by how much admiration is accorded us. We develop a desire to be loved, not by loving in turn, but rather by dazzling, outperforming, seeking and holding the center of attention. Such false motivations alienate rather than attract, inspire envy and antagonism rather than love, but still the majority of people go through life humiliating others, trying always to beat them, forever insisting on their own superiority, then wondering why in the world they are not loved.

It is possible to win love under false pretenses, but it is not possible to hold it. One can, by dint of singular physical attractiveness, personal charm, or great talent, win from others a profession of adoration, but unless such adoration is met with sincere lovingness in return, it soon will die. It is strange indeed that millions of people become frozen, isolated in little prisons of their own making because they need to be loved and cannot find it, when all the while the tool of their liberation is in their own hands—all they have to do is love and they will be loved in return.

THE SILVER LINK

The desire for love, the very necessity for love, springs from the individual's sense of separateness and isolation, his subconscious memory of a greater, wholer, more complete state, and his desire to return to that state by fusion with others. God has entered into the material body, assumed a mask in which He appears far less than Himself. In order to *become* a particular manifestation, He must *be* that particular manifestation, and all during the masquerade there exists in the depths of each creature an ache, a longing to return to a pure and absolute state; and this yearning, this reaching out to encompass all things, this desire to return to a condition of wholeness, is the longing known as love. So it often is said that God is love; for in love, in true spiritual love, all things are united, fused, made one in the essence of their being, and thus they return to a sense of their original state, which is perfection and completeness and serenity, which is God.

Too many of us today are love-blocked. The channel through our hearts on which lovingness goes out has been dammed up so that nothing can get through. We make our way through life as though frozen, unaware of the divinity of our neighbors, of all those we meet. Where we reach out a hand to touch them, it is for sensation only, not to console or sympathize or lend strength, not even to determine what stuff they are made of. If we truly touch them, let ourselves go out in that touch, we soon learn that we not only have touched them but we have touched God. To open the doors of your nature and let the spirit of love soar through is to lend a touch of magic to everyone you meet, to everything you do. Life is most exciting, most rewarding to those who love, who really let the bars down and love. It matters not if their love is returned, life itself will return it. Life's law is that only the lover becomes the beloved; there is no other way. The man who allows the compassion and mercy of God to flow unimpeded through his nature, out to others, to all life, will be showered in return by the lovingness of life, in abundance, in vigor, in friendship, in joy and happiness, for he truly has attuned himself to God. By allowing himself to love, truly love, he penetrates the mystic meaning of existence, discerns by a kind of communal feeling the absolute unity of life.

> True love's the gift which God has given
> To man alone beneath the heaven
> The silver link, the silken tie
> Which heart to heart and mind to mind
> In body and in soul can bind.
> —Sir Walter Scott

The nature of love springs from the desire of the created individual to return to a state of primary spiritual unity. It is the longing of the soul to return to God. From this desire to unite, to penetrate, to mingle with, to lose one's identity in, spring the noblest efforts and aspirations of man. Men become explorers, researchers, students, writers, artists, philosophers, scientists, all because they seek to know more about, to better identify themselves with, the world they find around them and the world they find within. Love provides impetus for all, and the man who is blocked from loving is blocked from doing, for the wellspring of life is dammed up inside him.

LOVE-BLOCKED

Charles was the kind of man who obviously was out to take what he wanted. No path was too devious, no means too unethical to be used to gain the ends he sought. When asked what those ends were, he replied tersely, "I'm going to be boss. Nobody is going to tell me what to do. Nobody is going to push me around." Nobody did either. Charles was far too big, too tough, too mean for that. But the pushing around he gave himself was something to behold. He was like a man surrounded by a ring of wolves. He simply bristled with aggression. He obviously considered everyone an opponent and was out to win at any cost. He couldn't work for anyone. He couldn't muster that much humility. No one could have put up with his hostility anyway. As a consequence, he was always in business for himself; in fact, he was in life for himself. His businesses always fared badly. Everything would go well for a while, then pretty soon his customers would start leaving. Finally there would be nothing to do but close shop and start looking for something else.

Eight successive failures had only increased Charles's hostility. By this time he was convinced that there was a conspiracy afoot to thwart him. He never had a kind word for anyone, never seemed to like anyone, actually seemed to dislike all company unless he could find a way to turn it to his profit. As far as Charles was concerned it was obvious that he dwelt in an enemy camp, that he was deathly afraid he might be found out at any moment.

When his last business folded and he had neither the capital nor the friends to get him started in another, Charles had come to the end of his rope. He locked himself in his house and wouldn't answer the door. One day the police came and took him to jail for a series of petty thefts that he had committed at night in order to be able to eat.

"I only took what they owed me," he told the judge.

"They've stolen from me, tricked me, forced me to live without food. I was only taking what belonged to me."

That was not the way the judge interpreted it, however, and Charles was sentenced to six months in the county jail. He cracked completely at this last outrage, had to be taken forcibly from the courtroom and restrained in his cell. The court ordered psychiatric treatment.

When Charles was discharged from prison six months later, he had changed, but hardly for the better. No longer did the edge of his aggression and hostility stand out; instead he seemed absolutely beaten, bereft, without the will or the urge to strike back. He searched desultorily for a job, but he didn't seem to really want one. He lived meagerly on donations provided by a welfare fund.

It was winter, and in the chill evenings Charles grew accustomed to taking walks. The exercise and the fresh air stirred him from his lethargy and he began to notice things, how the smoke rose in stately columns from the factory chimneys, how the icicles hung like narrow teeth along the eaves of buildings, how the noise of the city seemed hushed by a snowfall. He was crossing a bridge over a small river one evening, on his way home from his usual walk, when he heard a cry for help. Peering over the edge of the bridge he saw the head of a child bobbing on the surface of the water. Charles threw himself over the rail, into the freezing river below.

He reached the child all right, and with his last strength managed to land him on the river bank. By now both would have lapsed into unconsciousness but for a small gathering of passers-by who administered first-aid and called an ambulance. Charles and the child were taken to a hospital and each recovered without mishap. The child's parents were overcome with gratitude. They pressed all sorts of rewards upon Charles. He smiled at each, but shook his head.

"I've found my own reward," he said. "I couldn't take anything more. I've learned at last that the only way to help one's self is to help another."

When Charles was discharged from the hospital he was offered a job immediately. He took it and since has performed it ably. But most important of all, he has learned to make friends. He reaches out to people; some dam in him has been opened and lovingness pours through. He is a happy man, his years of bitterness and discontent forgotten.

> To look up and not down,
> To look forward and not back,
> To look out and not in, and
> To lend a hand.
> —Edward Everett Hale

EROTIC LOVE

The most earthy and universal manifestation of divine love is erotic love. In the attraction between the sexes rests the underlying drama of life—the yearning of the differentiated parts of the Supreme to be integrated once again. The human being is both aware of himself as an individual and as a part of something greater. As an individual he soon finds little of permanence to cling to, and he casts about for the answer to his existence, seeks endlessly for his greater Self, the vaster existence in which he has his true being. The desire to unite, to fuse, to combine, is his great subconscious longing to become immortal, to return once again to a state of wholeness and completeness that is dimly and only subconsciously remembered. Such basic underlying motivation readily impels him to unite with a member of the opposite sex, seeking in that union a spiritual fulfillment in which the erotic portion is purely a symbol of the ecstasy and perfection sought by the soul. Sexual union reproduces the species, carries on the long string of differentiation of the eternal and infinite Divine. Each step in that progression is made possible by the individual seeking his greater Self through union with another, and thus the erotic aspect of sexual union has a deep and persistent spiritual drive which, if ignored, defeats sexual union altogether.

Meister Eckhart wrote, "God and I: we are one. By knowing God, I take Him to myself. By loving God, I penetrate Him." This insoluble spiritual mystery, of God inside one and yet outside one, of the longing to penetrate and be penetrated by, has its natural material solution in the sexual act. Yet no solution to spiritual dilemmas will be found there. The temporary union achieved by a man and a woman, no matter how perfect, no matter how tender and mutual, is a transient thing, an indication perhaps but only an indication of the rapture to be found when the soul unites with God. Nevertheless, the man who commits himself to celibacy in order to better find God and to better love God all too often cuts himself off from the primary outlet of human lovingness and thus suffers an emotional shriveling, a kind of shrinkage of the soul; and because he no longer has this common tie of lovingness with others, he fails to understand others, their humanity and their fallibility, and no longer can he feel and touch human aspirations and human suffering, no longer understand himself.

To be sure, one has only to visit the breeding pens of any farm to convince himself that there is nothing intrinsically beautiful or uplifting to the soul about sexual intercourse. The blind brute follows an impulse it neither understands nor cares to understand, unites with its mate and procreates the species. Yet even here the master hand can be seen, irresistibly guiding each created being into union with another in order to express a wholeness that is absent from each solitary thing. The force of union, that gigantic power that carries with it the tides of progress and life, is made manifest here on earth through the sexual union of male and female, as if God in his plan of infinite progression and manifold manifestation has laid his hand on the brow of each creature, saying, "Seek thou thine opposite; in union thou wilt be guided to thy true self."

THE SEARCH FOR THE BELOVED

Sexual union is the most rewarding and at the same time the most frustrating of all human experiences. We are drawn to it like moths to a flame, irresistibly, with a compulsion that lies deep in the subconscious memory of race and specie, and we can no more fight its force and drive than we can blot out the light of the sun, and we cannot deny it without living a lie. Each of us carries in his secret heart, perhaps without ever having examined it, the image of his beloved. Oftentimes it is a trite and unworldly thing, overly idealistic, unreal in the sense that it is impossible of realization, as when a young girl, for example, envisages her knight in shining armor. Yet each of us finds her knight in shining armor, his fair maiden in distress if only we are able to look upon God's created world as it actually is and not as it is distorted to us through the eyes of the ego. We are drawn to love in order to become whole, in order to find in union a completeness that we do not know in solitary existence. And for a while we find it, perhaps only for a moment, sometimes for a day, if we are very lucky for months, even years, but in the end it disappears, for we have fixed our lovingness upon the flesh and made it transient. We cannot finally be fulfilled in loving or being loved unless our ultimate lover and beloved is God.

The Don Juan who flits from woman to woman is not so much seeking endless conquest as he is trying eternally to find fulfillment in his quest for the beloved. Always in the sight of a new and attractive face, a kindly manner, an outgoing lovingness he fancies he has found that magic alchemy that will transform his life, give him a reason for existence, bolster his ego into the giant and invincible thing he would like it to be. He comes together with an object for his love, and in union he is deluded for a while that his search is ended, that the beloved has been found. But, alas, all too soon the magic deserts him; he finds the object of his adoration to be human too, imperfect, subject to sin and error and sadness, and he deserts her, takes up the quest anew, a quest that never will be fulfilled short of its being focused upon the Divine, short of its being a search for God. The pleasures of the flesh will not satisfy it, nor even provide forgetfulness for more than a moment, and the longing of the soul to be reunited with its entire being, with its true Self, with its Lord and Master, remains with the soul always until that longing is eased by divine union.

SEXUAL UNION

There is, of course, a physical side to sex. There is a basic biological urge in each male to inseminate each female, just as there is a basic biological urge in each female to entice all males to compete for her. Though these urges exist in subconscient and instinctive areas and to all intents and purposes are purely animalistic, it is no good throwing up our hands and saying that they are abnormal or denying that they exist at all. They exist for the purpose of procreating the species, and the manner in which they exist is to insure that the best and most hardy examples of the breed achieve union and have offspring. This method of choice is apparent throughout all nature; why should it not exist in the human also? Though it is obvious that giving free vent to such urges in our modern society could hardly result in anything but chaos for the individual, such sociological implications in no way invalidate the urges themselves or make them criminal or explain them away. Let us recognize that we climb the ladder of progress by restraint and by discipline, and that the same problems exist in the saint as in the sinner. The man who achieves sufficient control over himself to be able to channel his urges and energies into constructive action on the behalf of himself and society has learned the secret of success. All energies are God-given, given to express in the manifold individualization of the Divine a constant refinement, an ever-upward and ever-outward realization of a constantly sought perfection. He who gives over his works and his energies to God need worry no longer about being overcome by wrong action. His energies will be channeled along the path of the greatest good for all, and his security lies in his own faith and love.

All the things of the enlightened man's life take on new and heightened significance. He finds in the sex act a spiritual union that adds to the sum of its rapture, to the totality of its ecstasy by opening planes and areas of experience that before were only vaguely hinted at. Now he comes to his beloved in reverence, in humility, knowing as he penetrates flesh he penetrates spirit also, finding in possessing and being possessed a wholeness, a togetherness, a oneness, that increases his knowledge of the Divine. From the microcosm of the sex act he senses, radiating out on all sides into the outermost reaches of infinity, that power and permanence and rapture and joy that only can emanate from God. So he comes to his beloved spiritually as well as physically; he knows the Divine in his beloved as he knows the Divine in himself; the two mingle and are one.

> Thy soul I know not from thy body, nor
> Thee from myself, neither our love from God.
> —Dante Gabriel Rossetti

SELF-LOVE

The true nature of love is made manifest through God's love for man; and the yearning of differentiated parts to be once more integrated in the whole has its first outgrowth in the drama of male and female, in their coming together, in their union, in the procreation that results. But as the awakening self becomes more aware, develops ego, divides itself from others and from God, there is born that thing of vanity and delusion—self-love. Self-love is the preening ego parading before the mirror of its own vanity, posturing this way and that, examining itself from all sides, seeking its own approval by a standard of comparison with others. The ego seeks to assure itself that it is better than those it sees about it. Accordingly, its opinion of itself is never the same as its opinion of the next fellow, but always better or worse. Since it is not equal-souled to events, to victory and defeat, to gain and loss, it analyzes all things in terms of whether they benefit or obstruct. Thus it never sees things and people in their true light, but always in the coloration of personal vanity. Self-love blinds, deludes, narrows the world to the small egoistic self, is the most immature of all concepts. This absolute egoistic concern of one's self for one's self is natural only to infants. To be hung up in self-love, never to progress beyond it, is to be an infant for life, emotionally, mentally, perceptually.

Yet self-love is a natural and necessary step in the ladder of progress by which the Divine marches toward ever-greater and more complete expression as a created thing. Evolving life awakens to the knowledge of itself long before it awakens to the knowledge of its sustaining source, and seeing itself becomes enamored of itself, and ego and vanity are born. Vanity and ego may be deluding forms, hiding for the moment life's true meaning, but they are natural evolvements of the discovery of self, and the discovery of self is predecessor to the discovery of God. The enlightened man leaves behind self-love when he becomes aware that his surface nature is not his true self and his body is not his true self and that the animating presence which moves him to act, which thinks, wills, and exists within him, is common to all men, to all life. Knowing this, he abandons self-love, leaves the shell of the ego as his ripened soul bursts outward into a more universal awareness, and his sustaining and nurturing fount becomes the love of God. So he abandons the small self and takes up his existence in the great Self.

Self-love is the love of the awakening infant enamored of his image as reflected in the eyes of others. He is the center of all attention, and his little world revolves around his every need. From this concern with self he grows to understand others, for only by knowing his own feelings is it possible for him to understand their feelings. In this way he matures, his love grows outward from the limitations of his egoistic nature and encompasses the outer world as well. Then he seeks an object for his love. Then he finds his mother.

MOTHER LOVE

In this first outpouring of love from the self to something other than the self the growing child finds a pure object of adoration, uncritical, never rejecting, accepting, yielding all. This sense of being loved despite his faults, of being desired no matter how poor his performance, how ignoble his actions, leaves a deep psychological mark on the growing child, so that in adulthood, perhaps long after mother and home have ceased to be, the mere mention of either, in conversation or song, can bring tears to the eyes of a hardened sinner. He recalls a time when he was loved for himself, not for what he might become or promised to be. He was the beloved, and he had nothing to do but accept that love. He loved in return, of course, but only according to his mood or according to how much love was tendered him. The simple fact of existence was all that was necessary to be loved; he had no tasks to perform, no walls to scale, no citadels to storm, nothing to win. He was loved because he was alive, and this condition, he falsely assumed, would be his permanent status in life.

Nothing on earth is more necessary in the evolving scheme of things than the love of mother for child; constant care and uncritical devotion are essential in getting the helpless infant to a state of independence. But where the child is unable to shake off the psychological need for his mother's love he is unable to mature to adulthood, cannot find the resources within himself to cope with the problems and vicissitudes of life. Because he feels that his share in life is to be uncritically loved, he cannot bring himself to make the effort required to earn love, to merit it because of his behavior toward others or because of tasks performed in their behalf. Consequently he spends a great deal of time bewailing the fact that he is ill-treated and nobody appreciates him and people keep doing him bad turns. It is he himself who is out of step with the world; if he is not loved it is because he loves nobody but himself. He is like a sponge, drawing in endlessly all affection but yielding none back. He supports no one, seeks always to be supported. He is a lichen on the tree of energy. He attaches himself like a parasite to those he knows and feeds upon the free flowing of their affection until natural imbalance causes a cessation.

> The two kinds of people on earth that I mean
> Are the people who lift and the people who lean.
> —Ella Wheeler Wilcox

Be a lifter and not a leaner. Give over your strength and energies to the Divine; love Him, love His created things, love your fellow man. You will be loved in return. God will love you, and in that love you will find such warmth and joy as will buoy you to the zenith of the heavens. Seek not to hold on to that which must be let go. The uncritical love of mother for child must not be carried into adult life, but gradually must be replaced by a mature love between individuals, one that can be sustained only by a sincere affection on both sides, each meriting the other. And seek not to inject mother-love into adult relationships; such relationships are doomed to failure for they are based upon unreality. Love lives only by being both given and received, and soon dies if either movement is withdrawn. For essentially love is a borrowing from God of a small part of His nature for use upon earth. It is a coming together of spiritual elements that in fusion exceed themselves. It is a borrowing and a lending of strength and energy, the better to build the race. It is aspiration and achievement, hope and fulfillment, longing and union. It is the Divine revealing Himself in humanity.

TOO MUCH MOTHER

Two people were truly concerned about Tom—his wife
and his doctor—but his mother thought he was wonderful. She
just couldn't understand what the fuss was about. So what
if Tommy drank a little and had some trouble holding
jobs? He was young yet, he'd get it out of his system. Why, it
only showed he was spirited, independent, that was all. She
was bitter at his wife for not upholding his actions, at his
doctor for suggesting psychiatric treatment. Tom had been
cited twice for drunken driving, had nearly killed an aged
pedestrian, had been fired from seven consecutive jobs,
holding the longest ten months. He was thirty-four years
old, the father of three children.

His case was a classic example of arrested emotional development. He had revelled so long in his mother's love
that he just couldn't face a critical world. Each time he met
any attitude other than complete approval, he was provoked
immediately to temperamental displays of sulkiness, bitterness, and retribution. One of his superiors said of him,
"He's capable all right, but such a child. He rages and broods
like a two-year-old. During the time he was in my department we were in a constant state of upheaval. I simply had
to get rid of him."

Everybody had to get rid of Tom. Only his mother could
stand him. Even his wife was fed up, standing by only out
of compassion. When Tom's doctor suggested psychiatry,
Tom told him to "go jump out the window," seemed pained
when the doctor didn't. At last Tom came to trial for driving while drunk and seriously injuring an elderly lady. The
evidence was incontrovertible. He was found guilty and
sentenced to eleven months in jail. His doctor intervened,
however, and suggested that Tom was willing to undergo
psychiatric treatment if put on probation. When questioned
by the judge, Tom agreed, and sentence was suspended.
Better the head shrinker, Tom told his wife, than eleven

months behind bars. He settled down to psychiatric therapy three times a week. He had no job, no friends, and his wife was on the verge of leaving him. He thought everyone was mad—except mother, of course.

Mother stayed right by his side. She insisted he come live with her, and when the psychiatrist flatly refused his permission, she inveigled Tom's wife into putting her up in their home. The psychiatrist realized he had lost the first skirmish, but he doubly resolved to win the war. He made it a mandatory part of Tom's therapy that he spend three afternoons a week at an athletic club. No mamma's boy, he assumed, could manage such a program unchanged.

One afternoon Tom was invited into a handball game. He had a partner, and they played two opponents. When the game went badly, Tom accused his opponents of cheating. When his partner remonstrated with him, he accused him of being in a conspiracy to make him look bad. Nobody could calm him down. The three others went quietly to the showers, Tom following, shouting recriminations. He challenged the smallest of the three to a fight, and when the fight was declined, struck him anyway. In the ensuing struggle he fell against a wash basin, striking his head and losing consciousness. When he failed to revive, a doctor was summoned and diagnosed a brain concussion. Tom was removed to a hospital where he hovered on the brink of death.

Both Tom's physician and psychiatrist were in constant attendance at the hospital, but there was little either could do. Tom's breathing was raspy, his pulse irregular, and he did not regain consciousness. A blood clot on the brain was causing increasing pressure and seemed certain to bring death eventually. A surgeon was called in to perform an operation. Tom was removed to the operating room, where, just before the anesthetic was administered, he sat bolt upright on the operating table and stated quite clearly, "I made a mistake. I'm equal. Not better, not worse, but equal." He lay back on the table then and relapsed into unconsciousness. The operation was performed.

Three days passed while Tom's life hung in the balance. On the fourth day he showed a definite improvement, on the fifth he was pronounced out of danger. Thereafter his improvement was rapid. For some time he showed a tendency to slur his speech, but gradually his articulation cleared. More than his physical improvement, his remarkable mental and spiritual transformation was apparent to everyone. No longer did he complain, recriminate, sulk, appear bitter or morose, but presented a pleasant face to all, exhibited a compassion and concern for others he had not shown in his whole life. When his mother attempted to monopolize his time, soothe him, placate him, sympathize with him, assure him of his bad fortune, he shook her off. She was uncomprehending, couldn't understand what had happened.

"Don't you love me anymore, Tommy?" she asked.

"Yes," he said. "I love you, mother. But I love God even more. When you're close to dying I guess you see things clearly, and for a while I understood that God was in me and in you and in everybody, and that all I had to do to become immortal was to love Him. That's what I'm doing now, loving God, in everybody I see. I want your love, mother. I want to deserve it. But I don't want to be protected. Can you understand that?"

She didn't quite understand it, but she sensed she couldn't change it. "I guess so, Tommy," she said.

He smiled at her. He didn't need it now, but at last he had her permission to become a man.

BROTHERLY LOVE

So the growing child matures beyond the egoistic sense of always being the beloved into an awareness that the world is peopled with others a great deal like him. He sees that in each of them exists a consciousness possessed of like urges, desires, problems, a consciousness which, though invisible, he senses to be the same as his own. Seeing this, he opens the doors of his own nature and reaches out with spiritual hands to meet others. When he does, his egoistic sense of isolation is shattered forever and he realizes once and for all that he is striding across life in the company of many brothers. Brotherly love closely approaches divine love, for it is a gathering together of the Divine's differentiated spirit, it is a beholding and an awareness of self by self, a mutual knowledge of common kinship with the master spirit of all creation. Who loves another gets outside himself, feels the vaster reaches of his true spiritual being and thus is able to perceive God more clearly in himself as well as others.

True brotherly love does not relate from surface to surface but rather from center to center. Outwardly your neighbor is a great deal different from you—taller, shorter, thinner, fatter, of different ethnical extraction, perhaps different religious training. But these physical characteristics, these mental characteristics, and hereditary traits are surface things, a cloak only, a sort of outer wall that conceals the real person from view. You never will truly love another by seeking desirable surface traits. The surface man is a false man, does not even exist, and in attempting to relate to him you face the completely frustrating task of establishing rapport with a ghost. He is there today and gone tomorrow, and he never returns in the exact same way you knew him today. People who establish relationships from surface to surface forever are being wounded by a loved one's betrayal. They seem unable to realize that their relationship was false to begin with and that there was no betrayal at all but simply an acting in accord with the true nature of the individual, a nature they never realized existed because they never had penetrated beneath the surface. Our divorce courts are full of people who have established relationships from surface to surface. The only true and lasting love between people comes from their relating center to center, from spirit to spirit, and when this happens, each in the other perceives himself, perceives the Divine.

RELATING SPIRITUALLY

Brotherly love is a love between equals, and one who relates from surface to surface never achieves it. He is always in the position of fancying himself better than or inferior to those he meets, and with his fancied inferiors he is haughty or arbitrary or condescending, while with his fancied superiors he is fawning or belligerent or frozen. Occasionally he makes what appears to be a friendship with someone far inferior to himself. The gulf between such people is extremely marked, is typified by the romantic cowboy and his dull but devoted sidekick. Western writers unwittingly have made the romantic cowboy an egoist who relates from surface to surface and cannot make lasting friendships with anyone but an inferior who will accept all and endure all to receive his favors. The man who relates from surface to surface is afraid of equals, at the very least is extremely uncomfortable around them. To him they are always competitors, and his immediate and only reaction to them is how to beat them or in other ways prove himself their superior. Small wonder he makes few friendships.

In any case, equality never is perceived surface to surface, for true surface equality does not exist. Only a relationship from center to center unmasks the spiritual sameness of people, allows them to perceive their brotherhood. In Exodus, God reveals his name to Moses, "I am becoming that which I am becoming," and this characteristic of the Divine, that He enters into each of His creations and becomes that thing, complete and entire, gives a basic spiritual equality and undifferentiated spiritual sameness to everything that exists. Know that there dwells in your neighbor the same animating Presence that resides within yourself, an ageless, deathless, birthless sense of "I," always the same in all creatures, not altered by entering the body, not changed by conflict, victory, or defeat, but witness only, triumphant always, untouched by the moment, never completely at home in the body, but existing truly in infinity, in eternity. Who sees the immortal in every creature loves every creature as he loves God.

> To love is to know me
> My innermost nature
> The truth that I am
> Through this knowledge enter
> At once to my being.
> —Bhagavad-Gita

DIVINE LOVE

Divine love is mature love, the most refined feeling and highest spiritual understanding possible to man. To accept God is to know God, and to know Him is to love Him. In love for the Ineffable, in self-exceeding through divine seeking, the individual arrives at a position of spiritual wholeness with all life, a place of peace and perfect equality that "passeth all understanding." Here is the true Kingdom of Heaven, a kind of divine consciousness that descends into the soul by special dispensation of the Supreme, a gift restricted to those who love God with all their hearts and all their souls and all their minds. Here is the divine alchemy that transmutes human clay into something noble and indestructible, that makes from baser substance a precious spiritual distillation, lending new color and form to the entire world, to all existence. Here is the key, which, when known and understood, unlocks the secret door in the wall of separateness and allows the Self to circulate freely through all existences. Thus through divine love does the soul mold itself into an image of its beloved, achieve infinity and immortality inasmuch as its perception of the Divine is clear. By breaking through the wall of separateness the soul mingles and absorbs, takes on a new and greater identity, forsakes the limitations of the delusive ego and begins to expand its awareness to meet the Supreme. This spiritual maturation is the end and the beginning, the alpha and omega of existence. Nothing more is going on in life than that God's created existences, lost in nature and absorbed in their limited being, should find their way back to Him. Love is the path and the way; not the limited self-seeking love of the individual for the group, but rather the love of the person for his Creator, the individual for the Divine, the man for God. Only in this manner does the true import and significance of love manifest in the life of the individual. Only in this way does its inner alchemy transmute the entire existence into a divine fire with a divine purpose.

PENETRATING THE WALL

In all things, then, the individual must attempt penetration of the wall of separateness that stands between himself and others. He must turn his eyes away from the delusiveness of surface differences and look beyond this veil into the inner core of spiritual being. There he will meet himself, there he will find that one infinite, eternal, animating presence that resides in all things, that is not different from being in different bodies but inhabits all with the same spiritual equality; for only one Creator has made all things from His substance, and nothing is lost or destroyed when created things vanish.

To arrive at this state of spiritual identification with others is to truly know the love of God. This divine love is apparent always in the life and affairs of the person who has cast off the deluding mask of ego and with humility but with a sense of destiny has aligned himself with the Divine. When a man looks into his most secret heart and examines the contents there, he soon shucks off the useless trappings of his little self, establishes a new spiritual center of gravity, sees his brotherhood with all men, his sonship of God. There in the recesses of his being, in complete retreat from the world and its strivings, he discovers himself anew.

Even as he has left the world to find himself, soon he redis-covers the world, as though it were created especially for him.

Strive to break down the artificial barriers between your-self and others. Relate to each person from the center of your being to the center of his being. Turn your mind and heart away from surface differences and discover the spiritual oneness of yourself with others, of yourself with God. This discovery will fill your life with divine love; your entire existence will be changed.

WINNING FRIENDS

Perhaps more than any other single human endeavor each of us strives to win friends and social acceptance. Human activity falls mostly into group activity, and almost as soon as we are out of our cradles we are associated with various groups. First, there are the neighborhood children, later the nursery school, the various higher schools, then the company we work for, the clubs we belong to, our city, state, nation, church, family. Always we attempt to win approval within each group, always we attempt to make of certain members our "fast" friends so that we may have confidants for our troubles and sharers for our triumphs. The man who has many friends and has won the acceptance of his fellows invariably is a happy man, while he who is ostracized by his group suffers pangs of loneliness and self-doubt. This is not to hold a candle for conformity or to extoll the virtues of presenting a constantly pleasant face to one's neighbors. A man must follow his own flame. Each of us dances to the piper, but each of us hears different music. To attempt to mold one's self in the image of one's fellows is not only foolish but impossible. Only by finding one's own self can one win true friends, true acceptance. All else is hypocrisy and is bound to be recognized sooner or later.

We all have known people who have cultivated fluent

styles of speaking, who are able to throw themselves into any role they choose and play it convincingly while all the time they feel nothing but the desire to please, to charm, to command the center of attention. This person is an actor on the stage of life. He is amusing, often charming, seems to radiate vitality and energy, but on knowing him better we are disappointed. We find his whole effort has been bent on creating an impression, and now that we have been admitted behind stage he no longer seeks to impress us. Underneath that poised and entertaining façade we find a total blank, a nothing, for he is never himself but only an occasion, an occasion which constantly is different and in which he dons whatever role is there for him to play. He plays so many parts he has lost himself among the characters. He is not himself for he does not know what he is. Such a person often is a talented actor on stage, screen, or television, but almost inevitably the breakdown comes, the total diffusion of a personality spread too thin. Adhesion is lost, and wholeness, and the individual skitters about, victim of every wind that blows, his divine quality of decision gone.

FIND YOURSELF

We must be what we truly are, and what we truly are is a question to be settled only between ourselves and God. Mistakenly we often set up patterns which are foisted upon us by fear, ambition, jealousy, or acquisitiveness, and in following them we lead false lives. We cannot truly attract friends and social acceptance when such motivations lie at the bottom of our activities. They are bound to show through, bound to alienate. But when we let go of personal avarice and ambition, when we turn our lives over to the Divine to do with as He sees fit, then we find that we are a power doubled upon itself. We begin to see the Supreme in everything we do, and everything begins to represent the Supreme. In a divinely authentic action, through the completely true being that we have become, we send out tendrils of spiritual connection to all those we meet; we know them as ourselves, they know us as themselves. Friends are ours and social acceptance, though we be on the surface different from every human that lives. In that difference itself our spiritual oneness with God is apparent.

It is, of course, foolish to think that we are going to want everyone for a friend. We may have an underlying spirit of love for the tiger, knowing that he is a creation of God and that God dwells in him, but when the tiger is loose and we are in its path it is wise not to dwell too long on that love. The tiger is only being a tiger when it kills. It is a magnificent instrument for destruction, and we may admire it, even understand our spiritual brotherhood with it, but we do not have to like it. The same with people. There are the saints and the sinners, the wise and the foolish, the great and the small. They are what they are because of the infinite variety that God brings to the world through the unfolding of His nature, and our spiritual brotherhood and basic underlying unity is a fact. But in this world of flux and fall, of strive and conquer, of danger and refuge, we need not like everyone or even almost everyone, not as desirable companions, associates, friends. Each of us plays his score on a different spiritual frequency, and those with whom we are attuned we choose as friends, companions, loved ones. The spiritual emanation is the thing. We are attracted to those who are like us, often repelled by those who are different. But we will come a long way in understanding others when we realize finally that we often attribute to them those very faults that lie within ourselves, that we conceal from our own eyes, from our own false vanity.

> Search thy own heart
> What paineth thee
> In others in thyself must be.
> —John Greenleaf Whittier

FINDING THE RIGHT MATE

Even as we desire to win the approval and friendship of others so do we yearn to find the one completely understanding person who will shower us with tolerance and affection and to whom we may open the floodgates of our being, confide all, give all, receive all. When this meeting of spiritual mates is accompanied by sexual union, there is achieved the most blissful state known to material man. Love between man and woman is like love between man and God. In the complete givingness, in the absorption, the fusion, the particular mental and physical alchemy by which two people break down the barriers of their separate existences and become one, there is played out on a minor scale a duplication of the process by which man finds God, loves God, becomes one with Him. The highest spiritual existence that comes to each of us, short of enlightenment in the sight of the Divine, is sexual union with a mate we love and have chosen out of that love. Surely the surging power of the universe pours through two such ones, lifting, elevating, making them into an image of their Creator, splitting off from their union other expressions of the indwelling Divine.

The search for the beloved of the opposite sex usually takes up a minor portion of each of our lives, but if perchance fulfillment escapes us, all life is lived under the shadow of this frustration. No man can be whole and entire without the experience of union with another, and this experience is only possible through finding the right mate. If fufillment escapes us it can only be because of something in our own consciousness, so that we do not see others as they truly are or have blocked out our own lovingness so effectively that we can neither give nor receive. In either case we continue our search, endlessly, peering into each passing face, wondering if perhaps tomorrow will bring into view that joyous one whose simple beholding will right all our wrongs, set all our doubts and fears to rest. But the longer we search the more futile our quest, for time instills fantasy in place of fact. Like the sudden discovery that God is within, so the quest for the beloved only is ended when we recognize that his image is also within and is not to be found outside. When we realize this we can let another into our hearts with tolerance and understanding, and the perfection of the image will not be tarnished but will adjust and mature until the one who has entered merges with it.

THE UNATTAINABLE LOVER

Adele had been an attractive girl and now she was an attractive woman, but though she was in her mid-thirties she still was unmarried. "Oh, it's not that she hasn't been asked," her friends said of her. "It's just that she's choosey, maybe too choosey." Undoubtedly they were right. Adele had been engaged seven times. Each time, only a few days before the ceremony, she had called the impending marriage off. "I know it seems like a pattern," she said. "And it probably is very odd. But when I finally knew each engagement was wrong, what else could I do?"

"You might have tried going through with the ceremony," she was told.

"Why?"

"Because your husband and your ideal lover may have merged."

She looked up alertly. "What do you know about my ideal lover?"

"That he is unattainable. Seven men have been left waiting at the altar because of him, but still he will not come. He is unreal, a product of your wishes, your hopes. When you marry, you must marry an imperfect, aspiring, erring human just like yourself. You will love each other only if you support each other. If you keep trying to escape that support, no one will love you. All is not moonlight and romance and sexual culmination in life. The law of nature is that we be necessary, that some cause, some event, some human being need us. If we satisfy this law, we love; if not, we neither love nor are loved. To know the bliss of a perfect mating you must suffer its imperfections, for what is perfect is but a moment, and what is imperfect is but a moment, and aspiration fills all between."

"But you can't know how desolated I am," she said. "Calling off each marriage was like accepting the end of everything. I didn't want to, but I knew they were wrong, and I just couldn't help myself."

"Adele," she was told, "marriage, like everything else in life, is exactly what we make it. If you feel a sense of incompatibility with all prospective husbands it is because that incompatibility is in yourself. Think. Have you truly accepted yourself?"

She hesitated. "Perhaps I haven't," she said finally.

"Do you know why?"

She shook her head.

"Have you accepted God?"

She looked startled. "What's that got to do with it?"

"Perhaps a great deal. Have you?"

"No, I haven't."

"You don't believe in God?"

"No."

"Then you think you're just an accident, that everybody is just an accident, that the world itself and everything in it are just accidents?"

"I guess so."

"Then I have a cure for your loneliness and your failure to find your beloved. If you will follow it faithfully, it cannot fail."

"What is it?"

"Prayer."

It took some time to persuade Adele that she wasn't being hypocritical in praying to a God she did not believe in, but she was told that God would reveal Himself if she would persist. She was given a simple prayer to repeat thrice daily in the seclusion of her room. She said she would see it through for one month.

Seven years have elapsed since then, and Adele still prays three times daily. She is married, the mother of four children, an active member of her local church. Speaking of that first experimental month of prayer she says, "The very first time I got down on my knees and said those simple words, my heart opened and tears streamed down my cheeks. God was there, I knew it was He. All bitterness and resentment seemed drawn out of me, and I was clasped around as if with loving arms. When I left the room the whole world was changed. A few weeks later when I met Edward there was no wall between us. Some barrier, some restriction had been removed, and we got right through to each other. It was a case of love at first sight."

THE GREATEST COMMANDMENT

This, then, is the manifesto that the indwelling God decrees, that we can change our lives through love. No road is too strait, no journey too far that our burden will not be immeasurably lightened through being carried with love. When we have allowed divine love to permeate our being and everything in our lives, we cannot fail to witness a transformation of all things from the common clay of material existence to containers of the divine spark, the divine Presence. By subjecting ourselves to the divine will, by loving God and perceiving we are beloved of Him, we finally attain to a skill in works that delivers us friends and loved ones and a serene and effective place in the human scene.

When we love, we allow God into our lives, and according to how our love is purified by selflessness we become recipients of God's power and His mark is apparent in all our affairs. Who attains to divine love has taken a great step toward mastery, even as Jesus advised, "This is the first commandment—thou shalt love the Lord thy God with all thy heart and all thy soul and all thy mind; and the second is like unto it—thou shalt love thy neighbor as thyself."

SEVENTH MEDITATION

I affirm my love for God, and in that love I perceive the truth of God's eternal love for me. I affirm the presence of the Divine within me, and in the knowledge of that Presence I sense myself secure forever, enfolded in everlasting arms. The nature of love is the nature of God; it is the eternal longing of His parts to be integrated once again into One. Accordingly, my knowledge of God depends upon my love for God; and inasmuch as this love possesses me, I possess it and am illumined. Therefore I consecrate my life, every fiber of my being to the Divine. I give all, ask back nothing. Yet what I give from my small self, that which is incomplete and finite and microscopic, must in the end be returned to me a hundredfold from that which is whole and entire and infinite. All about me I perceive the manifold forms of the Divine, and I perceive Him dwelling in each. There are no different selves in the universe, but one Self only, one sense of being, one awareness, one I, which is always and eternally God. When I love another, it is God I love. When I perceive in each form the Presence that inhabits all forms, then I know the Divine and in that knowledge I love all and my love is complete. No longer do I rail against loneliness, for God is within me. No path is too solitary, no way too deserted that I may not take it with the joy and knowledge of the companionship and comfort of the Divine. He guides my every step. He leads me in all ways. His love working through me draws my mate to me, cements our relationship, crowns our union with joy. His love working through me attracts friends, makes of my life a testimony to His warmth and everlasting compassion.

8 SUCCESS AND ACHIEVEMENT

Hast thou searched the far reaches of space
For a chance at a coveted role?
Chance cometh to him who perceiveth the face
Of the indwelling God in his soul

LIFE PRINCIPLE

It is a competitive world we live in. Everything occupies a position, and each position is open to challenge by all who aspire to it. Someone wants our job, our money, perhaps even our wife or husband. Nothing we possess is secure against the constant onslaught of human aspiration. Each of us daily defends his citadels, attacks others. The Supreme has laid His mark upon us by making life challenge and conflict, aspiration and effort, victory and defeat. Through aspiration we grow, through challenge we develop, through flinging down our all in the ring of conflict, win or lose, live or die, we temper our natures to their finest, hone the edge of our being to its sharpest fulfillment. Competition is God's mandate for life; through it He constantly evolves His manifestation toward an ever-greater perfection. When we compete, when we constantly strive to be better, to be greater, to exceed ourselves as well as others, we are living in accord with one of life's greatest commandments, and constant progress is ours.

Some people assert that it is cruel to compete, to attempt to beat someone, that such a psychological principle bred into people will produce a race of warriors, without sensitivity, without tolerance and understanding, without love. As in the Bhagavad-Gita when Arjuna, about to ride into battle, is overcome with repulsion that he must kill to win victory, so these people turn away from life and cease being what they truly are in order to live in the light of a false ideal. They need the advice of Krishna reassuring Arjuna that he is fulfilling the will of the Almighty by fighting, by playing his part, by being true to his nature. For God is the dweller in every creature and does not die when that creature perishes; nothing is destroyed, nothing lost, no cruelty is involved, no matter the conflict.

GOD-PRINCIPLE

Even as competitiveness is the essence of nature, so creativeness is the essence of God. We are involved in nature and absorbed in the ego when we act solely in response to outer stimuli, when our reactions are simply competitive. Only when our awareness breaks through the limits of ego-consciousness do we admit the divine power of creativeness into our lives and begin to originate things rather than react to those in existence. Competitiveness is life-principle, making dynamic the first stirrings of consciousness in matter, underlying the ever-evolving spirit as it refines itself through conflict. Creativeness is God-principle, freeing spirit from matter altogether, making of consciousness a paean of praise to the originator of things. Creativeness is that endeavor of consciousness that places human mind and spirit on the exact same plane as God's, no matter how briefly, no matter how imperfectly. An act of creativeness is a spiritual act, performed by a soul attuned to the Divine. It is a calling down of the powers of heaven to take form here on earth, and he who performs it performs a sacrament. Talent is a breaking through ego of a portion of universal mind, so that the power and beauty of the Divine is manifest. Those possessed of talent think of themselves as trustees and perform their creativeness through special dispensation of an acknowledged greater power, whether they call it God or not.

Competitive we are by nature, and to deny our competitiveness is to deny our humanity, to weaken our dynamic, to frustrate and falsify our purpose in life. But if competitiveness is sole ruler of our consciousness then we forever are prisoners of circumstance, tied to every conflict, to every storm around us. If we seek victory and achievement only, then our lives must be lived in constant rounds of disappointment and defeat, for victory and achievement are transient. All things come to all men, and their value is in their ability to inspire spiritual growth, not pride of possession or ego satisfaction. It is in aspiration that we fulfill ourselves, and aspiration is best satisfied by attunement with the Divine, not by seeking victory over others or dominion over created things. We find our greater selves through aspiring to the heights, but only when such aspiration is spiritual, a seeking inwardly and outwardly for God.

> Ah, but a man's reach should exceed his grasp
> Or what's a heaven for?
>
> —Robert Browning

A MAN ON FIRE

Harry was a live-wire, a real go-getter; he was like a man on fire. Whatever he did, he did with explosive energy. He seemed possessed of only one idea—to make money; and he dedicated all his waking hours to realizing that end. He seemed always to have a dozen ideas, to be shaping the ends of many enterprises. But somehow the money he sought just didn't materialize. By the time he was approaching middle-age he had held a half-dozen jobs, had started three businesses. Each had been an outright failure, and the money that Harry had dedicated his life to had not been forth-coming.

Nobody could understand it. "It's just bad luck," one of his friends said. "Lord knows if anybody is ever going to make a fortune, Harry is." But that was just the trouble—the Lord didn't know. What appeared to Harry's friends as bad luck had been simply the inescapable working of the law of being. Harry had isolated himself from the roots of his divinity. He lived entirely in his ego and saw himself as sole mover of events and people. Since his ego was not sufficient for such a concept, the enterprises undertaken by him were doomed from the outset. He had neither the expanded consciousness nor the humility to invite God in as his partner.

After his third business entered bankruptcy, Harry changed abruptly from a dynamic and enterprising executive into a lethargic and frustrated man. He couldn't understand why fate had treated him so badly. He looked upon the world through confused eyes, puzzled and uncomprehending at the stalemate he seemed unable to avoid. No longer could he summon the initiative and energy required to undertake another enterprise, to seek another job. Worried and desperate, he sought help.

"I guess I'm beaten," he said. "Much as I hate a quitter, I guess I've finally quit."

"Good," he was told.

Harry looked up belligerently. "That's an odd thing to say!"

"Maybe not. Ask yourself what you've been fighting, what you're giving up to."

He thought for a moment. "Life, I guess."

"Are you sure you haven't been fighting yourself?"

He looked at the ceiling, nodded slowly. "Maybe I have."

"You can't possibly gain anything by beating yourself. It has to be a good thing that you've given up that fight."

He smiled a little. "Maybe so."

"Think about it this way. Instead of visualizing life as

a battle, try thinking of it as a concerted effort by One Being who assumes countless forms to accomplish His purpose. His purpose will manifest through you if you let it, but instead of fighting it, you must do the opposite—you must submit."

"Now that *really* sounds like giving up," said Harry.

"It does now. Later, when you have begun to perceive the forces loosed by allowing God's will to work through you, then you will understand that you were really giving up when you were fighting. Will you try it?"

He shrugged. "What have I got to lose? I was ready to quit anyway, so I might as well do it this way. When do I start?"

"Right now. Start by getting down on your knees while we pray."

Harry had a tough time with this. He got down on his knees all right, finally managing that much humility, but his cynicism was deeply rooted. He just could not resist glowering at the entire human race. Instinctively he regarded everyone as an enemy, and in every competitive situation he fairly radiated hostility. Nevertheless he adopted a schedule of meditation designed to attune his consciousness to the Divine, and gradually, as he came to realize that a vast force lay dormant in some secret corner of his nature, he began to expand in awareness, to let go of ego-will, to allow the purpose and power of God to permeate his life. There came a day when he had achieved enough selflessness to be able to open a business without deep apprehension about the outcome. Naturally, things went well.

A former associate said to him, "What's happened to you, Harry? You don't rush around, get in a stew anymore. By golly, you actually seem calm!" He looked around the store. "And your business seems to be doing fine, too."

Harry smiled. "It ought to," he said. "God runs it."

The great lesson we all must learn is that there is opportunity every minute of every day through all our lives. It does not cease to be present simply because we do not see it. Failure is in our minds, in our hearts. We can quit and retire into the ego, or we can give over our lives to God. In the latter course we will find the answer to all our aspirations, to all our dreams and hopes.

For all sad words of tongue and pen
The saddest are these: "It might have been."
—John Greenleaf Whittier

ENTERING INTO LIFE

It is through letting the creative power of the Divine into our lives that we truly prosper. It is through softening the edges of competitiveness by spiritual oneness with our neighbors that we arrive at the zenith of our powers. When we turn over our lives and our aspirations to the Supreme, we are guided to undertake the work for which we are best suited, the enterprises that best fulfill our natures and our spiritual growth. But when we involve ourselves in the ego, absorb ourselves in the mechanics of nature, we can search the wide world over without finding a work to call ours. We all have seen victims of the stumbling ego, led this way and that, blown willy-nilly by every wind, never able to find a suitable job, always dissatisfied with the one that comes to hand. Such a person had best step down from the pilothouse of life and allow a surer hand to take the helm. In our limited minds we cannot see the whole scheme of things, the infinite plan, so if we act in the ego we act falsely. Since we do not see the thing to be done, chances are we do something else, and in that doing we are thwarted, in that frustration we suffer. Yet even suffering is not bad if used toward the end of enlightenment. Even defeat is good if it leads in the end to spiritual illumination. For we must find God if our lives are to fulfilled. We must turn over to Him our limited selves in order to realize our greater selves, our immortality, our power.

Finding the right work is not so much a matter of common sense and application as it is entering into the immense activity that is life. Those who stand by the wayside, who peer and debate, shuffle and retreat are tempted and repulsed, cannot possibly be vessels of that surging force of nature which aspires to the peaks and depths and widths and lengths of the universe. Nothing in life is small except to those who view it from a distance. If you will enter into things, become a participant, you will find that the entire drama of creation is played out on every field, however tiny. You cannot exude too much, create too much, participate too much; the Divine rewards you for every movement made in the direction of life. Those who retreat, who withdraw, who fail to find in mental and physical expression a symbol of the underlying significance of life, cannot achieve the enlightenment that is mandatory upon all who would arrive at mastery. "Abandon all past conduct and take refuge in me," cautions the *Veda*. Those who aspire to a regime of living that assures success and serenity in all ventures will wash from the slate of the past each experience that contradicts what they, through spiritual perception, know to be the truth. All experience is for the purpose of growth and never for the success of the individual. If you become immersed in past failures you live life's greatest lie. What is past is done; you cannot bring it back; you cannot change it. To live with it in the present is to be cursed with a condition you cannot alter. Each day to each individual is a new life to do with as he please. His is the fresh opportunity to choose each morning from countless spiritual by-ways the one path that he will take in search of his true self, in search of God. This expansion, this moving upward toward the infinite Self that lies behind creation is possible only to one who has cast off the bondage of the past and found his salvation in the mutable present, in changeable today, in alterable tomorrow.

The Moving Finger writes; and having writ
Moves on; nor all your Piety nor Wit
Shall lure it back to cancel half a Line,
Nor all your tears wash out a word of it.

—Omar Khayyam

THE GUIDING STAR

A truism that surely can be remarked of every man is that each has his special talent, his own particular and innate ability to interpret for a segment of humanity some impression of the Divine. This talent need not be overt expression such as art, music, science, but may take less obvious forms such as kindness, understanding, courage. Indeed, everything that is done well, mastered in any degree, is only done at the behest of the Supreme, who has descended into the material body in order to work out His continually progressing unfoldment. Talent is a filtering through the distorting mask of ego of a portion of the power and potency of the Divine, so that the artist is aware of being possessed by something greater and finer than himself. He feels a sense of holiness in relation to this talent, as if he, himself, were a vessel and the talent a distillation that must be dispensed with care. He understands that his greatest work is done when he gets himself out of the way and lets a power within him take over completely, do with him as it wishes. Thus he lets God through, and there is wrought through his hands a work of such power and scope that everyone who views it or uses it is touched with a bit of its magic.

Finding the right work is not so much a search as it is a following. Let not the symbolism of the guiding star escape you. Even as the wise men of long ago followed its rays across the sands of Israel, so each of us when he turns over his affairs to the Divine is guided across the sands of life to spiritual maturity. It matters not the paths we take, the work we do, the results we achieve. All these are in the hands of the Divine, and we may rest assured that the tasks given us are those best suited to our spiritual elevation and progress. There is implacable justice in life but it does not operate on the plane of matter and only the most negligible of its results are to be found there. All things originate in and return to spirit, and matter is only a spinning out on one of many planes of a particular aspect of spiritual meaning. Everything we see, hear, touch is incomplete, a partial truth only, a bare hint of something greater, highly changed, intensely significant.

MAKING HARD JOBS EASY

The materialist, by the nature of his limited perception, eventually meets frustration and failure. He does not see things as they truly are nor is he aware of their real potential. He attempts to move things on the material plane of life, as if they were chess pieces and he a player; and when his most brilliant moves do not achieve their calculated ends he is confused, stricken with fear and impotence.

There is a spiritual resolution to all tasks, and we find the work to fulfill our natures when we seek expression of the indwelling God. We do this not by passing tasks that have no apparent significance, but by turning our strength and energies to everything that comes our way. Nothing is insignificant in the eyes of the Divine. All things have an equal universal importance, are irreplaceable in the scheme. The tiniest event, one that occupies no more time than a twinkling of an eye, no more space than a square inch, can be the hinge upon which an entire eon swings. Never shirk the opportunity to serve, never withdraw from expressing your abilities. Do whatever comes your way, do it as well as you can, and you will find yourself being led into ever-greater realms of expression, ever-greater areas of performance.

The engineer surveyed the magnificent bridge that joined two peninsulas, that thrust its delicate arch into the air over a huge inland sea.

"What is the secret of building such a thing?" he was asked.

He thought a while, then answered, "There are two. First, learning that one and one are two. Second, wondering what two and two are."

The greatest, most vast, most moving of human achievements are made simple through the faithful following of the secret of the engineer. Each of God's laws is simple enough in itself, and each leads us inexorably to the next, and the next, so that in the end we have accumulated both tools and vision to perform acts so far superior to our human clay that we can only be positive that they emanate from God.

> Take hard jobs in hand
> While they are easy
> And great affairs too
> While they are small.
> The troubles of the world
> Cannot be solved except
> Before they grow too hard.
> —Lao Tzu

THE TOURNAMENT

Life, it sometimes appears, is a tournament in which each of us is a gladiator, and we measure our success by how many battles we have won. On the surface it surely seems that all that is going on is winning and losing and that to assure our complete happiness all we need is an effective method of winning. We often see that there are winners who are unhappy, but we assure ourselves that if such fortune comes our way it will find us more appreciative. The truth is that winning and losing have little to do with human felicity. Combat is built into nature, into the struggle for life, into every being extant. Each area of human conflict has those more fit to win than others, but that fitness does not automatically mean awareness, spiritual consciousness. Conflict is not for the purpose of giving spoils to the victor, but to refine and temper each human soul through exposure to effort and pain. Through each of us the Supreme is effecting his emergence, and His purpose in every arena of conflict is to make the soul aware of its unity with Him. The lessons we have to learn often are much concerned with winning and losing, for the ego aspires always to be victor and can conceive of no other battle than that waged on the material plane. It is the subjugation of the ego to its greater Self that is coming to pass in life, a kind of spiritual transformation wherein the individual abandons selfishness and takes up a new existence in the Divine. To that end victory and defeat are twin spurs, the one nourishing the ego, the other tearing it down. Adrift in this constant flux the ego eventually turns away from self-satisfaction and seeks a more stable refuge. Then it finds God.

Nevertheless in the contest itself, in the effort and courage and steadfastness required, are learned those spiritual qualities that expand the individual nature beyond its limited awareness. A man is molded of untempered metal the quality of which never emerges until he has been subjected to fire. All that the human soul is capable of is disclosed finally only through the stresses and strains imposed upon it in the crucible of conflict. We approximate most nearly to the nature of life and the mandates of the Divine when we throw ourselves headlong into every area of activity as if it were an arena and we fighting for our lives. In this manner the forces that lie behind our nature are allowed unimpeded progress through our being, and we are driven to perform feats that normally we would be incapable of. To enter into things without reservation, without giving or asking quarter, bravely, with full energy, is to call down from heaven an increased power that leads to great performance. Divine energy is dynamic, full of fight and fire and movement. By getting negative blocks out of the way and allowing that energy to course freely through our nature, we achieve, in a manner, its irresistible force.

Courage is the key to a complete giving of one's self to one's activities. Subjection of self to the thing to be done is the secret of heightened performance. This abandonment of self is made possible through an overcoming of petty fears and anxieties and apprehensions, through a complete surrender of vanity and conceit. There then enters into the individual nature a fierce boldness, an almost unearthly bravery that maintains its fire against all odds and against which no opposition can prevail.

ACHIEVING PEAK PERFORMANCE

People want to know the key to winning, as if the tournament of life hides a secret which, if known and understood, would allow its possessor constant victory. The head of every team strives to learn this secret, whether in the arts or sciences, business or sports, civilian or military, and he lends most of his waking hours to a perusal of that particular brand of psychology that he fancies best suited to inspire his team to peak performance each time it takes the field. Largely, this psychology has taken the form of the "created obstacle." Something lies in the way to the goal; it must be overcome, annihilated, disintegrated. It is a fearsome thing, wily, vicious, untrustworthy, a predatory enemy. Only the greatest effort of the team will guarantee survival. Each has to give all, every last ounce of energy, every last particle of skill; he has to throw himself into battle, kill or be killed. Such a keying up of emotional pitch into a frenzy of effort raises the standard of team performance, all right. It produces in the group a kind of unthinking hysteria wherein reaction to outer stimuli is reduced and the individual is completely involved in his own feelings, bent only on a single aim, to destroy, to win. No doubt this is the calculated effect which Adolf Hitler sought to bring about in the

German people and in which he often was successful. But in the end such motivation defeats itself through emotional surfeit. The team becomes listless, uninspired, dulled to all emotional stimuli through having been exposed too much and too long.

The way to achieve peak performance is through girding one's mental and physical powers to meet the oncoming test, all right, but such peak performance is consistently possible only to one who manages to get outside himself, to rid himself of selfish concerns and narrow boundaries so that he can expand all his powers within the scope of an unfettered imagination and an unencumbered drive. Some part of a man who performs his best must remain detached, so that he can see himself as he would view another, so that he can view his problems and tasks and efforts and victories and defeats as the bumbling but heart-warming efforts of an energetic child. In this manner, through keeping one spiritual leg in infinity while the other copes specifically with the problems and trials of an intensely finite life, a man achieves that equal-souled quality that allows the Divine to enter into his affairs and manifest His presence through a perfect working and a supreme poise. So it is said that one always can recognize a champion, that there is in his bearing a subtle quality of confidence that marks him as an emergent victor. It is the Divine shining through the mask of the individual; it is the Divine's perfect working and sure power that exudes through ego with an equal-souled quality to gain and loss, victory and defeat.

BEATING FEAR AND COMPLACENCY

Two things shut out this power in the end: one is vanity; the other is fear. Vanity is a swelling of the ego to the point where the power is cut off from manifesting above that level. Fear shrivels and immobilizes the power, tightens and restricts it, reduces its flow to a dribble. In all contests the crown rests precariously on the head of the complacent champion, even more precariously on the head of the fear-ridden one. The task of a leader is, first, to rid his team of fear; second, to instill a sense of humility, an instinctive and ever-present recognition that each task encountered requires all-out effort. This is the molding task of the coach, the manager, the general, the president, but it is equally important that each of us be his own taskmaster and banish fear and complacency from his life.

They seem opposite poles, these two, fear and complacency; yet they are merely different profiles of the same face. Complacency is the inflated ego; fear is the deflated ego; and both fathead and coward may be excised from your life by the simple expedient of abandoning self and taking up existence in the Divine. The enlightened man enters into the fray with complete assurance that he will perform his best, that the thing God has become through him will reach its full maturity in the heat of competition. He seeks to prove nothing by victory, he seeks to avoid nothing in defeat. He is equal-souled to both, as spiritually willing to accept one as the other, realizing full well that each is a lesson to be learned along life's way. And just because he does not fear defeat, just because he does not need victory, he does his best and his best is usually sufficient. His path is marked with winning, and even those defeats observed by the outer world are not defeats to him, for how can there be defeat to one who has allied himself with God and to whom each event marks the inexorable progress of the Divine toward His goal?

Jack was a fighter; he made his living with his fists. As a professional boxer, he met opponents seven or eight times each year. For this he was paid well, being proficient at his trade. He had embarked upon this career when he was well into his twenties, which is late for a boxer, and he never had bothered to pick up many of the refinements of his craft. Nevertheless he was very successful. He was asked why. "Fighting," he said, "is all heart. You don't have to learn tricks to do it. What's inside is all that counts."

What's inside is all that counts! If ever life were summed up in one sentence, Jack managed it. Whatever we set out to do, whatever tasks we undertake, whatever goals we aspire to, we need not search the world for the tools or the money or the help. We need only strengthen ourselves inwardly, deep inside, where God lives. What's in there is all that counts.

There is a way to make big jobs easy, to make all enter-prises, however vast, seem child's play. There is a power which we can hitch on to that cannot fail to carry us to victory. There is a dynamic force in nature which we can direct through us by a simple switch of consciousness, so that we are transformed from ordinary men into giants on the earth. The universe itself, all its stars and galaxies and infinite space and time, are part and parcel of this power. By unloosing it through ourselves we attain to a degree of its universality, its omnipotence. "Narrow is the gate and strait is the way," said Jesus; but it is available to each of us. We need only knock and the door will open; we need only ask and en-lightenment will be ours. The nature of being is such that by allying ourselves with the source of all being we tend to become like that source. By inwardly seeking union with God we find our lives reflecting that inner union.

THE POWERFUL WEAKLING

Ernest was an early failure. He undertook the operation of a small business when he was in his late twenties, and the business plunged him into bankruptcy. There had been a need for the business, it had been adequately financed, Ernest himself was a highly intelligent, industrious young man. No one could understand it, least of all Ernest. He suffered a nervous breakdown, entered a sanitarium. He was plunged into the depths of despondency.

"I guess I'm just a coward," he said. "That's probably why the business failed. Everything seemed so important that I just couldn't bring myself to make decisions, and nothing ever got done. I would come to my desk in the morning, after a sleepless night mulling over problems, but the minute somebody asked me what to do, I just couldn't make up my mind. What's the matter with me? Am I that much of a weakling?"

"Yes," he was told.

He hadn't expected that answer, and he looked up sharply. "Oh? Well, what's to be done about it?"

"Nothing. Just recognize it, that's all. Then you'll know you need help."

"What kind of help?"

"The best."

"How do I get it?"

"Just by asking."

"Asking who?"

"God."

Ernest thought that over for some time, then he said he didn't see what God could do about it. He could understand God being displeased and marking down in His book some demerits against the day that Ernest sought entrance through the Pearly Gates, but he just didn't see what God could do about Ernest being a coward.

"Nobody said you were a coward," he was told.

"You did, just a moment ago."

"I said you were a weakling."

"What's the difference?"

"A great deal. A coward has turned his back on his divinity. A weakling has just appealed to it."

"I don't think I understand."

"A coward is all wrapped up in his own personal abilities and faults. He cannot look outside his little world because he cannot see the forest for the trees. Conversely, the man who has admitted to himself, as all men finally must admit to themselves, that alone and without support he is a weakling adrift among vast forces in unimaginable space, by that very admission has resigned allegiance to his ego and is actively searching for something permanent and powerful to adhere to. This is the situation you find yourself in today. You could not have arrived at this crucial point in your spiritual development without first having been forced to the admission that you, by yourself, are a weakling."

"What do I do now?"

"Ask help from God. Seek Him in everything you do, in everyone you meet. Dedicate every moment of your life to union with Him. You will find strength and peace you never thought possible."

Ernest followed this advice faithfully, not so much because of intellectual conviction but because his sense of being had separated from the ego and inevitably was gravitating toward the Divine. In a few months he was discharged from the sanitarium. Before the year was out he had embarked once again on a business enterprise. His whole attitude seemed to have changed. He was decisive, brisk, seemed never to hurry, got everything done. He had put on a few pounds, appeared stronger, more vibrant.

"I've got a secret," he confided to a friend. "I do nothing by myself. I just hitch a ride on inner power."

> Our doubts are traitors
> And make us lose the good we oft would win
> By fearing to attempt
>
> —William Shakespeare

FALSE YARDSTICK

Money to most of us is the yardstick of success. We use it to measure ourselves against others. Without it we feel insecure, unworthy, a failure. Yet money itself is only a symptom of service and not a completely accurate one either, since in a vested sense it represents physical things, lands, buildings, minerals, etc., and therefore can be passed on from generation to generation, so that the holder of it today, at his own disposition, may not render any service to society whatever. The things he possesses render service, of course, and he is entitled to a fair return on their use. Any other system of ownership is bound to revert to an autocratic statehood, and therefore all freedom-loving men prefer an economic system based on private ownership of the instruments of production, for regardless of injustices in such a system, freedom remains, and a man's services to the group are fairly rewarded and he maintains a voice in the conduct of the affairs of society.

The mark of a man cannot be measured in terms of money. Insofar as the individual's aim in life is to establish an inward rapport with the Divine, money is only incidental to his goal and never synonymous with it. The seeker after enlightenment can be found in all economic walks of life. He may live in a rude hut on the wind-swept slopes of the Himalayas, in a comfortable suburban home on a midwestern university campus, in the luxurious splendor of a far-eastern palace, it matters not. If his aim is true and his focus is on the inner world of consciousness, enlightenment will be his, illumination will come, he will be united with the indwelling God. Jesus said that it is as difficult for a rich man to enter the Kingdom of Heaven as for a camel to go through the eye of a needle. He also cautioned, "Seek ye first the Kingdom of Heaven, and all things will be added unto you." It is focus on material things, obsession with possessions, habits of acquisitiveness that keep a man's consciousness limited to created things and prevent him from seeing the truth behind them. To such a man illumination is difficult, but many rich men have turned away from preoccupation with possession and found enlightenment. Similarly, the man who expands his consciousness so that his being is pervaded by universal mind becomes part and parcel of the will and power of the Divine, banishes forever from his life all lack and limitation. His cup overflows, he knows an unlimited abundance that springs out of the infinite creativeness of the Supreme. To see behind all the forms of nature the sure and painstaking hand of the Divine, to perceive the hidden purpose and magical potential of all things by their inherent relationship to God, this is the way to true wealth.

THE SECRET OF ABUNDANCE

There is a secret of abundance that provides one the spiritual equivalent of having a money tree in his own back yard. This secret occasionally manifests in men of small spiritual enlightenment, but it never resides permanently in any except the truly illumined. It is not a thing that readily lends itself to being put into words, for it is an abstraction, a method of perception that goes far beyond normal vision. Who enjoys this thing is able to look upon objects and events and receive a hint of their future use, their coming significance, so that he, with a kind of infallible action, is able to profit from what they become. Such a man might look at some real estate, debate with himself, run down endless bits of information, analyze all, wind up buying the land. On the surface it appears that his own background, the things he learned, the reasoning he applied to his information were the basis of his action, but actually some inner sense, some third eye is what prompted him. Subconsciously he perceived the buildings that one day would rise on the land, and thus he was led to make the purchase through an infallible sense of the future. All economic enterprisers, all successful businessmen, all speculators are the same. Possessing an inner sense that perceives the potential of things, they instinctively place themselves in position to profit from coming events. This is the money secret; not only the money secret, but the secret of success and achievement. "There is a tide in the affairs of men, which, taken at the flood, leads on to fortune," wrote Shakespeare, and from Ecclesiastes, "To everything there is a season, and a time to every purpose under heaven." The enlightened man unconsciously perceives coming events, attunes himself to them, prepares himself, then performs in the midst of them as if he were directing them, forming them. From inner attunement to the purposes of the Divine, he appears to mold the world.

Anything that is worth doing is worth doing well, and that thing upon which all others hinge is the discovery of our true nature through spiritual enlightenment. One does not set about seeking this enlightenment casually, deciding perhaps to devote an hour a day to study or research or meditation. Devoting all one's working hours to it, perhaps by joining the clergy or becoming a teacher of philosophy, still is not enough. If one truly and without reservation seeks spiritual illumination he must concentrate his entire life, all that he is and hopes to be, to this aspiration. Only in this manner will enlightenment come; only in this way is illumination possible. Work is the road, consecration and dedication are the vehicles; these taken and used, all else will follow.

> The heights by great men reached and kept
> Were not attained by sudden flight
> But they, while their companions slept,
> Were toiling upward in the night.
> —Henry Wadsworth Longfellow

THE INVISIBLE STOREHOUSE

Through spiritual identification with the Supreme comes automatic perception of the infinite abundance of nature. All created things are the handiwork of God and but a bare indication of His manifold creativeness. All things are possible; the moment their possibility is recognized, they become probable. There is a storehouse in the invisible mind of the Divine whence all things proceed and in which all things exist in infinite numbers and varieties, pending appearance in the material world. Form is only a shaping out of matter of an idea called forth from universal mind, and each thing in our lives, each event, circumstance, and object, comes to us from out of the limbo of universal mentality, called to our side by the force of our mental and emotional projection. We literally are surrounded by and living in the midst of our ideas, half-formed, preconceived, sometimes born out of emotional conflicts, but ideas nonetheless, given form by our magical tie with universal mind.

Once we perceive the immense and staggering creativeness of the Divine, we no longer live in fear of lack, apprehensive of limitation, anxious about restriction. We see that these negations do not exist except in the limited world of the ego, and because we have abandoned ego and taken on universality in thought and perception, the Divine returns our mental world to us in material life and we live in the midst of bountiful abundance. The mental perception that comes to the enlightened man usually compels him to devote his life to other purposes than the pursuit of money, though it is sometimes true that he cannot avoid becoming wealthy while engaged in his chosen work. Usually, however, he is content to take from God's abundance only that which is required for his personal living and the obligations of his position, all the while devoting himself to serving the purposes of the Divine. He would be as happy without a penny as with untold wealth, for neither truly matters. He sees money only as a man-made symbol of God's bounty, and he does not need its assurance to believe in that bounty.

It often is true that men with a great sense of abundance, who truly know peace of mind and a stable security, possess little money, indeed, have small use for it. Some men pursue their chosen work as if they constantly are listening to divine directions. They are seekers after silences, longers for solitude, yearners for union with that which has sprung them into existence. Money they barely recognize; it passes through their hands but never touches them. All things come to them and depart from them in accord with a universal flow, a kind of cosmic flux, which they constantly seek to join and never to oppose. Such is their inherent perception of the basic scheme of things that they see the infinite abundance that surrounds them in spiritual reality, and they could not possibly conceive of living in the midst of it in a state of lack. Deep in the recesses of their souls resound the words of the Master, "Ask, and it shall be given you; seek, and ye shall find; knock, and it shall be opened unto you."

TRUE WEALTH

The illumined man can make money. In fact, he cannot keep from making money. It is only by adherence to his primary purpose, union with God, that he averts going along entirely with the economic potential of things. Now that he has the secret of making money in hand, money itself no longer holds meaning for him, and he would consider it ridiculous to devote his energies to amassing it. And because he is freed from enslavement to money, he becomes a magnetic pole for it; it comes to him from all sources, from all his contacts. Just because he holds little regard for it, it holds high regard for him.

Alas for the egoist who loses his money. He is shattered, desolate. Since he has no spiritual resource to sustain him, he is but a bubble on the frothy sea of life, tossed this way and that by whatever current seizes him. The only security he knows is that symbolized by his possession, and if perchance those are stripped away, he loses all. Such a man often takes his own life in economic emergency or embarks upon other measures of self-destruction such as alcohol or drug addiction. But once the light of spiritual illumination has penetrated the ego, one cannot possibly be anxious or fearful about money. He perceives that true wealth lies in his relationship with the Divine; in that relationship is an abundance that money cannot buy.

> Loss of wealth is loss of dirt
> As sages in all times assert;
> The happy man's without a shirt.
> —John Heywood

MAGIC ELEMENT

We see the truth of things only when we are able to look upon them in a detached manner, without coloring them by our emotions and without projecting ourselves into them. Spiritual detachment is not possible to one who lives in the ego. Such a man constantly seeks to compare himself, to prove himself, and projects into all things his own insecurity, constantly attempts to wrest victory from a world peopled by enemies. He cannot see the purpose of things because he transfers his ego to each, he analyzes all in terms of pleasure and pain, without regard to their inherent nature. Only by the greatest coincidence is he able to assemble things into a sequence that produces the result he desires, for since he does not correctly evaluate the parts, it is sheer accident if he correctly appraises the whole. Seeking money and possessions, he is inevitably frustrated; and if by some chance he does succeed in achieving his end, the eventual loss of everything is certain. One cannot hold onto that which he does not understand, for only in understanding is there control.

Spiritual detachment allows one to see things in terms of the one great power which is working out its ends here on earth, rather than in terms of personal desire. Spiritual detachment is an alliance with the Divine in which the individual subjugates self and allows his consciousness to move upward and outward in a great encompassing movement that vastly increases his knowledge and perception. It is good to work hard, to become absorbed in whatever we do, to devote ourselves to our interests with heart and soul and mind, but a part of us, somewhere deep inside, must always remain aloof from the most furious movement, the greatest pleasure, the most excruciating pain, always remaining the observer, the chronicler, the judger, never involved, never hurt, never touched. Only in this manner is it possible for the individual to retain within himself that core of truth that descends directly from the Supreme, a magic element which, when activated, reveals directly the possibilities inherent in all things. This, above all, is a quality common to all successful men, that they see things as they truly are, that they see things as they inevitably must be, that both qualities are apparent because of their attunement with God.

THE TRUTH ABOUT MONEY

In the year book of his graduating class, Stephen was prophesied as "Grant High School's first millionaire," and indeed, he made no secret of his ambition in this regard. He was a handsome young man, dark, lithe, with a quick warmth and a barely contained energy. Grant High was situated in the middle of the working district, and Stephen often told his classmates, "Working is for squares. You want to be a big man, you got to do big things. Think big, act big, deal in figures, ways and means, and always think about money. How *you* come out, old number one, that's what's important."

Stephen took his first job in a print shop. In a few weeks he saw the possibility of a local advertising paper. He organized it, then another, afterwards another. When he was twenty-four years old, he bought the print shop and the three papers he had organized. A year later, all failed. But he was undaunted. Without a moment to bemoan his fate, he launched himself in another business. This time he was attracted to radio, went around to new stations and sold them on the idea of letting him handle their advertising sales. In this manner he came to represent six and in a few years had achieved a nice income. He decided to expand. Radio stations, he felt, were all right, but there were plenty other advertising media to represent. He expanded from coast to coast, taking on dozens of clients. In seven years he was bankrupt.

By this time he was considerably older and this setback had a deeper effect on him. He sought advice.

"What's stopping me?" he asked. "I seem to have every-thing—health, energy, intelligence, desire—but something is holding me back. Whenever I get to the point where I'm just about ready to make it, everything folds up. I can't understand what's wrong."

"What is it you want?" he was asked.

"Money, what else?"

"Why?"

He shrugged. "To be a big man, I guess. You know, right clothes, right car, belonging to the right group, things like that."

"That's all money means to you?"

"Power, maybe. That's about it."

"Stephen," he was told, "the reason you have failed in business is that you have blinded yourself to the possibilities inherent in money. Since you seek it only for personal pleasure, you fail to see that it truly represents the labor of others. When you have money, you are trustee of their energies, time, and effort. If you fritter these away on per-sonal pleasure it is small wonder that your businesses fail. Only by directing money at the production of goods and services, only by constantly envisioning it as representative of effort can you truly gain a perception of its divine quality. Money is work, and work is love made visible."

Stephen thought about that. "To tell you the truth," he said finally, "I've often felt guilty about constantly seeking money. I guess I've really felt it was selfish. But somehow money has come to represent security."

"Then take your eyes off it altogether. If you can find within yourself sufficient humility to surrender your life and work to God, you will find such security as you never dreamed."

"I'll try anything," he said, "but I don't think I quite un-derstand this surrender bit. What do I do?"

"Give over the running of your life to God. Pray for guidance. Listen to your inner voice. Follow it. Above all, understand you are serving something greater than yourself."

Stephen followed this advice well. He is not a rich man today only because he literally gives money away. His business is highly successful.

"Funny thing," he says. "Now that I no longer want money it seems to shower on me. I can hardly manage to keep it moving, it comes so fast."

Bertrand Russell wrote, "It is preoccupation with possession, more than anything else, that prevents men from living freely and nobly," and, indeed that man who devotes his life to grubbing for money without ever lifting his eyes to the stars, without ever allowing God into his heart so that the grandeur of the universe and the vastness of its concept can transform his consciousness, has not truly lived, only existed. Life is most exciting when we take on big tasks, when we keep striving at goals that make us grow, when we find within ourselves resources that carry us undaunted through all setbacks, through all reverses. This is the path by which the soul constantly increases in stature.

> To endure to greater than to dare;
> To tire out hostile fortune;
> To be daunted by no difficulty;
> To keep heart when all have lost it;
> To go through intrigue spotless;
> To forego even ambition when the end is gained—
> Who can say this is not greatness?
> —William Makepeace Thackeray

◇◇

EIGHTH MEDITATION

There is a power within me which I can use to overcome all obstacles, solve all problems, a power that
flows from the farthest reaches of the universe, out of
the infinite, omnipotent mind of God. I give over my
work, its progress and path, to Him. Only He knows the
real purpose and actual nature of the things I do and
the goals I aspire to. Only He can chart a perfect course
to the destined shore. No longer do I allow my little
self to direct my life and work, for in such egoistic
blindness there is only suffering. It is knowledge I seek,
and joy, and I find them through serving the Divine.
No matter the negations I encounter, I see beyond
them, perceive their other face. All serve a purpose,
each is a step in spiritual development, each may be
overcome by an inner perception that springs abundance
out of lack, expansion out of limitation, success out of
failure, victory out of defeat. I know that God is all
things at all times; therefore I affirm the positive. By
divine alchemy I call forth good from evil, not because
I will it, but because I perceive it, because I know that
God reveals to the individual soul that which his consciousness is able to perceive. My consciousness surpasses the limitations of ego, soars out to encompass all
beings, all life. I affirm my knowledge of God's manifold
expression, and I accept only good as befits my spiritual
stature. Success is mine, victory, progress, abundance,
and joy.

◇◇

9 CREATIVENESS

Creative torrents seek out the mind
Of the man who lives in God's grace
Surge through his being, leaving a kind
Of thought-world laid down in space

GIFT OF GOD

The only true experience is the act of creation. All usual action and thought are not truly action or thought at all, but only reaction to the stimuli of nature. People go through their lives as sleepwalkers, responding to things about them as automatons, never opening their beings to the imagery and force of the Divine so that new things can be called into existence through their own consciousness. The process of creation involves juxtaposition of finite mind with universal mind, so that the former pours into the latter as a lake might pour into a river. Proper relationship between universal being and finite being makes the individual a vehicle for the expression of the Divine. People sometimes are born this way, grow into renown as possessors of great talent—writers, painters, sculptors, musicians. Others, by dint of enlightenment, achieve this spiritual elevation and reveal to aspiring humanity some new facet of the Divine's nature. This creativity all of us can learn; through learning it we fulfill ourselves and our spiritual growth is made complete.

The movement of the Divine is restless, full of surging

force and barely contained energy. Always He seeks outlet, through whatever instrument available, to express some aspect of His infinite nature. For this purpose each of us is called into being, not to satisfy our sensual natures through pleasure, not to satisfy our egos through possession and victory, but to express in the unfolding drama of humanity that greater idea, that larger concept of the meaning and depth of life. To that end we best fulfill ourselves when we shift the living center of our being from the little self of our transitory nature and seek out the bosom of our originator; then by a sort of fusion with Him we express Him on the planes of matter and movement.

HITCHED TO A STAR

We are quiet when the Divine uses us for His purposes. Inwardly we are serene for we have subjugated our sensual nature to His spiritual prompting. Our actions and ideas proceed solely out of an inner attunement to the nature and being of God, and we are without turmoil, without strain and strife. Yet how different is our outer aspect! That which has been admitted into our consciousness is lightning and thunder, energy and force, builder and destroyer. It seizes us in its torrent, kneads and molds us into useful form, works us mercilessly. The man entrapped in divine current is a man possessed. He can no more stop himself from performance than the onrushing river can stop itself short of the sea. The Divine is using him to effect on the plane of matter a manifestation of truth, and use him He will, to the very end, until his body and brain and ego-mask are all used up and there remains of him nothing but God.

It takes courage to open yourself to the forces of nature, to allow the gigantic tides of universal mind to roll and echo through your being. All of life is changed by the spiritual decision to allow God to rule your consciousness. Truly, then, you have hitched your wagon to a star, a shooting star, a speeding comet that by its very momentum will plunge you ever deeper into life so that vistas of pain and pleasure, of subtle meaning, panoramas of infinite design and feeling will open before you, and you will become alive, truly alive, where before you barely existed. It is this faculty of baring their souls, of fully exposing themselves to the spiritual force of God that brings to some individuals the talent for creativeness. We know them and recognize them wherever they are. Their presence is an explosion of production, and what they produce is useful, beautiful, the Divine expressed and made coherent.

All people are born with receptivity to God, from whatever walks of life, of whatever intelligence and education. But this receptivity becomes stultified by over-reliance on material forms, by satisfaction with the world of created things, blindness to see beyond it. We all have the talent of God, intrinsically. It will express itself through our natures, in the particular form that our nature gives it, if only we open the doors of our being without reserve and allow the power to flow through. Whatever has been done before we too can do, and even greater things, for when we unite with God His mantle is ours and He is without limitation or restriction. We can do anything our consciousness can conceive of and accept. It will be done by the Divine, through us, we need only invite Him.

> Lives of great men all remind us
> We can make our lives sublime
> And departing, leave behind us
> Footprints on the sands of time.
> —Henry Wadsworth Longfellow

CREATION IS GOD-WORK

Creativeness is never a mark of the individual, but of God instead. It is the Divine manifesting through the mask of individual being a particular one of His many aspects. Respect and admiration are accorded those whose talent is great, who create works of beauty and utility that make life more understandable, more comfortable, but it is not they who deserve our admiration for they are instruments only; the one to whom our homage belongs is God. He creates all things from his own substance. Nobody else is creative but He. Strive and strain, sweat and toil as we may we never produce one single thing or thought unless He works through us. All creation is God-work. The entire task of the individual is to get himself out of the way and let the power of the Divine move through him.

To the degree that a man resigns himself to God, God makes him a perfect vessel. The work done through a man molds him, tempers him, gives him whatever qualities of the Divine are inherent in the task ahead. Thus the individual becomes like his work, the artist like his creation. Carl Jung writes, "The work in process becomes the poet's fate and determines his psychic development. It is not Goethe who creates Faust, but Faust which creates Goethe." *Time* magazine reports of Pablo Casals, the cellist, "It is not possible to watch any part of Casals while he is playing—not his face, not his hands, not even his cello. It is only possible to watch the whole of him, and this for the simple reason that the parts apparently have no existence independent of the whole. Indeed, Casals himself, while he is playing, seems to have no existence independent of the music. Watching him, it is quite easy to imagine that if the music should stop, he would disappear."

The entire process of creation is the relationship between finite mind and universal mind, a kind of "plugging in" of individual mind into God-mind. What results is creative, for something dynamic has been done, a power has been unloosed, it must come out, something must be produced. The nature of God-mind is creation, the nature of individual mind is instrumentation. Each man is creative only as much as he becomes an instrument for the works of the Divine. If the ego rules his life, if his consciousness is focused on created things and he lives in reaction to the outer world rather than by impulsion from the inner, he warps away his divine power and shuts off the flow of his natural creativeness.

PSYCHIC POSITION

Arthur wrote a best-selling novel when he was only twenty-four. Critics hailed him as a new discovery, a light that would burn in the literary firmament for many years. He was compared to Conrad, London, Hemingway, Maugham, Melville. He seemed likely to develop into the greatest American novelist of all time. He was treated as a lion in literary circles, feted, dined, made obeisance to. Everyone waited for his next book. They were a long time holding their breath.

Oh, he made lots of starts. He even finished a manuscript or two, but they were rejected by his publisher as they should have been. By the time he was thirty years old, Arthur still had not published another book, in fact had not published so much as a short story. People were beginning to say that he was a "one-book author." He had burned himself out, they said, by writing a good book so young.

Well, Arthur didn't think he was burned out. He knew something was wrong, all right, but he couldn't put his finger on it. He didn't waste any time lamenting it, though. He stayed hard at work, and while he produced nothing worthwhile, he constantly expanded his craftsmanship. Finally, however, discouragement seized him, and he sought advice.

"Sometimes it seems as if I'm back on the beam again," he said. "I'll write a page, even several pages, and the words rush out my finger tips so that I hardly can keep pace with them, and I think that now I've found it again and it will keep on coming. Then, just as suddenly as it came, it leaves, and I sit abandoned in front of the typewriter, each word a labor, each sentence a monstrous effort. Only the page that came easily is there to remind me of what I could do if only I could get myself into the right psychic position."

"How did your first book come, hard or easily?" Arthur was asked.

"Easily. It just flowed out, actually seemed to be the work of someone else."

"It was."

"Whose?"

"God's."

Arthur thought this over and then he said that he could see the point, that there was no doubt in his mind that when he was writing well some greater power had taken over. It interested him that this power might be God. He had thought of it only psychologically, never spiritually.

"What can I do to keep this power with me?" he asked.

"Make a shift in your point of view. Realize that all books are written by one author working through his chosen instruments, that all you have to do in order to insure that He will work through you is subjugate your will to His. Cease struggling, cease trying to form, simply listen. Be still and wait. You will hear Him speak to you. Everything you are to write will flood into your consciousness, impelling you to put it on paper. You will do this without strain, for something else will be using you, doing the work. You will not even be conscious of effort, so great will be the energy that pours through you."

"That's it!" said Arthur. "You describe it perfectly. But will it stay with me?"

"It will stay with you as long as you maintain the proper relationship. Remember that you are not the thinker, the originator, the doer. It is. Simply open yourself to it, listen, allow it to use you. As soon as you take over the reins, attempt in any manner to do the driving, it will leave as suddenly as it came."

Arthur departed with a purpose. During the weeks that followed he worked at achieving the proper spiritual relationship with his Muse. Several times he telephoned to say that he had had it for an hour, even two, but each time he had shut it out by taking over the words and their pattern. One day he called and said, "I've got it," then he called no more for some time. Next spring he published a novel. This book was not the sales success of his first, but it was a greater artistic and critical success. From that time on, he became a regular mill of production, publishing a novel every year, dozens of short stories.

Arthur tells no one of his secret, however. "It's too personal," he explains. "I feel it is something that concerns only me and God, that somehow I might dissipate its psychic force by talking about it."

CALCULATION VERSUS CREATION

Creation by means of personal calculation almost never occurs. Amongst artists only Edgar Allan Poe maintained he could produce or not as he chose, but there is reason to doubt his testimony in this regard. Poe was not wholly himself when much of his work was done, was, in fact, often withdrawn from his surroundings, an almost perfect description of the semi-trance state in which the subconscious mind takes over entirely. He might easily have felt that this particular state was self-induced, but once in it, it is certain that he had no choice other than to create. Most artists report of their most productive states a kind of withdrawal from sensory awareness of their surroundings into a world of pure thought and conception. This living in the midst of primary force, this residence in an area of spiritual movement seems to be the cause of their creative dynamic. Allied with a force above and beyond them, they are led to do as it wishes. It uses them, does their work, so that they, later surveying the result, are inclined to feel that it has been done by another, as indeed it has. It has been done by God.

Any calculated effort to create, any contrived manner of authoring a work shows immediately in the work; it has no freshness or originality in its composition but seems a copy of countless things that have been done before. Contrivance and calculation simply will not produce art or invention, for both are ego efforts and universal mind does not respond to ego but flows through the individual only when the ego is out of the way. Calculation is a blockage, actually damming off the power that makes invention possible. The entire effort of the artist or of anyone who seeks to create must be to subjugate ego to universal mind, to seek through surrender that state of heightened awareness, of immensely increased perception and understanding in which he is almost completely absorbed in his Creator and thus is expressing his Creator by means of identification. Thus a kind of spontaneous and involuntary production occurs, an automatic functioning which invariably produces works far above the normal powers of the individual, for they proceed out of the mind of God.

THE UNTRAVELED ROAD

People sometimes argue that complete self-surrender borders on lunacy, that absolute giving up of control by conscious mind and resignation to the impulses of the subconscious might easily lead to disastrous conduct on the part of the individual rather than have any noticeable effect on his creative output. But the very opposite is true. When the ego, through notions of inadequacy, through being encysted in emotions such as hate, jealousy, envy, bitterness, retires inward into the subconscious and grows there like a cancer, it squeezes God out altogether. Control goes, rationality goes, and the individual is swallowed in the maw of impersonality. So insanity comes, so feeble-mindedness. What has occurred is the complete involution of the ego, not its surrender. Far from surrendering, it fights twice as hard, grows twice its size, inside, where it cannot be seen. It cuts off completely its ties with God, destroys all power of the individual, leaves him impotent and bereaved of his divinity.

Surrender takes courage. Subjugation of the self to the Divine is not easy. It represents, to most of us, an awesome departure into the unknown. Inadvertently we cling to the stuff of the ego, fearful to let go. It requires faith and strength to cut off the ties of our old securities, even though we know them to be inadequate. We have to be bold and determined to walk alone into the vague and vast realms of the spirit, but alone we must go, for what we seek there involves only ourselves and God. If we live totally in response to mandates of the past, to digested and regurgitated opinion, to mores and taboos and standards that are foisted upon us by others, then we do not truly live but are mere ciphers, statistics; our reactions are totally predictable and we are not divine at all but merely a kind of vulnerable machine. Only when we throw off the ego and begin to create do we begin to fulfill our divinity and individuality. The path is open to all with courage and daring and aspiration. It is not well marked, not even well traveled, but none has set his foot upon it and ever been lost from God.

ACTION VERSUS MOVEMENT

All psychic life, all contemplation, all spiritual aspiration, far from being conditions of quietude, are conditions of intense activity. Ernest Hemingway is quoted as saying that one must never confuse movement with action, for movement is simply physical transfer through space, while action is the cause of a result. All of us seek action in whatever we do, but all too often we settle for running around, doing this and that, hustling, bustling, never getting anything done. True cause stems from spiritual sources, from a psychic force pent up in the bosom of the individual that impels him to accomplish his aim. This, no doubt, is the reason that Hemingway states that he will not discuss any work in progress. No doubt he has experienced the sad fact that discussion of the work dissipates the psychic energy that is impelling its creation.

The artist cloisters himself with his Muse. No one is involved but these two. The Divine bursts through the instrument of individuality with a manifestation of the meaning of life. Set down on paper, on canvas, in stone, something of the grandeur, significance, and drama of the emerging God is caught by the artist, transferred to his audience. This is a work of art.

Each of us is an artist whether or not he paints, sculpts, writes. Each of us can accomplish creative ends in life when he learns to cloister himself with the Divine and listen. If we can only achieve a spiritual condition of complete self-surrender, we have taken the largest step possible toward allowing the power and purpose of God to flow creatively through us. Such self-surrender is the *sine que non* of all creative effort, and exceedingly difficult to achieve. Life is so vital in all of us. The senses constantly beat at the window panes of our attention. Things are pleasurable, painful, desirable, repugnant, and most of the time we are making decisions solely in response to sensation. When we attempt to shut out the material world so that we may gain an insight into spiritual things, we find a thousand distractions. We may make a little immersion, a slight surrender, then something, a little thing perhaps, a slight noise, an unfamiliar odor, recalls us immediately, and we have gained nothing, only a sense of futility, and the Divine whom we seek is farther away than ever.

CONCENTRATION

Concentration is the mental tool we can use to implement our self-surrender. It is an axiomatic spiritual truth that whatever we set our mind on tends to enter into the deeper realms of our consciousness and from there, by divine impetus, gradually to make its appearance in the physical world. If we undertake to do things by willing them to happen or in any manner girding the forces of our individual ego, we then oppose ourselves to self-surrender and make it impossible for the full force of the Supreme to work through our nature. Only when we concentrate our entire purpose and total will on the Divine is it possible for us to know the full meaning of universal being. Only when all things are shut out of consciousness but the longing of the heart to know its Maker can the sweetness of self-surrender encompass one with its warmth and energy. We reach deeper, ever deeper, through layer after layer of consciousness, through planes of perception and meaning, all the time expanding the nature of our awareness, until at last that fathomless point is reached where we fuse our being with the being of the Divine. All that we are, have been, can ever hope to be is focused on this point. We have entered into a state of such concentration, such absorption, that to the outer world we appear to be in a trance. We can be spoken to and not hear, we can be touched and not feel. In some deeply mysterious way, we have withdrawn from the body while still remaining in the body, could, if we desired to, perceive ourselves as we would perceive another. We are detached from all sensation, are involved in and have become one with the thoughts and images that cross our mind. We dwell for the moment in a world of pure spirit, of psychic forces and meanings, and here we would as soon dwell forever, such is its bliss, its joy, its freedom and serenity.

Such is the magic state of divine fusion entered into by the individual when he is used as an instrument of creativeness by the Supreme; such is the cleansing and purifying action used by the Divine to properly temper and adjust His agents of manifestation. Every artist knows this state as the one in which his work flows effortlessly. Every thinker, creator, builder has experienced it as a field of increased vision, of magnified awareness. It is not something that just happens to people because of some peculiar functioning of their glands or because of some strange environmental condition. It is the soul's response to its Creator, its longing for return to a state of unity, of primary oneness; it is a report of the joys and the significance of that state, and it invariably manifests through one whose mental and spiritual powers have been consciously or subconsciously turned over to something spiritually greater than himself.

> Around the man who seeks a noble end
> Not angels but divinities attend.
> —Ralph Waldo Emerson

PATIENCE

Of all the virtues most difficult to apprehend by one who seeks divine union and creativeness through that union, patience stands alone. She often seems to desert us completely, leaving us ravaged by restlessness and dissatisfaction that gnaw at our very souls. Once having tasted of the union that now is the hourly quest of everything we are and do, we cannot tolerate the unspeakable impotence and solitude that we experience without it. We want it with us every minute, literally demand that it be with us every minute, and the blockage afforded by the exertion of our will isolates us from it, and we are enraged, bitter, desolate that we cannot find that which has become so dear. Creativeness is gone, inner joy and peace have fled, and our impatience keeps them from returning.

Oh, impatience is a common thing amongst those who experience the spiritual act of creation. Nearly all mental and spiritual activity transpires beneath the level of consciousness, and when we are not moved to perform, to act, to plan, to make decisions, we feel that nothing is being done. Something always is being done. The nature of our existence is that we are spiritual beings, and our physical bodies are but the smallest representation of what we really are. Like the iceberg, far more of our self is hidden from view than is exposed to the world. And what transpires in this hidden part of our nature is the real work, the meaningful action upon which all the circumstances and things of our life depend. When we expect everything to happen in the area of

our consciousness, we cannot help but be impatient, for what
is absent from consciousness appears not to exist, and so we
fail to perceive the intense action that is going on in deeper
planes of our nature.

When we are quiet, with the serene quiescence that is
the mark of spiritual perception, it is then that we are most
truly active. When we have thoroughly learned this remarkable lesson, impatience will trouble us no longer.
We may have a flash of insight, even a look into the original
center of things, an idea for some work may strike us full
bloom, and for the moment we are caught up, impelled by a
power beyond us to get at this thing we have seen, to manifest it in the physical world. Then, perhaps when we are
half through or even barely started, the inspiration deserts
us, and we are abandoned on a bleak and lonely vista without
resources, without energy, without the vision to proceed. We
stamp our feet and shake our fists at the heavens, but no
amount of vituperation returns us to our inspired state.
We can only resign ourselves to this state of apparent in-
activity, accept it as evidence that something vital is happening in deeper regions of our being, for one of the laws of our
divided nature is that when the surface is active it is quiet
in the depths, and when the surface is quiet the depths are
active. Knowing this we are able to accept the cycles of work
and rest that are our lot in life, using each for its true and
best purpose, discontent with neither, discovering the inherent joys of each. And eventually we come to realize that
our greatest satisfaction lies in that time of quietness, that
point of rest on the spiritual journey where nothing is apparently being done but wherein we find a spiritual close-
ness, a tie with the Divine that stems directly from our
complete reliance on Him to move us when and as He will.

DIVINE TEMPERING

All great ideas, all strong motivations well up instantane-
ously from the depths, impel the accomplishment of some

work and seem to the onlooker to be perfectly spontaneous. Actually they are the result of lengthy and arduous subconscious thought on the part of the individual. That which he gestates as a whole and complete thing was a long time in conception. It is the result of everything he has ever learned, done, aspired to do, of the particular relationship he has developed with the Divine, of the work that the Divine has laid down for his spiritual maturation. Insight into the nature of things and inspiration as to their development are never the result of the isolated individual thinking out improvements on nature, but rather of the Divine manifesting through the individual His progressive unfolding. Therefore the process of creation depends entirely on the individual's complete surrender of himself to God. Only in this manner can he become a vehicle for the works of the Divine in the world. Any ego-centering makes him an amoeba, the smallest of the small, and nothing works through him, nothing carries him forward; he lives out his life in prison bars of his own making.

Surrender to God, concentrate on His purpose, listen to His instruction, act accordingly: these are the commandments of creation. Who follows them is led inexorably to creating new and exciting works. He will not necessarily do this effortlessly, but he will be impelled by a power greater than himself to overcome all suffering and pain, all obstacles encountered. Nature shows us that new life is born into existence through pain, and we must face the great creative fact that all new ideas, all inspiration are similarly brought forth. The Divine tempers His instruments by subjecting them to stress and strain, and when the metal is proven to His satisfaction He uses the vessel for the performance of His deeds in the world. But if the metal prove faulty, if it is left cringing and defeated in the wake of pain and effort, He casts it aside without concern, for it is only Himself after all, an unfit conception and one He has no further use for.

What we are led to perform, to bring forth when we are

allied with the creative power of the Divine is inevitably beautiful, for it contains a glimpse of Him who supports our being, hints of a magnificence and grandeur we long to know. Spiritual truth underlies all works of art, and it is this truth, even though obscured, even though barely hinted at, that makes them beautiful.

> Beauty is truth, truth beauty,—that is all
> Ye know on earth, and all ye need to know.
> —John Keats

ARTISTIC VISION

Beauty was an elusive ideal for Robert. He was a painter, and he had destroyed far more of his canvases than he had kept. He would sell none. "They're not good enough," he said. "They're junk. I keep them around only to remind me how far I missed."

"Missed what?" he was asked.

"The vision," he said. "The picture that was in my mind."

One of his canvases was a pastoral scene, a country road with eucalyptus trees lining either side, shading the road with their intertwined branches. In the distance a patch of sunlight shone where the road emerged from shadow. Light and shade were exquisite.

"Isn't this an actual scene?" Robert was asked.

He frowned. "An actual scene inspired it," he said. "But is a painter a photographer? If what he sees is worth anything it is in the way he sees it. This is no good because I failed to paint it the way I saw it."

"How did you see it then?"

"Like a cathedral. It seemed like a psalm of God."

There was no mistaking the fact that he had caught something of this feeling in the painting, but a hint only, a kind of subtle emanation.

"I think you manage to convey your feeling. The picture has a spiritual quality."

"To you perhaps, not to me. All I see is a parody of the perfection that filled my mind. When my hand moved with the brushes this was the result, a caricature, a burlesque. It mocks me, fills me with impotence, haunts my dreams."

"Nothing is one-sided, Robert."

"What do you mean by that?"

"Life is a great duality—the physical and the spiritual. The spiritual is the idea, the inherent perfection that lies behind life. The physical is the gradual unfolding of the perfection of spirit. Since it is unfolding, it never quite manages to capture the entire meaning and scope of the entity it attempts to represent. Thus the physical is always a profanation of the spiritual. Your picture to you is a spiritual thing. You sensed, felt, and perceived it in a spiritual manner. But when you brought it forth into the world something of its meaning and scope was lost. This is always the relationship of the spiritual and the physical."

"I cannot reconcile myself to that," Robert said. "The pictures that I see and feel inside me *must* come out. If I cannot give them form they are a torment and will not let me rest."

"It is you who give yourself no rest because you refuse to accept God's law of living. Do you think you know more than He? Is He not able to express as He wishes the meaning and significance of life? It is a great conceit to think that such interpretation rests on your shoulders. Let it go. Be content to express as you can the truth of your inner vision."

"That is very difficult to do," said Robert. "Beauty is an exacting mistress. She is not content to rest within, but must come out. I don't believe I can contain her."

"Don't try to. Let her come out as she will. Just don't strain. Put yourself in the hands of God, of your Muse, of Beauty. Let yourself be used, don't try to use that which possesses you."

"But what of my work? How can I tolerate my work?"

"There are truth and beauty in it. Each will grow as you yourself grow, but the work of any moment will never approach the spiritual vision of that moment. Be content to know that when you paint you leave something of truth and beauty on the canvas. That is enough for any man."

Robert returned to his work with tongue in cheek. He thought that if he failed to be critical of his own work he couldn't possibly improve. In the months that followed he turned out an increasing number of excellent canvases, several of which approached greatness. He destroyed none, let all be shown, sold those he could. He seemed happier, less taut, more content with life.

One day he said, "I think I understand. Who am I to say which of my works is true, which beautiful? Are my standards important? If a picture is given me to paint and I paint it, is even the work mine? How can I be critical or destroy the work of One who is greater than I? I am content now just to work. I have found peace in the doing itself, not the result."

> A thing of beauty is a joy forever
> Its loveliness increases; it will never
> Pass into nothingness.
> —John Keats

THE PRIMARY THINKER

Original thinking is the basis of all creativeness, but how difficult it is for most of us to achieve. How often we abdicate from thought in favor of reaction, how often we subordinate the mind to that which is told us, taught us, that which we read. We walk around, perform our duties, think of ourselves as being masters of our fate, when all the time we are only a mobile set of reflexes. Any good psychologist can predict exactly how we will behave in any given circumstance. But if we think, we are not predictable; only people who react are predictable, for they act only out of habit and thus prevent themselves from rising above circumstance. Original thinking proceeds out of a man's wiping the slate of the past clean, so that he neither is a product of it nor can it influence him in any way. Original thinking is made possible through a man's letting go of conceit, of ego-centeredness, of any conception or ideal that keeps his performance bound to limits in himself. Only by letting go of experience, only by letting go of self, is it possible for the individual soul to think in terms large enough to be an improvement upon that which has been thought before. You cannot become an instrument of the Lord when you cling to little islands of refuge, when you refuse to let go of beliefs and inhibitions and false ideals simply because what will replace them is unknown. You must throw off all bounds, all limitations, all restrictions, all finalities if you seek to be joined to the Divine. For when you become His instrument you must be open to all possibilities, all probabilities, however remote, however fantastic. Only by opening yourself to the manifold possibilities of God is it possible to know Him in your own nature and to manifest His power and goodness in life.

It always has been generally believed that talent is something a person is born with; he either has it or he doesn't; if not it is just too bad. That just isn't the case. It is true that the inherent relationship of the individual with the Divine is more apparent in some people than others; some appear to be more gifted through showing a greater aptitude for painting, music, writing, or other forms of creative activity. But the Divine does not tie some of us closer to Him than others; He supports each person with His entire being. Therefore when a man appears to have no creative talent it is because some facet of his own nature is blocking out his spiritual existence, some denial in his mental and sensory make-up is keeping divine power from manifesting through him. This blocking out of his spiritual existence, this denial in his earthly nature can be overcome through mental and spiritual treatment so that in the end he will undergo a great awakening of his underlying spiritual being, so that powers and abilities will stir and make themselves known in such a manner as he had never dreamed.

THE INFINITE ARTIST

All paintings are painted by one Painter, all books are written by one Author, all music composed by one Composer, all buildings designed by one Architect, all invention created by one Inventor. He is Rembrandt, Tolstoy, Brahms, Wright, and Edison, and He is in each of us, neither more nor less than in them. He will work through your nature to produce invention if only you school your sensual self to take a back seat in the direction of your affairs and turn over your thoughts and desires and life to Him. The very essence and nature of the Divine is creativity. Wherever He is, there the evidence of His presence is productivity. From the inexhaustible fount of His infinite and manifold nature spring ceaseless formation and invention. The life of a man who opens his soul to the power of God is a life lived on a bolt of lightning. He is used by the dynamic power that runs and sustains the universe, and his life takes on the potency of that power.

All artistic sensibility has universal meaning underlying it, a communication, as it were, from the soul of the artist to the soul of his audience, in which the two mingle and become one. So it is that the hearing of an extraordinary piece of music, the viewing of a great painting inspire in us the same reverential awe as do countless sharp stars on a clear night, the limitless expanse of the ocean, the rugged gorge of the Grand Canyon. By contemplating the works of nature we gain insight into the vast and almost incomprehensible being of God. It is the artist who captures this universal feeling, this glimpse of the infinite, molding it into form while retaining the meaning. All creation is a message from God, captured on canvas or paper, in brick or steel or clay, wrought at the behest of the Divine as a sort of rainbow to the soul tokening His promise of immortality to each of us.

SILENT TESTIMONY

The painter, the poet, the musician, the sculptor, the writer, each walks in nature, filling his heart with her sighing sound, the silent noise of her germinating fecundity, her immense and universal propensity for eternal growth. So there comes to him a storing up of creative power, a kind of charging of the batteries of the soul, which eventually results in the bursting through of a new idea, a new interpretation, a new perspective. The works of nature hold for the aspiring creator hidden truths, esoteric meanings that can only be divined through moving among them and probing at the secrets of their grandeur. The sea speaks to the man, and the man writes *Moby Dick*. The wilderness speaks, and he writes *The Deerslayer*. Nature stirs the imagination, inspires the heart, charges the energies; her silent testimony exists as a monument to God's intimate relationship with all created things.

> To him who in the love of nature holds
> Communion with her visible forms
> She speaks a various language.
> —William Cullen Bryant

Creative imagery grows out of the soul's relationship to the Divine. It may be visual and resolve itself into pictures within the consciousness; it may be auditory and resolve itself into voices speaking within; it may even be entirely automatic, possessing the individual so completely that he acts at the behest of something beyond his own volition. Without doubt the great identifying mark of the artist is the welling up from subterranean layers of consciousness of a power that possesses him and uses him and which is greater at all times than he. This basic spiritual relationship, however, sometimes is not understood by the artist himself, and he flies from his Muse in order to regain the sanctuary of his egoistic nature, thinking that it is weak and immature not to be exercising his own will but always to be acceding to something inside him. When he recognizes that the cessation of his own will is the spiritual culmination of all that is significant in life, then he becomes a truly great artist, then he ceases to act in the restricted sensual sphere of his own nature and expands his consciousness into the universality of God. Then he can truly communicate, truly see.

THE ARTIST INCARNATE

Creativity, then, is not a thing in itself, or even something that is restricted to certain men. It is simply the overt manifestation of the soul's union with God, a sure sign that the ego is not the director of the actions or the ideas, but the Divine instead, for it is the mark of God and never of man when works of progress and power, new and revealing, make their way into the world. In some men this subordination of the ego to the Divine is an unconscious thing. It is a relationship developed so early in life that they are unaware of any struggle, of having made any decision, but are led always from within. These are men with intense dedication, immense preoccupation. They spend their lives listening to inner voices, watching the play of imagery in the mind. They appear to have gigantic powers of concentration, so effectively do they blot out the stimuli of the world. Actually they are not focused there at all, but within. And it is this shift in valence from normal centering in the material world to a centering in a world of mind that gives rise to our geniuses, our Mozarts, Shakespeares, Michelangelos, Jesus Christs.

Talent is not possessed by the individual at birth, but is only the power and glory of the Divine shining through. When encysting layers of ego and isolation are removed from the spirit, then it penetrates the mask with expressions of its true purpose and ultimate meaning. These expressions resolve themselves into creative effects, give the impression of being the result of a talent possessed by the individual, when in truth he possesses it not at all but is possessed by it, for it comes from beyond him and is greater than he. The same talent exhibited by our geniuses lies dormant in every one of us. All we have to do is abdicate from the presidency of the partnership that exists between ourself and God. As long as the ego is in control, our affairs are being conducted by the junior partner and our lives are frustrated through being encompassed by narrow horizons. But once we step down and let the senior partner take over, we awaken to new powers and an immensely increased scope of awareness.

> Thou art become my greater self
> Small bounds no more can me confine
> Thou hast my being taken on
> And shall I not now take on thine?
> —Jalalu'd Din

Each of us is the Artist incarnate. Each of us, by finding his true relationship with his Creator, inevitably must manifest in the world of created things those expressions of the master spirit that are an inspiration to all. Thus great bridges and buildings are built, first rockets probe into space, epics of literature and masterpieces of art come to us. The soul of the artist is the soul of God. It is He in all creators who does the actual creating. Artists are only instruments, can only be artists through being instruments, and no man can be creative in life without first surrendering himself to the Divine, giving himself over completely, to be used as God sees fit.

Inspiration seldom comes to the listener in the form of thunder and lightning. More often it is a small voice speaking in the depths of the soul. But it moves him with a force and purpose he never has known before. No matter the quietude in which such inspiration comes, it comes as irresistible truth, as the manifested word of God. Heeding it, following it, working to effect its ends becomes the primary purpose and the sole motivating force of the enlightened man. So it is that everything he creates bears the imprint of the emerging Godhead, touching the soft core of emotion and feeling in all who behold it, for what it symbolizes above all else is the spiritual unity of all beings and their umbilical tie with the Divine. The glory of this conception, regardless of how vaguely hinted at, is what makes art art, creation creation. Without it, all artistic endeavor is a child's scribbling.

THE SEARCHING SOUL

Harriet had fine perceptual sensibility, a deft touch with her hands, an inherent understanding of line, light and shadow, perspective. She worked well in water colors and oils, was even an exceptional draughtsman. She went several years to art school, then decided on a career as a dress designer. She apprenticed herself to one of the leading commercial houses and spent several years under tutelage. When finally she asked for greater responsibility, however, she was denied. She insisted upon a reason and was told that she had no creative sense, that she must be content to do the artwork on other people's ideas; designing work of her own was out of the question. She was deeply upset. She quit her job at once, determined to find another.

But jobs in the dress designing business were difficult to come by, especially when her previous employer was not inclined to recommend her, and Harriet found only closed doors. Finally, she took a job as a sales clerk in a department store. Now she was convinced that her previous employer had been right, that she had no talent. Her goals seemed destroyed and she existed from day to day. She began to drink heavily, sought gaiety in the party life of the big city.

Harriet was an exceptionally attractive young woman, and she had no difficulty finding escorts. In attempting surcease from the ache of her disappointment, she carried on several love affairs during the ensuing year. One day she found herself pregnant. The hopelessness that had been creeping up on her now engulfed her completely. She decided to take her own life. She took a large overdose of sleeping pills and was discovered unconscious when the maid came to her apartment in the morning. Harriet was taken at once to the hospital where she hovered on the brink of death for twenty-four hours. Gradually she began to recover. Friends sought help for her. She was taken to a religious councillor.

"I don't want to live," she said. "I'm tired, things haven't worked out right. I'm ready to go."

"How old are you, Harriet?" she was asked.

"Twenty-seven."

"That seems rather young to die."

"Not when there's nothing to live for."

"There will be the child. Won't that be something?"

"I don't want it. I don't even consider it mine."

"Perhaps not, but God considers it yours."

"I don't believe in God."

"That doesn't obliterate Him, Harriet. He is there whether you believe in Him or not. He runs your life whether you allow Him to or not. He is molding you here on earth, tempering you by pain and ordeal so that you will awaken to your true spiritual birthright. All who attempt to run their lives in accordance with the motives of their own vanity eventually meet desolation, for this is a spiritual law. God sees the soul on the wrong course, and He places obstacles there. Like a river rechanneled, the soul boils and rages, but eventually takes the new course, serener now, quietly proceeding to the sea."

Harriet looked interested. "You mean you believe in predestination?"

"Not predestination for the things of the flesh, but rather predestination for the things of the spirit. Each soul undergoes its own ordeal, an ordeal designed only to refine and purify its understanding, and this ordeal is only between the soul and God."

"Then you believe that what has happened to me *had* to happen to me?"

"Yes. It has been the way chosen by the Master Spirit to awaken you to your true spiritual self. Your suffering is largely over, for even now you are glimpsing that greater Self, finding a hint of its meaning."

"What am I supposed to do?"

"Ask God. Go home and get down on your knees and ask Him. He will answer, and in that answer your life will be rejuvenated."

"I don't think I can."

"A few days ago you tried to take your own life. Is it more difficult to get down on your knees?"

She nodded at this, said she would try. When she left, there was a hint of purpose in her bearing that had been missing before.

Harriet had her child, a boy, and she gave him her own surname. During the months of her confinement, she worked out several sketches for new dress designs, and she was startled at how they turned out.

"It's almost as if someone else is doing them," she said.

"Someone else is," she was told.

Morning and evening she prayed. Tension left her. She grew peaceful and poised, able to work long hours without fatigue. She returned home from the hospital with her child to find that three of her sketches had been accepted by a leading dress manufacturer. Today she is one of the most able designers in the industry, successful, secure, married, with two more children. One evening in a discussion at her home she was asked how she managed to successfully combine both home and career.

"I let God do it," she said.

THE UNSEEN LIGHT

Alfred Lord Tennyson wrote, "More things are wrought by prayer than this world dreams of," but the kind of prayer that get results is not the will of the prayer-maker exerting itself to effect some material solution to his problem.

The kind of prayer that gets results is the prayer for guidance, for illumination, a pledge that completely submits the soul to its Creator, to the will and the working of God. This is the path to heightened powers of creativity, this is the avenue by which every man can awaken within himself the latent Artist whose brush paints all pictures.

Creativity then is a by-product of spiritual illumination, the mark of a man whose center of consciousness is spiritual and not material. It is an end obtained not so much by devotion to a particular activity as it is an inner devotion to an unseen light.   All efforts of the man who aspires to creativeness must be directed toward the end of achieving unity with God. He must seek within for the power and purpose to expand beyond himself. When at last there comes into his soul a kind of silent joy, a serene bliss, a letting go of all personal problems, then he will know that God is there, sustaining him, guiding him, working through him. His soul will become a shrine then, a place of inner sanctity, a haven of reverential fusion. Here he meets all life, from here all proceeds. He senses this inner center as being both alpha and omega of existence, as being directly connected to the original determinant of things. God's house lies within him. The Divine himself dwells there. Now he is aware that all things happen out of an absolute purpose and delicate design which He not only is able to perceive but actually seems to direct.

> We two will stand beside that shrine,
> Occult, withheld, untrod
> Whose lamps are stirred continually
> With prayer sent up to God
> And see our old prayers, granted, melt
> Each like a little cloud.
> —Dante Gabriel Rossetti

NINTH MEDITATION

I search the inner depths of my consciousness for that haven of refuge where God and I meet and become one. The noises and insistencies of the clamoring world fade away, and I retreat ever deeper, through planes of being and awareness to a place of utter repose, of absolute bliss, of complete unity, where all barriers are removed between myself and the Divine. I lose myself in Him, and in that losing I find my greater Self; He takes my being and makes it an instrument of His purpose and His power. Through my mind and spirit course the restless surging energies of God, ever unfolding, dynamically illustrating the manifold sides of His nature. Whatever impinges itself upon my awareness has a delicate and mystic meaning, and I am conscious that nothing is fully developed, finally complete, but that each thing, event, idea is but a partial revelation of a hidden and magnificent truth. To the emergence of this truth I dedicate myself, for I know that concealed in the heart of each creature is the incarnate God; through expressing Him I discovery myself. To be is to be a part of God; but to grow is to become God. To that growth, to that becoming I consecrate my life. The apparent duality of my being I surrender as partial truth. I know that my true self is the Self of the Divine, the one Self that pervades the universe, that inhabits every being, that looks out of the eyes of every man. Through allowing this Self to work through my nature I truly become creative. I am instrument of the ultimate artistic sensibility. I know that each soul aspires to union with its Creator, that each seeks for a sign of that union through beauty, knowledge, love. By knowing the Divine and loving the Divine I am assured that His power will work through me to illustrate to the world the divinity of man.

10 STAYING YOUNG FOREVER

Spirit is the mold and flesh is the cast
And flesh is donned like a gown
Styled to fashion and not made to last
Cleave not to flesh for all lay it down

AGELESS SPIRIT

Our concept of age arises from our relating ourselves to a physical body, to its birth, growth, maturity, eventual decay and death. Ego-centeredness naturally brings with it such idenification, and as the body decreases in vigor with passing years, so does the spiritual inhabitant fall into a state of decline. The enlightened man knows that he is spirit alone, birthless, deathless, and ageless, that his very being is synonymous with life, that according to divine law he can only grow, never go backward, never die. His roots are not in the physical body or even in the material world, and he is not affected by what happens in that world. It cannot age or injure him or stay his developing consciousness from union with God. His true being is always expectant. Each day is a rebirth into increased awareness. He is detached from his body, sees it only as an instrument of expression, is content in the end to lay it down, passing serenely on to greater experience.

How sad it is to see the great spirit of the ego-centered man grow old. The cranky, short-tempered, irascible elder is an all-too-familiar character. Within a fleshy prison of his own making his spirit is confined, and as that prison shrinks, so does his spirit shrivel. Yet it is not residence in the body that reduces spirit to the ills of the flesh, but rather the failure of the individual to perceive that he is not confined to the body, that his roots are in eternity, that his liberation is in his own hands. People sometimes argue that the latter years of a man's life are bound to be beset by aches and pains because the body mechanism is running down and its resilience becomes less and less. This premise is accepted without question by ninety-nine percent of all oldsters. They grow feeble and bent, fall prey to all manner of ills, live out their last years as slaves to thermometer and pills. But there remains a glorious one percent of rare individuals who have conquered fear, who have opened themselves to the Divine and in whom divine energy courses. They die, yes; they lay down their bodies, yes; but while they live they *live*. Life flows in them unchecked, unhampered, unrestricted, and they are as vigorous, as expanding, as full of interior growth in the years of senility as most people are in adolescence.

TRIUMPH OVER FLESH

What an inspiring thing it is to see spirit triumph over flesh. Something within us stands up and applauds, for we have been shown the meaning of life itself. Winston Churchill in his eighties writes masterpieces of literature, leads his nation as elder statesman; Bernard Baruch is consulted by world leaders; Bernarr McFadden made parachute jumps; and the whole world is liberated a little from bodily ties, has an instant of enlightened understanding, sees that the strength of man is not material but spiritual instead. The body is only an instrument used by the spirit an instant in its pilgrimage through eternity. It is not possible for this body to block off the growth of that spirit, but the man who identifies his vigor solely with the body lives in the ego and grows old there. The man who surrenders himself to the Divine is always growing; he aspires, wonders, learns, tries, follows a light that is perpetually new. He is not made old by having lived so long. Wisdom is his glory, and the passing years bring it to him. He accepts no word as final, no boundary as absolute, no fact as indisputable. He sees life itself as a state of flux, and he joins it, aspires with it, grows with it. God guides him to new areas of mind, heart, and soul. He is an adventurer in the universe.

FOUNTAIN OF YOUTH

Lester was old before his time. Though he was not yet fifty he was thin and haggard, walked with a stoop, was listless, devoid of energy.

"I've worked too hard all my life," he said. "I guess it's finally caught up with me."

"Hard work is a builder, not a destroyer," he was told. "There has to be another reason."

He was willing to explore this possibility, but it was difficult to get him to take time. He was tied to a million loose ends and was forever trying to tuck them neatly in. Three or four businesses that he long ago had disposed of still presented him enough problems to take care of a normal working day. He had been married twice, had had children by each marriage, and was constantly fretting over one child or another. Though he was retired he had problems enough for a man with three jobs.

One day Lester was persuaded to go on a fishing trip with a religious councillor, and the two men journeyed by horseback to a remote lake in the High Sierras. There they made camp with a guide and settled down to fish.

The lake was rimmed by snowcapped mountains with a single pass through which the trio had entered. In the mornings the sun shone dazzlingly on the ridges, while the waters of the lake below were placid and deep blue. The air was brisk and cold, warming lazily at midday, turning cold again at night. Fishing was wonderful, the exercise invigorating; appetites were rapacious. Nights around the campfire were a perfect setting for Lester to discuss his problems.

"Time is a funny thing," he said one evening. "I think I've always been scared to death by it. It's like sand slipping through my fingers. I can't hold on, and pretty soon it will be all gone and that will be the end of me. That's why I've tried to work so fast, because there's so little time."

"So little time for what?" he was asked.

"So little time to live."

"Lester," he was told, "as long as you think you only live here and now and in the body you find yourself in, you have no choice but to run. But you cannot escape. There's no time at all for the man who is bound to the flesh. He can't even count on the next minute."

"Exactly. So what's the solution? We're bound to our bodies, all right. I'm inside mine and nowhere else, that's for sure."

"Is it? Are you so very positive that you are nowhere else? Do you really think that you came into existence from nothing and one day will go back to nothing?"

"I'm an atheist, you know that. I don't believe in God and I don't believe in a hereafter. What's that nonsense get you?"

"Strength, Lester. Spiritual strength that keeps you young."

He snorted. "The fountain of youth, eh? And all you have to do is believe in God?"

Wind had sprung up over the lake. It made a low moaning sound against the rocks along the shore. There was a faint clatter of pots and pans as the guide cleaned up for the night. Lester's words seemed to echo.

"Well?" he asked impatiently.

"That's right. All you have to do is believe in God."

There was no more conversation that night. Lester obviously felt that there should be some further explanation, but the fact that none was forthcoming seemed to stir him. He fidgeted before the fire for some time, finally made his way to his sleeping bag.

Next morning he hooked a beauty, an eight-pound rainbow trout which he played for twenty minutes. His eyes glowed as he held it up for all to see. It was a beautiful fish.

"Do you think that is an accident?" he was asked.

"What do you mean?"

"Do you think that fish is an accident. Or is it possible that some supreme intelligence made it?"

He put it on a stringer, obviously thinking.

That evening, again seated around the fire, he voiced his feelings.

"How can believing in God keep a man young?" he asked.

"Believing in Him enables you to perceive Him, and when you perceive Him you discover Him to be your true self. Since He is birthless, deathless, and changeless, so you take on those inner qualities yourself."

"That sounds tricky," he said.

"It does now, because you are outside looking in. Once you are inside, participating, it will seem like the simplest of truths, and you will be amazed that you have not seen it before."

"How does one get inside, then?"

"Just by letting go. Whether you know it or not, Lester, you have a 'do it yourself' attitude toward life. You've been ever so busy trying to run things yourself. Well, step down now. Don't try to run anything. Put yourself in God's hands and see what happens."

Lester was fortunate at that mountain lake. Set down among the dwarfing works of nature, he relaxed, let the tensions slide from him. He made a strong spiritual effort, and God partially revealed Himself. Lester was ecstatic, would have stayed in camp for weeks but for the assurance that his new spiritual awakening would go with him. Today he is in his late sixties. "Sixty-seven years young!" he says, and he is too, a vigorous, adventurous young man. In the last seven years he has undertaken four new enterprises, all successful. He hasn't had an ache or pain in years.

> For every man the world is as fresh
> As it was at the first day
> And as full of untold novelties
> For him who has the eyes to see them.
> —Thomas Henry Huxley

SPIRITUAL HERITAGE

Through growth we live, through stagnation we die, and the enlightened man, aware of this, never rests for long on any plateau. Upward, onward, outward, expand, seek, improve, those are the laws of life. Adhering to them a man stays in the stream, always young, always growing. Dare and challenge, hope and aspiration spur his energies, focus his intent, concentrate his purpose on unfolding the hidden Godhead. This is his goal and his fulfillment, his sustaining spiritual resource; to this he consecrates his life. Used by the Divine for the purposes of the Divine, he takes up his residence on earth by special dispensation of an omnipotent and ageless spirit which gives him its own nature, provides him the qualities of its own consciousness. And so he stays young forever.

Enthusiasm and purpose, concentration and growth, those are the marks of the man who stays young, but he does not acquire them as separate things, rather as a group, for all are symptoms of his spiritual identification with the Divine. No man can remain young while identifying himself with the body, with past experience. As he perceives the signs of bodily aging, as experience floods his memory with explicit recording of the passage of time, he begins to feel that he is growing old, feels he is mortal, feels he will die. Nothing can dispel this sense of death and annihilation except the sure and certain knowledge of immortality. If a man believes that he is mortal, that he will not survive the death of the body, then the aging of the body withers and bends him, cracks and dissipates his spirit. But if he identifies himself with God, if he sees that he is not truly body but is spirit instead, that his spirit existed in the dimmest beginnings of time, before the formation of the earth itself, then he cannot grow old with the aging of the body or the passage of a lifetime that is the barest fraction of second in relation to his total existence.

IMMORTAL SELF

Knowledge of immortality is the key to never growing old. The enlightened man does not struggle or guess or wonder at eternal life. He lives in, by, and through God, and as God is eternal so is he. The spiritual certainty engendered by surrendering the ego and turning over one's life to God produces in the individual the knowledge of immortality, acts as a magic potion, keeps him young forever. No ghostly finger from the beyond need beckon him. No voice of a departed one need speak. He needs no sensual evidence to furnish proof of life beyond death. He has discovered it already here on earth. By separating himself from ego and identifying himself with God, he has achieved immortality even while residing in a mortal body.

> Strange is it not? That of the myriads who
> Before us pass'd the door of Darkness through
> Not one returns to tell us of the Road
> Which to discover we must travel too.
> —Omar Khayyam

There is only one life, one mind, one being, one self in the universe. It is He who inhabits all creatures, it is He who is your very self. He is not made multiple by residing in many bodies, but remains always one and indivisible. He appears to be different according to the form He has entered, but once He sheds that form He returns to His true and mystic Self, the uttermost and final Being. This in each man is immortal, not the ego, not the body, not accumulated experience, but the Divine dwelling within. The ego itself does not cross over into spiritual life. How then can it return to tell of what exists there? The ego is a temporal thing, manufactured of separateness and isolation, and has no place in the complete unity and oneness that exists in spirit, in the heart of the Divine. Thus the man who identifies himself with ego renders himself mortal and subject to growing old, while the man who surrenders the ego and identifies himself with God achieves immortality and remains young eternally.

Some people harbor exceedingly odd ideas of the hereafter. Their questions revolve around such issues as—will we be old or young there? will we have the same bodies? what will there be to do?—as if the hereafter is a projection of earthly life and the things enjoyed and possessed here are to be enjoyed and possessed there also, only more so. Some even believe that individual spirits will return to inhabit discarded bodies on a central judgment day. That ought to be a grisly sight. In any case, it becomes apparent that few people are prepared to envisage a hereafter in terms of a purely spiritual existence, but insist on bringing along some kind of body. They either want the same body they had or else a better one, and they don't want it to be too old or too young, and they want it to stay that way. They want to eat and drink and live off the fat of the land because all their pleasures are of the flesh and their identification with the ego. The enlightened man sees the hereafter in terms of the central Intelligence that is molding and directing the universe, and he knows that he is the very Intelligence himself. He has put off all bondage to flesh and ego and perceives them only as instruments for his expression, things he uses but which remain only tools. His true self has an indivisible oneness with all things, all creatures, with

God. Deep in the subterranean depths of his own nature he has met and fused with the Divine; his horizons are the infinite reaches of space; his time the ends of eternity.

> For I am the Brahman
> Within this body
> Life immortal
> That shall not perish
> I am the truth
> And the joy forever.
> —Bhagavad-Gita

FEAR OF DEATH

Fear of death is a stronger motivating factor in most men's lives than they generally care to admit. Many exhibit the greatest nonchalance toward it, but their attitude usually conceals an inner turmoil that they cannot always suppress. It is not merely the pain associated with the termination of life that inspires fear of death; it is the impending annihilation. The ego senses its eventual dissolution and becomes frantic to escape; it jitters, cowers, and rages, and inasmuch as a man is tied to it, so his psychic health is affected. The founders of modern psychiatry have made sex and fight the principal motivating factors of the human psyche, but until fear of death and desire for immortality are included, psychiatry will never become an exact science. Death is the final, towering enigma of human existence. It stands as a gaping maw across every path, and there is no escaping it. Men climb mountains, jump from airplanes, plunge into the depths of the earth and sea, journey into space, all to assert the principle of life against death, to flaunt the courage of spirit in the face of the frailties of the flesh. They do these things not because they are unconcerned with death, but rather because they are over-concerned with it, because they fear it.

Now it is foolish to fear the inevitable, but this solid psychological fact is small solace to the man who faces death without spiritual resource. There is in all of us the knowledge of immortality, but when the evidence at hand disputes this subconscious knowledge we become victims of a paralyzing inner fear. We may go about daily tasks with apparent assurance, keeping the hours with outer serenity; then something happens that breaks our routine, that in one single stroke shatters our security, and panic seizes us; the demon we have contained so long and so well escapes its bonds, and the mortality of all created things engulfs our consciousness, obliterates the security of the ego. We are adrift on uncharted seas then. We either find out true spiritual selves or perish in the ensuing storm.

Some people may go so far as to take their lives over such an inconsequential matter as losing their money, becoming completely unhinged at the loss of a security they never realized was false in the first place. One might assume that a suicide fears life more than death, but the strange psychological fact is that a person in the grip of panic usually runs right into the arms of the fate he fears. Everyone knows the reaction of the cornered animal. The man jumping off the top of a building because the exigencies of life have brought him to bay is reacting in the exact same manner, throwing himself into the maw of death because it is death he fears so much.

The enlightened man has no fear of death, for he knows he does not die. All that is perishable in body and mind are but tools he uses, not part of him, not affecting him, as easily shucked off from his true being as a butterfly sheds the chrysalis. He is not ego-centered, his consciousness has no bondage to material things. Nothing that is truly himself is changed by the changes of the body. Nothing that is truly himself dies with the death of the body. His true self is the divine spirit, entered into the body to work out its purpose, not limited by the body, not affected by its birth and growth and death, serene always, encompassing all, manifesting its nature for the pure joy of expression.

If the red slayer thinks he slays
Or if the slain thinks he is slain
They know not well the subtle ways
I keep, and pass, and turn again.
—Ralph Waldo Emerson

SHEDDING DELUSION

Courage to face death stems from a man's realization of his immortality. What does he lose then but a delusion donned to please himself? He is not attached to this delusion. He knows that it came into being with the growth of his body, that eventually it must be lifted. The ego is a subtle thing, a thing of mental qualifications and even with some spiritual significance, but nevertheless part and parcel of the body, built of the experience of the body, built of the delusion that arises from the apparent separateness of created things from their Creator.

False sense of self is responsible for nearly all human suffering, and it is the shucking off of this self into a realization of inherent Godhood that is the purpose and destiny of life. As a consequence of ego, there is no growth without pain, and mankind lives life as a footrace against death, a race the ego cannot win and one in which it dares not look over its shoulder for fear of seeing its pursuer. The psychological implications of such a situation are all too apparent in our modern society. Youth is worshiped as if it were God Himself. The advertising of various medicaments assures the prospective purchaser that they will contribute to his youth and desirability and in some mysterious way protect him from the ravages of age and death. The ego-centered man lives like an ostrich with his head in the sand. He accepts the blandishments of those who seek to entice him by appealing to his selfish core, and at the same time he realizes the mortality and futility of that core itself. Small wonder that psychiarists' couches are filled and churches overflowing with those who seek surcease from the constant bludgeonings of being disoriented from the spiritual center of things.

The enlightened man lives in the knowledge that he is God Himself. An inner attunement to the original cause of things enables him to know the purpose for which he has entered into the particular form he occupies. Within the scope of his own nature he constantly seeks to fulfill his destiny by keeping his inner ear attuned to the directions of the Divine. He knows that his present form is a temporary thing, brought into existence for a particular moment and purpose, that when that moment and purpose are fulfilled his form will disintegrate and his spirit reunite with God. He takes no thought of his eventual physical demise for this is no more an incident to him than was his birth; each is but a step in the progressive unfolding of the Godhead. His life, because he is centered in God, is eternal. He is not bound by the body because he is not of the body. Therefore he does not fear death, is ready to return home when the Divine calls him, whenever his work is finished.

> If God in His wisdom have brought close
> The day when I must die
> That day by water or fire or air
> My feet shall fall in the destined snare
> Wherever my road may lie.
> —Dante Gabriel Rossetti

HELL AND THE HEREAFTER

Cecilia was afraid of the dark. She had a naturally sunny disposition that always was transformed by the setting sun into an attitude of apprehension and gloom. She often would remark to friends, "It's like a pall settling over me when night comes. The whole world is narrowed, limited to what I can see, and I feel trapped, cornered in a tight little room from which there is no escape. Out there in the dark, unseen but watching, something seems to be waiting for me." She refused to go out of the house at night, always slept with the lights on.

Her problem was not dealt with when she was a child as it seemed only a quirk of character, and it was not until she was nearly thirty that it began to influence her daytime behavior. She grew nervous and fitful, deeply apprehensive. She could not hold a job, was forced to break off her engagement to a young man who sincerely loved her.

It was obvious at once that Cecilia's subconscious problem revolved around an inordinate fear of death. Her phantasms of the night and her unconscious identification of darkness with the grave were telltale signs.

"Do you believe in hell?" she was asked.

"Of course."

"What do you think it is like?"

"Dark except for fires, and very hot, and there are screams from people who are burning."

"Do you think of hell often?"

"Yes."

"When?"

"At night."

"Every night?"

"Even when it is not night, for I know that night must come."

"You are afraid of death then?"

"Nobody wants to die."

"Perhaps not, but some people are able to think of death as a sort of going home."

She smiled wistfully. "It's nice they can be so sure they are going to heaven."

"They don't think about hell at all. They don't believe there is any such place. They believe everyone goes to heaven."

"Then they're wrong."

"What makes you so sure?"

"The Bible says so."

"The Bible says a great many things that are not to be

taken literally. Perhaps by hell the Scriptures mean the spiritual condition of being separated from God. If that is so, then hell is right here on earth, for only here, in life, can the soul be separated from its Creator. After the death of the body, it reunites with its Maker."

She looked up. "I like that," she said.

"Cecilia," she was told, "there is only one true life, one true mind, one true sense of self in the universe. This is God. He makes all things from Himself, dwells in each as resident spirit, adopts all forms, all manners in manifesting His infinite possibilities. He has become you. He is your very life, your very self. He underlies your consciousness, sustains you, guides, supports, and nourishes you. Do not think for one moment that He plans to punish or torture you. What profit, what pleasure could there possibly be from His punishing or torturing Himself? If you make mistakes, if you fall from the path of your resolve, it is for the purpose of spiritual growth, it is so that you will find within you the divine spark and realize that your true existence is God's existence. Sin and error have no other purpose than fulfillment of life's mandate that there shall be no growth without pain. Have no fear of hell or the devil or death. They simply do not exist."

"Death does not exist?" she asked.

"Death does not exist. All forms wither and pass away, and so it is with the body, but the spirit within is imperishable. Its life is eternal, its domain infinite, its home the bosom of God."

Hope had dawned on Cecilia's face. Tension was visibly drawn from her. She was given a few simple meditations to memorize and a few days' respite to mend her spiritual fences. At the behest of several of her close friends she was directed to a church that taught a loving God and omitted the doctrines of hell and the devil. Within a few short weeks she was back at work, her daytime problem clearly solved.

It took somewhat longer to clear up her fear of the dark.

So strongly had torturous visions of Satan and purgatory been implanted in Cecilia's subconscious that only constant assurance of the lovingness of God and her own immortality finally were able to break down her fear. But eventually she was able to go out after dark, even to sleep with the lights out. She married, and one day she said to her husband, "I finally know why God is called Father. I can feel his arms about me, holding me, assuring me. It is into His arms we go when we die." That day she was cured.

> The grave itself is but a covered bridge
> Leading from light to light
> Through a brief darkness.
> —Henry Wadsworth Longfellow

REINCARNATION

Personal survival after death means survival of the ego to the unenlightened man; to the enlightened man it means awakening to the real nature of his being. The deluded man expects that he will carry on a life in the hereafter that parallels but exceeds the one on earth, while the enlightened man expects no similarities whatever. Upon his return to the spirit and being of God he expects to live in the spirit and being of God.

The attempt of the unenlightened to understand eternal and indestructible spirit has thrown much obscurity upon the doctrine of reincarnation, so that today people search for indications, even manufacture evidence that the ego persists from one lifetime to the next, from one body to the next. There is only one spirit that incarnates and that is the spirit of God. Indeed, all of life is nothing but successive reincarnations of this spirit, for the Divine enters into each creature and becomes that creature. There is only one sense of self in the universe, only one "I," one sense of being. It does not belong to Henry Jones, Tom Brown, Alice Smith, but remains always the exclusive property of God. Jones, Brown, and Smith are but masks the Infinite Spirit has donned to work out the possibilities inherent in Itself; and Jones, Brown, and Smith are not real, but illusions only, concealing the indwelling God.

The whole end of spiritual enlightenment is a shucking off of personal ego and a subsequent identification with the being and self of the Divine. When such enlightenment descends on the individual it is as if he were touched by the hand of heaven. He attains to power and skill in works, for his will and God's are one. He attains to eternal youthfulness, for he truly dwells in a place where time is not. And he attains to immortality, for he is not attached to the body or to any created thing. The illumined man knows the true meaning of reincarnation, that it is the basic underlying activity of life and that it does not concern the ego which is only a blossom on the eternal tree of being and becoming.

Arguments are frequently made in favor of the ego persisting from life to life, body to body. Cases are pointed out where persons have recalled previous lives, spoken languages they never have learned or heard, remembered in detail previous deaths. Many data have been accumulated, nearly all of it from persons in a trance-like state, either under hypnosis or in a reverie of their own induction. Under such circumstances the conscious mind is cut out of the circuit of awareness and there is exposed the great subterranean layers of consciousness which for the purpose of convenience are called subconscious mind. This subconscious mind, or at least some part of it, is universal in nature, belongs to no one person alone, but is a community possession of all beings that live, of all beings that ever have lived. It is able to span space and time, actually seems to be everywhere at any time, giving good reason to suppose it is both infinite and eternal in nature. No other conclusion is possible than that it is the mind of God. There the lives of all are indelibly recorded and available for recall. Complete contact with universal subconscious mind may one day produce in detail the entire history of mankind. This universal mind is the central Self that inhabits all beings, that incarnates endlessly in manifold expression of its infinite nature. This is the one true Individual that encompasses all individuals, to whom the doctrine of reincarnation truly applies. This is the Soul that stands invisibly behind every person.

SOULS TOUCH IN THE CENTER

The Divine in His wisdom enters into the body of each creature, and by His presence life ensues. That which is built up of worldly experience, of pain and pleasure, of aspiration and effort, is not a thing in itself, but simply a mask. We feel we know another person because we know his background and his behavior. We like him or dislike him according to whether he comforts us or provides us a threat. We cannot expose his spirit and ascertain it as our own unless we already have spiritually united ourselves with the Divine. If we act in the ego we never touch another person, never truly feel his presence, never know him for the thing he intrinsically is but constantly seek to confine him within the circumscribed bounds of a type of humanity.

When you touch another person you touch the living God, not by touching him with fingers, but by touching him with your soul. There is a center of spiritual feeling that exists at the core of every creature. To touch this center in just one other is to be united with the whole world. We are not little islands in a vast ocean of being, but rather consist of one entire mainland, and each of us is as integral a part of the whole as another. In order for God to become what He is to become, He had to become all that He has become, and each of us represents an absolutely necessary manifestation of His progressive unfoldment. Each man's life is lived under the direction of divine necessity, and each man is not just the man that he is, but he is God as well.

Human personality is precious not because of its completeness but rather for what it indicates it might become. The play of character upon character, the conflict of construction and decay are what give to life an underlying indication of that mysterious but never fully realized power for perfection that exists at the core of each creature. We are what we are only because we strive to be better, and when we cease striving to be better we become nothing at all. Through latching onto the rolling tides of creation and aspiration we center ourselves in the heart of life. By allowing ourselves to be thoroughly used, exalted or defeated, but always thoroughly used, we align ourselves with the Divine and His being fills the lonely hollow of our hearts. There can be no withdrawal, no retreat from life or a person dies inwardly, in his soul, where it counts. Death of the body is nothing, when it becomes part of the spiritual progress by which a man attains to eternal life. But death of the soul is a sad and lonely thing. And men do kill their souls, kill them with hard and painful thrusts, by allowing their wounded egos to strike out at God.

SALVATION

Pain and effort and hardship are for the purpose of spiritual growth. Life is not a soft and effortless thing. Blades of grass grow through concrete, fighting their way into the sun. The young in heart meet every challenge for a joyous testing of their strength, for the opportunity for growth that lies there. Victory or defeat, exaltation or humiliation are accepted equally by those who bear the mantle of God's enlightenment. There is no growth except through pain, there is no gain except through loss, there is no attainment except through sacrifice: these are the laws laid down for God's creatures, for their redemption from the errors of the ego and their salvation in the being of God.

And when a person departs this life, what of the memories left in the hearts of his loved ones? What of his countless deeds, his innumerable influences on the trend and the body of humanity? Do these depart with him or are they independent of him, God-like things, not of the ego or the personality, but forces disseminated in the world at the behest of the Divine. Each of us leaves behind his indelible imprint on the history of life. We seem to form such small links in an infinitely long chain that we often believe that omitting our little lives would have no effect upon the outcome. But each life is so important that if one of us did not live in the space and time allotted to him, the universe itself would cease to function. Everything in existence hinges on the central Being who pervades all. Nothing is wasted, nothing erroneous; everything serves a divine purpose, is absolutely essential in the scheme of things, otherwise it would not exist at all. We are immortal in spirit when we identify ourselves with God, for then we dwell in the long reaches of time, in the immeasurable spaces of infinity; but always we leave behind us the indelible mark of our existence, from one generation to the next, throughout the ages, regardless of how lowly our worldly position appears to be.

When the stream which overflowed the soul was passed away,
A consciousness remained that it had left,
Deposited on the silent shore of memory,
Images and precious thoughts that shall not die
And cannot be destroyed.

—William Wordsworth

"Nothing can come out of nothing, any more than a thing can go back to nothing," wrote Marcus Aurelius. Our bodies do not simply materialize out of a fathomless void and return to that same state after an allotted time. Bodies and personalities and egos are surface indications of a vast underlying being, one that encompasses all existence, one that supports our surface selves as bubbles on a sea, but which remains the entire Self of each of us. The Divine is ageless, always and eternally young. The man who trades in the incomplete and limiting ego and centers himself in God's grace takes on the properties of the Divine; the spirit of God supports him, keeps him young.

WINDOWS OF THE SOUL

Youth is a spiritual attitude and has nothing to do with the number of years a body has aged. Youth gushes forth in all its energetic splendor from a fountain of divine origin, and pervades and sustains every being that exists as long as his inner vision perceives it. "Any man's death diminishes me," wrote John Donne, "because I am involved in mankind." It is the knowledge that all of us are part and parcel of one central guiding intelligence that gives us the mental and spiritual scope to understand ourselves in relation to others, in relation to God. When we see that we are not isolated, that in spiritual essence there is no difference whatever between ourselves and any person that lives, then we begin to emerge from the cocoon of our egoistic isolation and attain to a vast unity with everything in existence.

The activity of life beats like a giant pulse. People are building, creating, working, loving, being born, dying every minute of every day. When an intense personality, vivid, completely alive, suddenly terminates, we are stricken to the depths of our souls. All of us face death long before we are personally called upon to journey down the endless corridors of infinity. We see it come to our friends, to our loved ones, leaving behind an abandoned body that once was the home of a personality we knew so well. We cannot see where this personality has gone, we only know it is there no longer, and something within us is frozen with ap-

prehension that it has not simply gone but has suddenly
ceased to be.

> Ah Christ, that it were possible
> For one short hour to see
> The souls we loved, that they might tell us
> What and where they be.
> —Alfred Lord Tennyson

The history of the evolution of man from primitive
primate to a creature aspiring to travel among the stars
is testimony enough that life is going somewhere, its destination yet hidden in the misty reaches of a coming awareness.
Purpose and destination can only be the result of a central
and guiding intelligence that sees at once the end and the
beginning and all the events between. God is not lost along
the way, floundering from one path to the other, puzzling
over various roads. Everything is ordered in its proper place,
each is equally important in the scheme. Every man's life
is a preparation, a kind of tempering by exposure to pain
and effort of the spiritual mettle within him. There are other
worlds, other planes of mind and spirit, other areas of
infinitely increased awareness. Hints of these come to us
occasionally in the form of intuitive bursts of insight, so
that for a moment we are able to look beyond the form of
a thing and see its true significance. In that mystical moment
the entire world is changed, and we know with a certainty
that heretofore has escaped us that life is a spiritual journey
and not a physical one, that what happens to us on earth is
only for the purpose of increasing areas of awareness in the
recesses of our souls. We exist in order that we may fulfill
ourselves in God, that we may understand who "I" is, who
God is, and the relationship between. There is no finer,
fuller, greater thing that can happen to any individual than
that the curtain of separation be withdrawn from the windows of his soul and the light of the Supreme illuminate him
with understanding.

DANGEROUS WITHDRAWAL

Too many defeats, too many disappointments finally reduced Donald to a state of apathy. He didn't care about anything. Everything was too tough, and he just wasn't going to make any more effort. He was angry, deep inside, where anger burns and spurs and never relents. His friends and parents were deeply disappointed, for Donald was yet a young man and they had held great hopes for his future. He was a gifted musician.

The house in which Donald chose to take up his hermitage was a small cottage perched on a cliff overlooking the Pacific Ocean. He took no notice of the sea, no notice of its innumerable vistas and constantly changing scenes. He kept the blinds drawn, had no desire to look out at all. He was totally concerned with the activity that went on within him. He had withdrawn into himself to the point where he existed as an entire world and there was nothing outside himself.

"Why don't you go out and see people?" his mother asked him.

"Why?" he asked. "People mean nothing to me."

"Don't you play the piano anymore?" she inquired.

In the corner sat a battered upright. Its keys were dusty.

"Play?" asked Donald. "I can't play, you know that."

"But you play wonderfully," she protested.

Donald looked at her in amazement. "You must be crazy," he said. "I can't play a note."

That decided it. Donald had had years of musical training, was a pianist of concert calibre. His mother sought the help of a religious councillor, who had some difficulty arranging a meeting with Donald, but finally visited him in his seaside cottage under the guise of having been a friend of Paderewski.

"What kind of man was he?" asked Donald at that first meeting.

"Paderewski was involved in a dream," he was told. "It was a big dream and a beautiful one. It reflected in the way he played and in what he tried to do with his life."

"Did he ever tell you of the dream?"

"Not in so many words, but I knew what it was."

"How did you know?"

"By his spiritual awareness."

"What was his dream, then?"

"Of a golden world. He saw every man a king."

"That's not possible."

"He thought it was."

"He must have taken an awful beating."

"He did."

"And that didn't convince him?"

"It only made him more positive of man's divine destiny."

Donald thought about this, then he said, "God, how he could play."

"That's why, of course."

"How do you mean?"

"You said, 'God, how he could play.' That's exactly it. Because of God, how he could play."

"Maybe I don't follow you."

"It's simple, really. Paderewski knew that his talent came from something beyond himself, something greater than himself. He gave over his life, his ability, his very being to the service of this divine something. His life and his playing were a sacrament."

Donald nodded. "It must have been a great satisfaction to him to be able to give such a talent."

"He didn't give it, he received it."

"But you inferred he gave his ability to God."

"His ability, yes. Himself, yes. But by that giving he made himself an instrument for the Divine. Talent poured through him, but it was not Paderewski playing, it was God Himself."

Donald's eyes sought the dusty piano in the corner of the room. "I wonder if he ever had doubts about his ability," he said.

"Of course he did. Don't think for a minute that some egoistic part of his nature didn't occasionally take over and try to do the job itself. When that happened it was as if the well had gone dry. Freshness left his playing. Command of technique and interpretation abandoned him. He had to stop, go somewhere by himself, freshen his spirit at some fount of his own finding."

"If only I weren't so critical," Donald said. "If only I could just play and not eternally listen in disgust because it doesn't come out the way it sounds in my mind."

"Give it to God. Let Him play. You will not criticize Him."

He liked that and smiled. "He'll have to be better than I am."

"Don't worry, He is."

Donald started to play again that night. He played for hours. Next day the blinds were open on his windows. He walked on the beach, seemed to drink in the air and sun as if it were giving him strength. Several weeks later he found the courage to contract for a concert. He practiced long hours for it, seemed to do so without effort. Gone was his brooding pessimism. In its stead was a kind of serene acceptance of all he was doing and all that might ensue. His concert was a rousing success. He embarked on a tour at once.

Some years later he addressed a group of aspiring musicians. "Don't ever forget," he told them, "that a musician is an instrument himself, for if he would play at all well, he first must allow God to play through him."

THE VISTAS OF ETERNITY

Youth is a primary condition of eternal spirit, and none of us grows old except that he inhibits his spirit by imposing upon it the hurts and wounds and defeats of the ego. A man stays young who has found his true relationship with the Divine, for he abandons all attachment to the flesh and allows God to use him as He will. His beginnings and ends are rooted in eternity. Deep in the recesses of his being whispers the voice of his greater self, "I am, I always was, I always will be."

And so immortality and an eternally young spirit mark the soul of the enlightened man. His illumination frees him from all restriction, all limitation, all ills, all aging. He truly dwells in a place where time and space are not, where all are joined together in the omniscient One, where joy reigns, where truth is triumphant. There in serene grandeur dwell the departed, free from all delusion, the veil drawn aside and the sweeping vistas of eternity revealed at last. There the enlightened man's soul is centered, from that place his entire life is guided, and when his earthly life is over, his spirit undergoes little transformation, but merely casts off the last fetters of illusion and strides foursquare into the reaches of infinity.

Only a little while now and we shall be together again
And with us those other noble and well-beloved souls gone before.
I am sure I shall meet you and them;
That you and I shall talk of a thousand things
And of that unforgettable day and all that followed it;
And that we shall clearly see that all were parts
Of an infinite plan which was wholly wise and good.

—Richard Bucke

TENTH MEDITATION

Youth is growth, and growth is the measure of receptiveness to learning. I therefore open my mind and my heart to the power for life that pervades the universe, I open my soul to God. He sustains my being, He uses me for His ends; in Him I center myself, through Him I attune to life's purpose. There is a place of pure spirit at the center of my soul that is timeless, spaceless, and ageless. I anchor myself there. I resign all attachment to body and ego. These are but instruments of the Divine. His spirit is not altered by entering a particular body, is not changed by the delusions of any ego, but remains always one and indivisible, above suffering and pain and effort and strife. Infinite serenity and omnipotence mark Divine spirit, and they are qualities of my potential self, for Divine spirit dwells within me. It is God in me who saves me from the flesh, who preserves me from death, who gives me immortality. It is God in me who is strong, wise, omnipotent. I clear the channels between myself and Him, displace the ego, make it subservient. My life takes on the luster of Him who guides it. Joy accompanies me on every quest for I know that I shall find growth and wisdom. What strain, what struggle, what pain and hardship can there possibly be in this life that is but an infinitesimal second in the eternity of my existence? Never born, never dying, never aging, the spirit within me keeps me young forever.

11 MYSTIC POWERS OF THE MIND

Winged thoughts that are loos'd in space
On planes that the eye cannot see
Shape coming events, appoint time and place
For the things that will happen to thee

EXTRASENSORY PERCEPTION

Mystic powers of the mind are mostly associated with the supernatural, a word that once was held in disrepute by all science but which gradually is being restored to accepted usage as a result of modern studies of extrasensory perception. And there *is* such a thing as extrasensory perception. It is not just superstition or legend or tall tale. People successfully have read other people's minds, perceived events at great distance, foretold the future. Such accomplishments have been so adequately documented that there now exists no doubt but what extrasensory perception is a quality of the mental or spiritual make-up of man. Chairs of parapsychology have been established at leading universities. Experiments are being conducted daily, seeking to establish by statistical analysis a realm of mental and spiritual being beyond the visible world, an area of increased consciousness wherein the individual no longer is contained by the body and its senses but rather exceeds all, attains to some new and exciting state of being.

272

Parapsychology experiments principally have dealt with thought transference, clairvoyance, and precognition. For purposes of definition thought transference means communication between individuals without use of the five senses; clairvoyance means the actual envisioning of an event that is happening or has happened elsewhere; and precognition means knowledge of coming events. Individuals tested under laboratory conditions have exhibited all these qualities, not one hundred percent of the time, not one hundred percent accurately, but so often and so accurately that the chances of pure coincidence are billions to one. Not all people tested have exhibited this ability, and most of those tested are more able one time than another. The conclusion is that it proceeds out of a part of man's make-up that is buried deep beneath the surface of his conscious mind, a thing he uses little if at all, and seldom consciously. Parapsychology has probed at this unknown something as if it were individually possessed, as a brain might be, seeking to uncover it in each individual, never finding it, never touching it, never even able to weigh, count, or classify it.

UNIVERSAL MIND

Now if one man can read another's mind, see events at a distance, foretell the future, there has to be some contact between one consciousness and another. In some mystical way, the man who reads another's mind must *become* that other man, and the man who sees a distant event must *become* that distant event, and the man who perceives the future must *become* that future. Some entirely new concept of being, some new and encompassing idea of awareness lies behind the field of extrasensory perception. Such a concept is answered by universal mind.

Universal mind is a vast and all-encompassing mental and spiritual being in whom all things and events exist. The principal quality of this mind is that it is just one, infinite in size, eternal in scope, and nothing exists outside it. It is an enormous sea of consciousness, pervading all, supporting all, and individual consciousness grows out of it. All things are made from it; it is rock, sea, bird, beast, man. All things in their true essence, then, are mental, or spiritual, and the rock itself is not a rock at all but merely an example of enclosed or restricted consciousness. Awareness is in the rock. Universal mind is there.

"Nothing is more certain," wrote Edward Carpenter, "than that worlds on worlds and spheres on spheres stretch behind and beyond the actually seen." We are so sure that the on-ward march of events hinges on our little minds that we seldom stop to consider the greater concept of a single mind in which the universe with all its galaxies and solar systems is enclosed. There *is* such a mind, and no amount of argument will disintegrate it. You may fly from it, struggle against it, but you cannot escape it, for it is your very Self. All ills and suffering are caused by being out of joint with it; mastery is attained by living in harmony with it. Do not plead the shortness of life, the blows of fate. Make the shift of being from ego to God and live eternally. All hardship will assume a mystical purpose with spiritual growth as its end. The very stars will obey you, the moon and sun do your bidding. Your will and the Divine will become one.

> Stand still, you ever-moving spheres of heaven
> That time may cease and midnight never come.
> —Christopher Marlowe

HEIGHTENED PERCEPTION

Human ego is the wheat and nature is the mill and God is the miller, and what is being ground is refined consciousness, expanded sense of awareness, spiritual union of the individual with God. The man who prides himself on making his own decisions, on being guided by his own feelings, on influencing the world because of the strength of his will, simply deludes himself and is the lowliest of tools.

He is the product of everything he has learned, every experience he has been exposed to, the quality of his nervous reactions, his mental capacity, his emotional stability. He made none of these and is a product of all. The moment he begins to assume that his little self controls its destiny, he immediately is moved around by nature at her whim and everything he does is reaction. But when the soul begins to unite with its Creator, when individual mind subordinates itself to universal mind, then the power begins to break through, then the miraculous capacity of God Himself manifests through human agency and the supernatural occurs, events come to pass that defy understanding, originating on some higher plane of existence.

Immanel Swedenborg, one of the world's great mystics, often exhibited powers of clairvoyance. He once envisaged a dangerous fire three hundred miles away. He told the precise time it broke out, the precise time it was brought under control, what it had consumed. Three days later his vision was borne out exactly when accounts of the fire began to come through!

Edgar Cayce, "the Miracle Man of Virginia Beach," documented thousands of cases of medical clairvoyance wherein he accurately diagnosed the ills of others while separated from them by hundreds of miles. To effect such clairvoyance, Cayce placed himself under auto-hypnosis. In trance he assumed another identity, erudite and worldly, far removed from his humble and uneducated self.

Daniel Dunglas Home, the celebrated Scottish spiritualist, levitated himself from the ground before unimpeachable witnesses. Mrs. Leonora Piper and Mrs. Osborne Leonard, in séance, were able to produce accurate details of the past known to no living persons and unrecorded by any known documents. Pearl Curran wrote dozens of books while in a trance-like state and under the influence of a psychic personality known as Patience Worth. William Blake insisted that credit for his works belonged not to himself but to "celestial friends." Jacob Boehme stated that when he was working he was the helpless tool of some power other than his normal surface mind. Clearly, some area of mental or spiritual existence, of immensely heightened perception, exists beyond and above man's surface personality and mind.

PRECOGNITION

Margaret first attracted attention by becoming distracted in her high school classroom. Her eyes would glaze and she would sit rigidly at her desk, staring into space. She would not answer when spoken to or respond to touch. On each occasion her teacher summoned the school nurse, but Margaret always returned to normal awareness before the nurse arrived. Nevertheless her behavior appeared so strange that her teacher reported it to her parents. Questioned by them, Margaret stated that she sometimes had "daydreams," but she denied feeling unwell or ever being out of contact with what went on around her. She was taken to a doctor, given a physical examination, found to be in perfect health. She was taken to a psychiatrist where tests revealed her intelligence and emotional responses as normal. Her parents decided that her teacher had been over-concerned, that Margaret was simply indulging in normal adolescent daydreaming and would soon grow out of it.

One night she awakened from her sleep and began screaming. Everyone rushed to her bedside. "Don't sit there!" she cried. She trembled with fright and covered her eyes with her hands. She obviously was talking in her sleep. Gently, her parents awakened her.

What had she been dreaming about? they asked.

It was about the restaurant where they ate on Fridays, she told them. It was about the table where they always sat, the one near the corner window. In her dream they were all getting ready to sit down when a car crashed right through the window, headed right for the table. She could still see it. They mustn't ever sit at that table again.

They told her they wouldn't. They smiled to reassure her. They told her to try to go back to sleep, not to worry.

The following Friday the whole family went to the restaurant. Margaret was in a state of great apprehension, but when her parents offered to take her elsewhere, she would have none of it. She had to go, she said. Once there, however, they naturally chose a different table. Margaret went to see the manager.

As dinner progressed, her father noticed that no one was sitting at their old table, even though people were waiting. He remarked on this.

Margaret said, "I told the manager if he let anyone sit there while we were eating, we'd never come in here again. I told him you'd pay him extra for keeping it clear."

"Did you, now?" Her father glanced up to see the manager watching them curiously. He started to utter some caustic comment. Suddenly there a scream, a rending crash, and the entire building shuddered. A heavy automobile had crashed through the corner window, disintegrating the empty table and chairs!

Margaret's father was not required to pay for keeping the table clear.

There were other incidents of precognition in Margaret, though none that pronounced. As she grew older, her disassociation grew less and less until her contact with a higher realm of consciousness eventually was broken entirely and she lived as others. Was she better off? She was more acceptable socially. But during those times when her visions had come perhaps she had stood at the very threshold of knowledge that might transform the entire human state. In any case, Margaret gradually taught herself to conform, and the door slowly closed.

Much on earth is hidden from us,
But to make up for that we have been given
A precious mystic sense of our living bond

With the other world, with the higher heavenly world,
And the roots of our thoughts and feelings
Are not here but in other worlds.

—Fyodor Dostoyevski

MAGIC ALCHEMY

A whole host of phenomena is available as evidence of the
constant functioning of the psychic side of man's consciousness. Materialization is another area of supernatural experience that has come to many and for which there is no logical
explanation. For example, John has a vivid dream that he
is visiting the home of his friend, Earl, in a city several
hundred miles away. He dreams he is sitting in a chair in
Earl's front room, reading a book called *Land of the Phar-
aohs,* when Earl comes into the room and stares at him in
a startled manner. John awakens and finds it is morning.
He can't get the dream out of his mind. Several days later
he receives a letter from Earl. "The other morning," the
letter states, "I arose from bed and went into the front
room. To my utter amazement, there you were, sitting in
my favorite chair reading the very book I had been reading
the night before, *Land of the Pharoahs.* I started to speak
to you and you suddenly disappeared. I realize, of course,
that I suffered an hallucination, but I simply cannot tell
you how very real you looked!" To make the matter even
more astounding, John remembers exact whole passages
from the book, which he had never read or even heard of
before!

People's lives have been saved by their receiving warnings
from the materialization of friends, loved ones, or even
perfect strangers. And one case is even well recorded of a
woman who set out to buy a house because she felt she had
lived in it before. Even when she learned it was haunted,
she insisted on purchasing it. As it turned out she had
nothing to worry about anyway. The tenants on first seeing
her told her that it was she who was the ghost, that they

had seen her many times wandering about the rooms! Some magic exists by which consciousness can be freed from the confines of the body, can go out in trance or even in waking to other places, act there and bring back its information. Universal mind provides us the means to circumvent restricted personal awareness and transfer onto a plane of consciousness that is everywhere at the same time and in which all things exist. The individual who sufficiently surrenders his ego-centeredness in trance or sleep is then existing in universal mind and thus in a mystical sense actually has become all other things, actually is existing in all other places.

There is an area of awareness that exists on a fine hairline between complete absorption in universal mind and retention of personal awareness. From here the individual is able to report his experience, i.e., a subject on the verge of going into deep hypnotic trance or a person attaining to complete lucidity just before falling asleep. Such reports are invariably of a new and completely changed world in which there is no such thing as an inanimate object. All things reveal a new and previously hidden meaning that cannot quite be grasped by the intellect but which makes a profound impact on consciousness. Objects that were thought to be inanimate are seen to be in a state of intense activity, of constant movement and flux and change. One sees consciousness in them, arrested, fixed under some kind of divine limitation, and one sees the possibility of liberating that consciousness, of changing, as it were, the thing perceived into something different through the simple act of perception. It is this higher state of being, this condition of higher consciousness that undoubtedly was experienced by Jesus in the performance of his miracles. Changing water into wine takes on an entirely different meaning when the possibility is seen of Jesus actually *being* both water and wine. Feeding the multitudes with a few loaves, stilling the waters, quieting the winds, raising the dead, healing the sick are all indications of an enlightened man who has attained to that higher plane of existence wherein he has fused his being with universal mind, wherein he has achieved identical consciousness with God. He affects all created things simply by perceiving in them the change he desires, for his will and the divine will are one.

> Deep in the man sits fast his fate
> To mold his fortune, mean or great.
> —Ralph Waldo Emerson

PSYCHO-KINESIS

Dowsing is a further example of the subtle contact between conscious mind and universal mind. For years the water diviner held a prominent place in all communities. Nowadays he is much more apt to be an amateur geologist and have access to subterranean charts, but there was a day when he wandered the earth with his forked hazel stick, dipped its nose to the ground, commanded, "Dig," and water was found. Many an oil well and vein of precious ore also have been discovered on such information, but with advancing technological progress the art of the "Dowser" has fallen into disrepute, and, indeed, those who are adept at the art have become so scarce as to be practically extinct. But the evidence is there, evidence that always points to a magical contact between the diviner and some consciousness inherent in water, oil, and ore, as if they were he and he they, and all the art of finding them dependent upon an invisible psychic process that had nothing to do with the hazel stick at all.

Spiritists, poltergeists, and mediums are additional evidence of the psychic ability of man to displace himself mentally in time and space and assume a different identity. Much trickery has been unveiled in investigations of professional mediums, but there remains a large body of indisputable evidence of materializations and rappings and levitations, solid testimony that certain individuals either have access to a supernatural power or are used by such a power to effect its ends. Spiritist Daniel Dunglas Home, through a lifetime of producing the most incredible phenomena, was never discredited as resorting to trickery. The James Hermanns are an outstanding and current case of poltergeistism. The "Haunted Hermanns" have experienced almost every kind of flying object. Bottles and boxes fly off shelves, cabinets fall over, corks pop out, mirrors crack, radios throw themselves across the room, chairs tip over, and always at the behest of some mysterious and capricious power that apparently acts independently and shows a definitely mischievous character. Investigation of poltergeists nearly aways reveals a teen-aged child in the family, but as yet has failed to show that such child is deliberately causing the phenomena. Perhaps the young have a closer contact with universal mind, and during periods of emotional upset their tumultuous feelings act on higher spheres, manifest in a topsy-turvy household. In any case, in poltergeistism, objects are set in motion without the intervention of any known force or any known human agency.

MYSTERIOUS MIND

For the most part men live unknowingly, without awareness of their umbilical tie with the power of creation, without being conscious of the vast reservoir of intelligence and psychic energy that is theirs to draw upon. It is perhaps necessary to this particular step in evolution that man should be absorbed in his own individual nature in order that he eventually be led to his universal nature, but now he is blinded to the higher planes of his existence by the restricted horizons provided him by ego. He feels isolated, alone, and his awareness and consciousness are hemmed around with this false notion. Yet his tie with the Divine is not altered. He is still a creature of God, is in spiritual essence actually God Himself, and the pain and suffering and effort required of him by life are to provide the necessary tempering of

spirit by which the individual soul exceeds itself and becomes the oversoul. It is the power and glory of that oversoul that breaks through the wall of ego as thought transference, precognition, clairvoyance, materialization, dowsing, levitation, and spiritual healing to constantly remind us
that our true existence is not in material bodies bound to
the earth but on some higher, heavenly plane that transcends
all earthly limitation.

> It is wisdom to know others
> It is enlightenment to know one's self.
> —Lao Tzu

Hypnosis has provided a tool for the study of universal
mind. Imperfect as its techniques might be, nonetheless it
has exposed for clinical observation the vast reservoir of
power and knowledge that lies below the level of consciousness. Psychology presupposes that each man possesses in
addition to his conscious mind an individual subconscious
mind. Sigmund Freud postulated three mental levels, the
Id, the Ego, and the Super-ego, where the Id was the subconscious accumulation of instincts and urges, the Ego a
sort of straw boss that kept the Id in check, and the Super-
ego transcendent of them both, being conscience. Anyway,
no matter how many levels of mind are postulated by modern
psychology, each is considered to be possessed by the individual as his exclusive property. Psychology admits that many
subconscious minds are similar, but it lays this to a kind of
racial memory, a sort of instinct that is transmitted from
generation to generation through the nerve and brain cells,
a kind of impression on protoplasm. That an overmind exists,
a sea of consciousness and intelligence that encompasses all
life and from which each individual mind derives its being
and its awareness has been to this point largely the exclusive
province of religion and speculative philosophy, though
esoteric groups have held to such belief since the dawn of

recorded history, witness the *Bhagavad-Gita* and the *Vedanta*. It now appears that hynotic techniques have brought universal mind into the laboratory, opening up an entirely new field of scientific investigation.

THE TRANCE

Hypnosis has come a long way since the days when Anton Mesmer displayed his peculiar healing method when he proclaimed that by means of animal magnetism flowing through the tips of his fingers he was able to draw pain and illness from sick bodies. Mesmer fixed his patients with the proverbial hynotic eye, made passes through the air over the affected body part, and startlingly enough made a considerable number of cures. There is evidence that he really believed magnetism flowed through his fingers; certainly he failed to realize that he had succeeded in blocking out the conscious mind so that the subconscious was exposed and respondent to suggestion. In any case, when his name was eventually blackened, so was Mesmerism, as his technique was called, and inasmuch as it was the direct forerunner of hypnotism, hypnotism always has had Mesmer to live down.

James Braid, a physician practicing in England in the nineteenth century, undertook to administer suggestive anaesthesia to his patients with such outstanding results that he wrote a book abou his findings, *Neurypnology,* in which he first used the words hypnosis and hypnotism, which he coined from the Greek work *hynos,* meaning sleep. For a while hypnotism became a fad to be practiced by the unaccomplished upon the uninformed at all manner of parties and gatherings. Stage hypnotists put on shows in theatres and halls, all aimed at producing startling effects rather than dispensing knowledge. As a natural result a reaction developed, and hypnotism fell into disrepute, though it was not entirely abandoned by the medical profession. Gently but insistently physicians used hypnosis for inducing anaesthesia. Even the development of excellent anaesthetics such as chloroform, gas, and novocain did not cause them to abandon it.

Sigmund Freud, himself, investigated hypnotism and even used it occasionally in psychoanalysis, but eventually he set his mind against it, unable to develop its technique to a science or even in the last analysis to determine exactly what part of the human psyche it dealt with. Hypnotism today is commonly used in the practice of medicine, commonly used in the treatment of psycho-neurosis, but still no one knows just what part of man's mental make-up it deals with, except that it lies below the level of consciousness.

Now essentially what hypnotism exposes is universal mind. When the conscious mind is in trance, the entire mental, emotional, and spiritual character of the man is changed. He no longer is the person he was or is he necessarily even the person he might be capable of being, but in some mysterious way responds so completely to every suggestion given him that he can even speak fluently in languages he does not know or understand. Edgar Cayce, an uneducated, almost illiterate man, made brilliant philosophical discourses while in trance, profound and perceptive medical diagnoses, yet while in his normal waking state he had practically no knowledge in these fields. The talent Cayce had was an exceptional susceptibility to hypnosis. In fact, soon after the first time he was hypnotized, he was able at will to hypnotize himself, and this auto-hypnosis was the direct cause of the miracles he performed at Virginia Beach. Cayce in trance became a physician and a philosopher even though such knowledge was not possessed by his conscious mind and even though he had not a day's training in either. The mental and spiritual quality encountered once Cayce's surface personality was out of the way was a tremendous power of becoming, an astounding ability of response that enabled the subconscious to become anything suggested to it. Only one conclusion is permissible from such evidence and that is that the subconscious is capable of becoming anything, that resident in it is all knowledge of all events and all procedures and all people, past, present, and future. This is universal mind. This is the mind of God.

> From every gulf the tides of Being roll
> From every zenith burns the indwelling day
> And life in Life has drowned thee, and soul in Soul;
> And these are God, and thou thyself are they.
> —F. W. H. Myers

CLAIRVOYANCE

Christine was only fifteen years old when she first experienced clairvoyance. She was walking down a country lane, on her way home to the vacation cottage she was sharing with her parents on the shores of a western lake, when suddenly her surroundings faded and she saw the living room of the cabin. On the floor lay her mother, unconscious. She has had a heart attack, thought Christine. She pulled herself back to her surroundings and ran to the village for the doctor. The two of them arrived at the cabin to find the scene inside just as Christine had described it. The doctor administered to the fallen woman, was able to revive her, and she was put to bed. Christine's father came in from the lake where he had been fishing, and he was told the story. Neither he nor anyone else doubted the authenticity of Christine's vision. It seemed like divine intervention.

A few weeks later, Christine dreamed there was a metal box buried in a corner of the backyard, containing money and other papers. Following her instructions, her father dug it up. The box apparently had been underground for some years, but the money and papers inside were intact. There were several hundred dollars in currency and a paid-up insurance policy made out by the owner of the property to his wife. An attempt was made to contact him and it was learned that he had just passed away. His widow has been frantically trying to locate his insurance!

Christine now was almost sixteen years old, and her parents, realizing the significance of these two occurrences of clairvoyance, had her submit to a thorough mental and psychological examination. The results were revealing. Christine possessed normal intelligence, but was inclined to be vague about what occurred around her. She might, for example, sit in the midst of conversation but be unable to recall any of it when asked questions later. It was apparent that the focus of her attention was on an inner world, but of its contents she would confide little. She just liked to daydream, she said. Most marked of all was her suggestibility. She followed all instructions docilely and to the letter, as if compelled to do so by something stronger than herself. She made no resistance, could not be drawn into an argument. If told that dogs were noisy and repulsive she would agree and think of something to say to confirm it. A short time later it could be suggested to her that dogs were lovable and loyal and she would agree and think of something to confirm this opposite idea. She seemed unaware of any conflict in these different attitudes and when they were pointed out to her she was able to justify both positions to her satisfaction. It was obvious she would be a wonderful hypnotic subject but her parents would not permit this and no amount of reasoning could dissuade them. In the end they were assured that their daughter was normal in all ways, but for a slight tendency to suggestibility, and that psychologically she was on the withdrawn side, an introvert, but well adjusted.

Christine had several other clairvoyant dreams, but they were not particularly significant. And as she grew out of adolescence into young womanhood, her ability gradually left her. It is interesting to note that later testing revealed that her degree of suggestibility had changed markedly and that her introversion had been reduced by the incorporation in her personality of many extravert qualities.

RELATING TO GOD-MIND

There is excellent evidence that extrasensory perception is at its height in children of adolescent age. Perhaps it is because such physiological changes are taking place within their bodies, such expansion is being met with in their mental horizons, that many of them unconsciously retreat within themselves, there to better hear whispered voices from other planes of mind and being. Shortly, however, their focus establishes itself in the physical world and they desert forever their intuitive relationship with the Divine.

A quality of universal mind is that it *knows*. The nature of its universality, its infinity, its timelessness, is that the answer is synonymous with the question, the result synonymous with the action, all independent of process. Mathematical geniuses are cases in point. Many of them are able to give in a moment the answers to problems that should take hours of labor with pencil and paper. When asked how they are able to arrive at such rapid results, they answer that they just seem to know, that the answers seem to come from some magical recess of mind and automatically project upon the screen of consciousness the minute the question is asked. In short, it is not they who do the thinking at all, but rather some vaster level of being, some higher and more aware area of consciousness, that they remain servant to and never master of.

If hypnosis is able to expose universal mind, and if the use of this mind lends immense powers to the individual, then why not become accomplished at auto-hypnosis, or failing that, receive regular hynotic treatments and thus expand immensely in effective living? Such a procedure is impossible without a consequent breakdown of individual personality and its disassociation with its surroundings. Occasional treatment by hypnosis produces beneficial effects not only in mental and spiritual realms but in body healing as well, but constant resort to such therapy is in direct an-

tithesis to the underlying motivation of life, which is the
growth of individual mind to complete understanding of
and integration with universal mind, not in the manner of
being absorbed but rather in the manner of consciously
blending with, so that the individual "I" becomes the "I"
of God. Complete immersion in the subconscious can only
produce irrationality, for universal mind can manifest as a
thing only through the window of personality. While ego
or individual self is to be surrendered as a proper relationship between the individual and God, it must never be
obliterated. Nothing remains then to manifest through, and
the whole purpose of life, incarnation of the Divine as a
finite thing, is defeated.

Auto-hypnosis, to a limited degree, is acceptable. Surely
the affirming of mental and spiritual goals and the affirma-
tion of the individual's relationship with and access to the
power of universal mind can produce excellent results.
But even here care must be taken. It is the peculiar relationship of the ego to universal mind that its affirmations are
often negations, that it says one thing and thinks another,
that it believes it is affirming health, while all the while in
the nethermost regions of its emotional blocks and subconscious pain promptings it is affirming disease and affliction
and restriction. That is why the most effective treatment of
any kind is from one mind to another. Detachment, above
all things, is necessary in effective spiritual treatment, in
effective prayer. Hypnosis illustrates that a perfect stranger
has more effective access to our subconscious than we ourselves have. Creative prayer is that prayer that deals directly
with universal mind, unimpeded by the twisted urgings and
subconscient promptings of the ego. Creative prayer, therefore, is that mental and spiritual treatment undertaken by
an enlightened man for the benefit of his neighbor. In short,
the thoughts of others in regard to you are the source and cause
of much that occurs in your life. Knowing this the wise
man cultivates the opinion of others in the same manner as
he cultivates his opinion of himself, by seeing his relation-

ship with the whole, his at-one-ness with all people, his at-one-ness with God.

THE UNSOLID WORLD

Life is a strange and wondrous thing. We seem to exist in a world of solid objects, of movement of things through space, and it is the reality that we give this world of things that makes us materialists, that causes us to be subservient to matter, to the world itself. Yet there is excellent evidence that the universe and all things in it are entirely mental. We gain our knowledge of an object by our sensory apprehension of its vibration. We "see" some vibrations, "touch" some vibrations, "hear" some vibrations, "smell" some vibrations, "taste" some vibrations. The variation in the frequency of vibrations picked up by each of the five senses leaves vast gaps between where tremendous amounts of undiscerned knowledge about the object lie, and, indeed, on either end of the high and low frequencies picked up by the senses lie an almost infinite number of frequencies containing hidden knowledge of the object. In addition, it is not the vibrations themselves that our senses pick up, but rather a mental and neural interpretation of them, for the vibrations impinge upon nerve endings and are transmitted to the brain and there transformed into perception by some central observer. In short, the sensual data we receive from the outside world are but the barest indication of what is truly there; a million times more remains untold about each object than our senses ever record. Perhaps there is nothing there at all in a material sense, but all things are thought-things, apparently laid out in space and time and interacting, but in reality only thoughts in the mind of God.

The most solid objects we know, rocks, trees, steel itself, are not solid at all but each consists of a certain number of imprisoned molecules with far more space between them than in them and each moving about with the speed of an express train, banging into each other and the limits of their prison. The molecule itself is not solid, but consists of a certain number of atoms with far more space between them than in them, and the atoms are partially confined too, though they may leave and reunite according to the laws of chemistry. Neither is the atom solid, but rather consists of a proton and a number of electrons revolving around it, much as planets revolve around the sun and with proportionate distance between. Vibrations from the outside may cause electrons to leave or to enter the atom, giving rise to the science of electronics, and the atom itself may be fissioned or fused, thus setting off a chain reaction in all surrounding atoms as protons and electrons seek new homes and a new balance in "at rest" energy. These atoms, these tiny worlds, cannot even be seen by the most powerful microscope, but are so small they remain in actuality only mental concepts in the minds of those who deal with them. We deduce that they are there because we need some theory to account for the behavior of energy, but perhaps they are not there at all and the world of the microcosm will finally convince us that the macrocosm too is in mind.

> Light and sound come to us in their gay dresses
> As troubadors singing serenades
> Before the windows of the senses.
> What is constantly before us, claiming our attention,
> Is not the kitchen but the feast;
> Not the anatomy of the world, but its countenance.
> —Rabindranath Tagore

INVESTIGATING THE UNKNOWN

The past one hundred years have seen such staggering advances in the world of scientific research that it is now quite apparent that man has arrived at the threshold of his dominion over the universe itself. Yet even as he prepares to embark into outer space, still he does not know himself, what he is, where he comes from, what his destiny is. It is

almost as if his Creator turned his senses outward so that
he could not see himself, and even when he finally has
settled and inhabited the universe still he may be ignorant
of his own soul. Surely he is not purely an automaton, performing all unknowingly the bidding of some blind will.
Surely the conquering of nature and her ultimate enslavement are not the goal and purpose of his existence. His
tragedy is his failure thus far to find his origin and destiny,
for until he is able to conquer the death of the body by
transcending it, until he is able to rise above material existence by achieving planes of spiritual being, then he is nothing
but a tiny link in an unending procession that marches
eternally from womb to grave. Science has not provided
answers for the eternally questing soul. Science has picked
the bones of the material world, and the animating Presence
still is hidden. It remains for the inner vision of mystic and
poet and saint to reveal to the weary wayfarer his kinship
and likeness to God. For it is in the Divine that we all are
Divine, and it is by spiritual union with Him that we per-
petuate ourselves, attain to immortality, dominion over
earth. It is through investigation of the worlds of mind and
spirit that man will fulfill his mission and himself.

Much groundwork in the investigation of other spheres
of consciousness has been laid by Drs. J. B. Rhine of Duke
University and S. G. Soal of the University of London.
Both Rhine and Soal have conducted endless experiments
with specially marked cards in which subjects attempted to
guess a card held by another person (telepathy), guess one
that would soon be drawn (precognition), or guess one that
was drawn by automatic means and not witnessed (clairvoyance). Results, tabulated according to the most modern
techniques of mathematics, have proved beyond any shadow
of doubt that a factor of extrasensory perception exists in all
persons. But how to approach it, how to develop it, is something else again. Neither Rhine nor Soal have found a solution.

The London Society for Psychical Research has accumulated over the years an amazing number of highly authenticated cases of clairvoyance, psychokinesis, and precognition, concerning all manners and types of people, some of them well known.

M. Maeterlinck wrote of an occurrence of psychometry (object reading) when once he took to a certain woman a handkerchief that had been sent to him anonymously. The handkerchief's sender was described to the most intimate detail. Maeterlinck stated that he subsequently investigated and found this psychometric reading to be absolutely true.

H. G. Wells often wrote of mystical experiences in which he was able to get outside himself and merge with something greater. Sir Oliver Lodge recorded many instances of extrasensory perception. Henri Bergson and Friedrich Nietzsche reported experience with the "other world" of consciousness. And the list of those with profound and moving knowledge of the invisible planes of existence is enormous: Jesus Christ, Guatama Buddha, Lao Tzu, Whitman, Wordsworth, Balzac, Boehme, Ruysbroeck, Dante, St. Paul, to mention only a few.

It is almost as if a crack occasionally appears in the hard rock of consciousness, admitting through for a moment a ray of light that bathes the world in a new glow, then the crack is sealed and the world returns to normal, but the memory remains; it entices us with its promise of things to come.

> Yet ever and anon a trumpet sounds
> From the hid battlements of Eternity;
> Those shaken mists a space unsettle, then
> Round the half-glimpsed turrets slowly wash again.
> —Francis Thompson

OTHER PLANES OF AWARENESS

We are quickly taught when we investigate the world of phenomena that there is in each thing essentially the same quality of being that exists in ourselves. A thing is not a thing just from being so big and so hard and so heavy and shaped a certain way as it is from fixed energy or arrested consciousness. Perhaps consciousness and energy are not exactly the same thing, certainly there appear to be differences between them; but there is evidence in the behavior of the very atom that it exercises choice in what it will or will not do, so that even if it does not actually have a will of its own it certainly is a vehicle for some other will. If there is intelligence in the atom there has to be intelligence in the rock, and if everything in the world is consciousness fixed into form through being arrested as idea, then we have an entirely new concept of being to contend with.

For in the end consciousness is consciousness; to be is to be; to know is to know; to be aware is to be aware. There cannot be different kinds of consciousness but only different degrees of consciousness, only limitations of complete consciousness, so that one degree might say, "I am conscious here and only here," and another might say, "I am conscious of this and only this," and each by the limitation it imposes upon itself isolates itself from the whole. Yet each continues not only to remain a part of the whole but in actuality is the same as and equal to the whole because there is only one consciousness. Now what this means to each man must be determined in the end by the degree to which he has managed to slip away from the grasp of the material world and to perceive the spiritual basis upon which everything is built and sustained. Light begins to dawn upon him when he becomes aware that all things are immersed in a sea of consciousness of which he not only is a part but in some mysterious way the entire sea. As this mystical insight begins to take possession of his nature he will look on created things and see behind their boundaries to the hidden idea that gives them form. Then it is that he is able by means of direct identification to actually become the thing he apprehends, to actually know it through expanding his consciousness to encompass it. This boundary broken through, all so-called laws of nature are superseded, are no longer restrictions to be observed, but each obeys him, his will, his thought, his desire, for that which he knows is innate in the thing he knows, and in a very real and actual sense he and each thing are one.

The enlightened man realizes there are no absolute laws, that everything is in a state of flux, that life itself is a creative thing and therefore must change constantly. He sees no permanence in matter but rather recognizes it as consisting of essentially the same thing as himself, consciousness only, and he perceives it not as an indication of an outer world but as an indication of the inner. He does not attach himself to the body for he realizes he is not the body, that his roots rest in some far-off place where he shall return when his moment of becoming is over. There are other worlds, other times, other planes of existence to which he aspires, and there he shall find his fulfillment.

A PSYCHIC CALL

Moments of mystical experience often occur in the lonely grandeur of primitive nature. John and Pete were men of vastly different backgrounds and somewhat different beliefs, but they had a common love for nature and a fondness for fishing. One spring they made a pilgrimage to Jackson Hole, Wyoming, and from there into the fastness of the rugged Teton Mountains. They traveled by horse, with two pack animals and a guide. Their goal was some of the more remote lakes and the indescribable thrill of matching wits with the fighting trout. They were not disappointed. The fishing exceeded their expectations.

On the fifth evening in camp, John announced that the next morning he would scale the north ridge and see what lay beyond. He'd had enough fishing for a while, he said, and besides he was curious about the waterfall. The guide couldn't tell him and none of the maps showed the headwaters of the creek that tumbled from the ridge in a misty fall to the lake below. He urged Pete to accompany him, but

Pete declined, preferring to fish. The guide, of course, offered to go, but John said the ridge was a challenge and he wanted no help. Pete, he laughed, wouldn't have been any help. And so it was settled.

John left before sunrise. He carried a small amount of food and water, and he grinned and said he guessed he'd be back before sundown but not to wait up. Both Pete and the guide expected him back long before then, but they didn't say anything. They waved goodbye and watched him disappear on the slopes of the mountain just as the sun tipped its top. All that morning they fished. When they came in for lunch, Pete searched the ridge with binoculars, but he saw no sign of John. They took a short nap and went back on the lake, and in the late afternoon Pete began to feel uneasy. Pretty soon he was seized by a kind of violent trembling and sweat broke out on his forehead. "Something's happened!" he exclaimed. "John's caught. He's trapped in some kind of hole and can't get out!"

The guide didn't wait to remonstrate with him. He had lived too long with the inscrutable telepathic ways of wild animals to doubt that Pete's feelings were authentic. They rowed immediately to shore, and even though the sun was low in the sky, they started up the slopes of the mountain. Night had fallen by the time they reached the ridge. It seemed senseless to go on. They might easily be killed or injured upon the treacherous rocks in the darkness. They made a small fire and huddled before it as the hours of night wore on.

The two men sat in a doze, their eyes fixed on the fire. The flames smoldered and leaped and flickered and danced. In ever-changing shades of orange and yellow the vision formed.

"I see him," said Pete at last.

The guide knew at once what he meant. "Where is he?"

"In a fissure in a big rock. He's wedged tightly in the bottom."

"Is he alive?"

"Alive but unconscious. There is pain in his left leg,

and his side hurts. He is very weak. He doesn't know whether
to hold on or not. He thinks it is hopeless."

"Tell him it is not hopeless."

"I'll try."

Pete peered into the fire.

After a while the guide asked, "Where is the rock?"

"Down the slope to our left. After a while there is a
stunted pine. Beyond it, perhaps two hundred yards, is
the fissure where John lies."

"We will go as soon as it is light," the guide said.

At dawn they set off. Within a half hour they came to the
stunted pine. From there is was a short distance to the fissure. Peering down into darkness they could see nothing.
One end of a rope was made fast, and the guide lowered
himself to the bottom. His voice floated back.

"He's here, and he's alive!"

The rope was tied to John, the guide climbed out, and
he and Pete pulled the injured man to the top. He was barely
conscious, but he grinned.

"I knew you were coming," he said. "I could see you. You
camped on the ridge last night."

John's leg was broken as were three of his ribs, and he
was suffering from shock and exposure. They managed to
get him back to camp, where they set the broken bones,
treated him with sulfa and gave him two days' rest. Then
they made the return trip to Jackson Hole. John recovered
completely. Neither he nor Pete will ever forget the complete
spiritual rapport they established that eventful night. Sig-
nificantly, it never again has occurred to either of them.

TOWARD A MAGIC MOMENT

Gradually the higher power of universal mind is breaking
through. This very day somewhere on the globe, some person, all unsuspecting, will be put in touch with universal
mind, and for a moment, perhaps even an hour, will transcend space and time and the limits of his body. This visita-

tion will leave as suddenly as it came, and he might never experience it again during all his life, but the memory of it will remain bright. That crescendoing experience will have shaken him to the foundations of his being, and he will be ever after a different man. Always he will be conscious of the higher planes of awareness that lie behind and beyond the visible world, and through knowing that he once climbed onto them, the entire yearning of his heart will be to re-experience that unutterable ecstasy, that range of easy and perfect power once again. So he will dedicate his life to a search for God, and so he will find Him.

All the power and perfection of universal mind is yours. If you will surrender your life and your desires to the Divine, become an instrument for the working of His will in the world, then sooner or later your consciousness will expand into areas of awareness and perception that will transform your existence. It is not what you are or what you do or where you go that is important, but the self within you. Meditate on that. See behind the series of little "I's" that are constantly performing their concealing dance in front of your true being. In some magical moment of complete repose you will see, truly see, and your illumination will have begun.

ELEVENTH MEDITATION

Behind the world of the senses are higher planes of consciousness where the true causes of things exist. I affirm that these higher planes are within me, that my destiny is to know them, that they will reveal themselves to me insofar as I surrender my being and will and purpose to God. I know that the truth of objects is not completely revealed by my senses, that there is hidden significance in all things. I know that in actuality there are no inanimate objects, that each thing consists of arrested consciousness. I know this consciousness proceeds out of the mind and being of God, and that in its pure form it is idea only, awareness only, similar, even identical to my own. Therefore I affirm my oneness with all things. In all I perceive the indwelling Presence. He resides in the tree, the flower, the bird, the beast, in my neighbor. He is the observer that sits in the center of each creature, who is never restricted by the restrictions of form. I am not I in a true and real sense, but my consciousness is the consciousness of God. Where I fail to expand to meet this awareness there I limit myself to the form and circumstance of ordinary life. Therefore I take refuge in the body and being of God. I stand apart from my own strivings and concerns and desires and am not identified with them, but watch them. They are not me; they are the warp and woof of life's longing for itself, the inevitable result of conflict and aspiration and effort and failure, and though I exist in the midst of all and participate in all, still I am not touched, and by that very detachment there is unloosed through my nature the power and the purpose of the Divine. His vaster being, His greater consciousness manifest through me.

12 MASTERY OVER LIFE

Stand not apart from the Maker of all
'Tis illusion for thee to be awed ·
By a spiritual Self that is ten miles tall
He is thee, thou art He, the indwelling God

THE SPIRITUAL FLAME

There is inherent in the void of space itself and in all apparently inconscient matter a spirit of all-encompassing light and wisdom, hidden there, gradually emerging, eventually to reveal itself as the Godhead. The unfoldment of the spirit through successive stages of space, matter, animal, man, and God is the very purpose of life. If existence were only a matter of chance, then sooner or later it would have become chaos. If it were merely a matter of the mechanistic working of blind forces, there could have been no progress, no evolution. The emergence of consciousness out of the inconscient, of supra-consciousness out of the conscious, can only mean that every step of the way is in the hands of a supra-mental being who, on the planes of matter, is slowly but surely manifesting his entire nature and complete awareness. God is, and He is in all, and even though hidden, yet controls all; and each thing exists only through Him and for a purpose that He alone fathoms, and each thing is in essence Himself and has no existence outside Him.

Life, then, is not for the sake of man, but for God. Man

himself is only an illusion that God has donned in the play
of expression He is engaging in while revealing His nature.
Man is a particular stage in the unfoldment of God-consciousness, a stage that has transcended the inconscient but is yet
short of exceeding the limits of matter and consequently has
not arrived at that supra-consciousness which reveals the
ultimate mental and spiritual being. Nevertheless it is God
who is man, God in man who is conscious, who calls himself
"I," who is bound by an illusion of His own making, who
through the sheer delight of becoming has involved Himself
in matter and now through that same delight seeks liberation from it. Thus it is you, yourself, who are God, not in
physical being, not in the limited sense of ego or conscious
knowledge or acquired skills, but in spiritual essence, in
sheer being, for in the depths of your soul, on another plane
of existence, a flame of being burns, no bigger than the tip
of the thumb, and you are it, and it is you, and both are
God.

Man's dilemma, then, is caused by his newly won self-
consciousness, his apparent separation from other beings and
the world around him. He sees events and people as existing
outside himself, as possessing a primary physical reality that
acts upon him and which he may act upon. He feels that a
force outside him is either something to be confronted or
acceded to, that he too may generate a force that either
must be confronted or acceded to, and so he sets his physical
being and egoistic sense of self to acting upon and reacting
to things around him. Thus it is that more often than not
he opposes his ego-will to the will of God and suffers pain
and defeat. This is his present evolutionary delusion. This
is his fall from grace.

THE DUAL WAY

The way to mastery is first to acknowledge the will of God
as the supreme working in the world. Once this very primary

spiritual decision is made a man no longer seeks to oppose his ego-will against events or people but rather seeks through expanding his consciousness to penetrate and understand them. Soon he sees God there, intuitively perceives the divine purpose, makes his will one with divine will and thus rids himself of suffering, pain, and defeat. The simple acknowledgment of the will of God as the supreme working is not the whole course to mastery, however. There are those people, and many of them are sincere seekers, who have so thoroughly immersed themselves in humility that it has become a kind of second ego and they cannot break out of its limitations or expand into the light of supra-mental power and action because they have imprisoned their growth in abasement. Complete death of the individual in a swallowing up by the infinite does not produce mastery. Mastery must be exhibited, must effectuate itself, must work in the world, not simply in some hidden realm of the spirit; otherwise it is not mastery at all but only isolated spiritual ecstasy and thus still bound to the ego. The individual must surrender himself to the Divine, true, must actually immerse himself in the vastness of the Divine being, but at the same time he must also expand until he is able actually to sense the Divine as being contained within him. Spiritual growth takes two directions: into the Divine as a matter of penetration, the object of which is to feel, to sense, to achieve identity; and outward as a matter of expansion so as to be able to contain the Divine and thus to know, to do, to effectuate. One type of growth without the other produces half-illumination. Only both produce mastery.

Take up your abode in His Soul!
Take up your abode in heaven, oh bright full moon!
Like the heavenly Scribe, He will open your heart's book,
That He may reveal mysteries unto you.
                                        —Jalalu'd Din

STEPS TO MASTERY

It is by becoming aware of the existence of God that we seek Him, and it is by seeking Him that we embark upon the road to spiritual illumination. Thus the first step to mastery is consecration, a total focusing of our intent and energies on uncovering the Godhead, on knowing Him. When we seek him, then sooner or later we must find Him, but only if we first surrender our egoistic will and seek to follow His intent in all things. Thus we learn to live in accordance with a greater plan, a more heavenly consciousness, and we inevitably grow senses attuned to the voices of the spirit. Thus the second step to mastery is surrender. We live in a world of competition and clash, reward and defeat, pain and pleasure, and the great temptation always before us that we think all thoughts, have all feelings, perform all acts out of egoistic desire. Desire for the fruits of our actions, for the applause of our fellows, the gains of our endeavor, must be exorcised ruthlessly from our nature, for desire keeps us bound to the ego, erects insurmountable walls around the consciousness, makes it impossible to grow. We overcome desire by offering our thoughts, our feelings, our actions to the Divine, giving all to Him without attachment to result. This is sacrifice performed upon the altar of the ego, that we might more clearly see God. We must perform it daily, even hourly, for sacrifice is the third step to mastery. Then and only then, these three steps taken, will the face of the Divine be revealed to us, and we perceive Him in all His power and glory, and we see our umbilical attachment to all created things. Then we love, and in that love we are fused with Him, and the light of His consciousness bears us upwards onto new planes of being, new effectiveness in living, for love is the fourth step to mastery.

These are the steps to mastery over life: consecration; surrender; sacrifice; and love. He who takes them with his heart and performs each as a living sacrament will find his entire being transformed, will awaken the sleeping soul of humanity with his magnificent illustration of the divine life.

> I want to teach men the sense of their existence,
> Which is the Superman,
> The lightning out of the dark cloud of man.
>
> —Friedrich Nietzsche

THE LIFE DIVINE

The end of mastery is the divine life, an earthly existence lived in fullness, joy, and complete effectiveness. There is inherent in our natures a perfect Being whose purpose is to unveil Himself in space and time. Insofar as we allow Him to totally possess us, that far His image shines through. And possess us He will in any case; use us He will in any case; but when we identify ourselves with ego and surface mind, His being is obscured and we struggle in the grip of forces we neither control nor understand. It is only by living through God that our lives take on significance. If we live in the ego we live for an ephemeral, mortal thing and we are saddened and frustrated. The divine life is not simply a spiritual realization that transforms a man's inner world and leaves the outer unchanged. Such realization would have but the barest meaning. Spiritual illumination that has not the power to effectively change the world is not true illumination at all, but only a kind of emotional and intellectual sham, a delusion of the ego still, and worse, one that chooses death instead of life. The enlightened man by special deputation of the Divine is granted the power to act directly upon things through the power of his consciousness, not through being opposed to them, but through being one-souled with them. Through this mystical superseding of the boundaries of consciousness, what he perceives is what each thing perceives, and his will and that thing's will are the same.

PURIFICATION

It is not into blown-up ego that the enlightened man elevates his consciousness. It is through abandoning ego altogether that he is able to perceive other planes of awareness. It is through a kind of dying, a complete letting go of his individual self and desires that he truly becomes an instrument of God and thus eventually is able to transcend the limitations of his earthly self. The will he has always known, desire-will, must be let go of altogether, for it is through this will that he often falls into opposition with God's will and thus experiences suffering and pain and defeat. The Divine purifies each instrument by threshing it in its individuality, by exposing it to the fires and elements of existence, then accepting it home again, expanded now, cleansed of its false sense of self, a worthy instrument for His own being. This is the purpose of life.

To be, to become, to bring into being, these are the surging forces that underlie all nature, that provide motivating force for everything that is done, everything that exists, every form of life. The great and awesome work that is going on in the universe is not under the plan and supervision of men, but of God. It is He in them who builds and conquers and explores and aspires. It is He in them whose sure hand can be seen bringing all things under dominion, removing inexorably the veil from space and time and cause. The great commandment of life is to be used, and we are only truly used when we offer ourselves as a living sacrifice to Him to do with as He sees fit, without tears or pleas, without anguish or remorse, but with joy and fulfillment. Let us then be what we truly are, become that which we are capable of becoming, bring into being that which we are capable of envisaging, all at the behest and under the will of God. Let us surrender ourselves to Him to be completely used in the fire that is life so that in the end the spirit may be

fulfilled and proceed to its destiny unencumbered by fear
or frustration or remorse.

> God is law, say the wise;
> Oh Soul and let us rejoice
> For if He thunder by law
> The thunder is yet His voice.
> —Alfred Lord Tennyson

THE TRANSCENDENT GOAL

To truly become ourselves is the thing to be done; and our
true self exceeds the outer body and surface mind. If we
salve the wounds and hurts of the ego, strive to understand
its gropings and desires and hates, in the end we understand
nothing, have appeased nothing, have dealt with nothing,
for the ego never truly exists but is only an infinitely changing mask behind which is hidden the one eternal and
omnipresent Self. It is this Self which is our sustenance and
our salvation. As long as we are separated from it by giving
false reality to the ego, we are prevented from expanding
our consciousness into universal mind, into God-being, into
cosmic awareness. But that very instant that we put aside
personal desire and seek only the will of the Divine, that
moment we irrevocably have placed our feet on the path
to illumination.

And the goals to be attained through enlightenment transcend all earthly things, have their roots in heaven, but
just because they concern the root matters of existence so
they affect all material things, and the final proof that the
spirit has undergone transfiguration lies in its works in the
world. Any other claim to mastery is false. Spiritual illumination that deals with the spirit only and does not free it from
its bondage to material existence is meaningless. Spirit is
involved in matter for the purpose of rising above it, to
become free of pain and defeat and death and decay. This

redemption gives life its significance, gives creation a meaning, gives purpose to the eternal seeking of created things for their Creator.

Directing the consciousness inward and living inward requires an extreme act of decision, a breaking away from the hold of the senses and consequent enamoration with the incessant parade of sensual stimuli. There is no other path to spiritual illumination. Inward the eye of the soul must be turned, there to discern the indwelling God, thus to exceed the limitations of the body and ego in a self-expansion coincident with the measure of the Divine. Under no circumstance must this going inward be identified with that painfully introverted egoistic retreat from the world that is the mark of the wounded ego. The introverted ego adds to its psychological illness by becoming preoccupied with the movements and memories of the little dwarf it considers to be itself. The dwarf has not the courage or spiritual resource to abandon self altogether, and thus, through surrender, open up the vistas of a new world. But behind the dwarf, beyond the perception of the ego, exists a supra-mental being of light and power and beauty and perfection, whose image we adopt as our own the moment we perceive Him.

> My Self supports all beings
> And constitutes their existence
> I am the Self
> Which abides in all.
> —Bhagavad-Gita

TRANSFIGURATION

In Nepal by Katmandu near the headwaters of the Ganges dwelt the blessed Sanjaya, chosen of God, bearer of the light, knower of the Absolute, worker of miracles. A rude hut on the slopes of the Himalayas was his home, exposed to wind and elements, beset by storms in the winter, insignificant on the mountainside but nestled in the lap of God. Many were

Sanjaya's years and far were his travels, and he had dwelt among all manner of men. Europe and Africa had known him, and America and Australia, and the light of his love and his learning he had dispensed at the will of God.

There came one day to his mountainside hut a man to whom the Truth had been revealed but whose heart had not accepted it, who had not yet resigned the dominion of the ego, who had not yet surrendered to God. The two men sat cross-legged before a small fire on the earthen floor of the hut, and outside the sinking sun set the mountaintops afire, left the valleys in descending night. This is their dialogue:

"There is an ache in my heart," said the seeker, "and a loneliness in my soul. Joy is gone, and hope. Man is swallowed in the unimaginable abyss of space and time, and God does not even know him."

Sanjaya moved his hand. "The spirit of man is grown around with flesh, and in order to break through into his true existence he must grow in two directions—inward into the heart of God; and outward to encompass the being of God. If he grows only outward he magnifies his ego and eventually is broken on the wheel of desire. If he grows only inward he loses himself altogether and is saddened at his weakness. It is there that your progress has been arrested. You have penetrated but not expanded. You have not fully opened your soul."

"How is it that I have not grown outward? I have sought God with all my heart."

"Perhaps you have not sought Him for His sake, but for yours. Action performed for the sake of desire is action performed for the ego, and if one acts in delusion one perpetuates delusion. You have carried the false boundaries of the ego-self with you, even though you have penetrated the heart of spiritual enlightenment."

"It is true that I have sought God for the sake of myself, for the sake of my inner peace and strength, but how else can one seek Him?"

"One can surrender to Him, perform every act for Him, think every thought for Him. Thus one eventually is led by His will and not by ego-will, thus one eventually expands to include His power and purpose."

The seeker felt the anguish of his heart. Then, as he peered out the open door at the darkened slopes of the mountain, something lifted off the shoulders of his soul and passed away into nothingness. He felt joy come over him. Ecstasy seized and possessed him.

"God has spoken to you," said Sanjaya. "It is written on your face. Now the limits of your consciousness are down. Now you are open to receive Him."

The seeker felt the world recede. Vistas of light and shadow and color opened before him, all hemmed around with sound that was not really sound but instead a kind of incredible harmony, mathematically perfect, but not cold, rather warm with lovingness and beauty. His innermost heart, long ago disappeared into impenetrable depths, returned to him, energized now with a vitality beyond itself, enlarged with a capacity that included all things.

Sanjaya stood and touched him on the brow. A current flowed between them, powerful, relentless, but still compatible and loving, and it seized them and shook them and they rose above themselves and stood atop the mountain and surveyed the machinery of the universe. And the seeker was awed by what he beheld and fear began to flood into him and he would have fled at this return of the ego, but Sanjaya gripped his arm and kept him faced into the countenance of God.

"You are being threshed now," he said. "The chaff is being winnowed from you so that the pure grain may grow and the ego trouble you no more. Let down the doors of your being and fully allow Him to enter. Grow! Not only shall He possess you but you shall possess Him. Peace, power, and perfect action shall be yours."

They stood, these two, guru and disciple, on the mountaintop that all aspire to; and as they surrendered to God so

God surrendered to them; and they knew that ecstasy, that indescribable wholeness and joy that comes of union with Him.

> I am a Lamp to thee who beholdest Me,
> I am a Mirror to thee who perceivest Me,
> I am a Door to thee who knockest at Me,
> I am a Way to thee, a wayfarer.
>
> —The Apocrypha

YOUR SPIRITUAL DESTINY

This evolution out of matter, this unfolding out of flesh of the Godhead in all its glory and power is not something that must be awaited through further centuries of evolution, but is upon us now, is fully capable of realization now, for the secret and universal Self is not gradually entering into His created existences, but is totally existent in the heart of each. God is entirely within you, all His power, and presence, and wisdom, and knowledge. You are not just a part of God; you are altogether God, and God is altogether you. For the purpose of this self-finding did He involve Himself in matter, absorb Himself in each of His separate existences, and as He evolves and unfolds out of each, so He discovers Himself, all aspects of His nature, and this is His delight, this is the salvation of each of us. We have only to let go of absorption with our surface selves, resign the ego and its bondage to desire, and the Divine emerges from us, transforms our lives with His presence and power and serenity. A supra-mental Being transcendent of the limitations of the flesh, of space and time, of pain and suffering and defeat and decay, is the purpose of evolution. Gradually the emergence of that being is taking place. Buddha was such a one, as were Moses, Christ, Mohammed. Each time an enlightened man arises from the bondage of ignorance, that much closer is brought the day when mankind shall march by tens of thousands toward spiritual fulfillment.

Now your spiritual destiny is upon you. The secret knowledge is yours. The Divine in His totality dwells within you. Abandon ego and bondage to your surface self and give over your life to Him. He will transform it into an image of power and perfection. You will attain to mastery through becoming one-souled with things, through becoming united with God.

I rest not upon my great task to open the Eternal Worlds,
To open the immortal eyes of Man
Inwards into the world of thought; into Eternity
Ever expanding in the bosom of God, the Human Imagination.
O Saviour, pour upon me thy Spirit of meekness and love.
Annihilate the Selfhood in me; be thou all my life.

                                     —William Blake

◇◇

TWELFTH MEDITATION

I resign the dominion of the ego and surrender my life to God. I renounce the priority of sensual stimuli and find within my own nature the power to originate thought, feeling, action. No longer do I exist as reflex to events around me, but now I take up that larger existence that descends from higher planes of mind and spirit. I ally myself with first cause, I identify myself with God. I make my life a living sacrifice to Him, surrendering each of my thoughts, feelings, and actions without desire for their fruits. No longer am I enamored of the vain desires of the ego. Fame and money and applause are not ends in themselves, and when sought as such are traps from which pain and suffering eventually ensue. I penetrate within myself to that core of consciousness that is pure being. There I take refuge, turning away from all strident demands of the beckoning surface self, yielding my identity to God. Yet I do not lose it. My "I" remains, is not engulfed, but now takes on greater awareness, an eternal significance. I expand outward from the center of myself, beyond all horizons, beyond all limitations, seeking to include that which formerly included me, so that I may know God not only by penetrating Him but also by containing Him. Thus I am led to a mystic resolution of myself with the Divine, and He and I become one. By special deputation from above I am forthwith able to live a divine life upon earth. I seek not to change that which is ordained, but only to understand, to possess identical consciousness with all, and in that identical consciousness to act in accordance with divine will, equal-souled to all results, existing always above the conflict, secure in the knowledge of union with God.

◇◇

Books by U.S. Andersen

THREE MAGIC WORDS

1. The Lock 2. Illusion 3. Mind 4. Form 5. Intuition 6. Faith 7. Attraction 8. Love 9. Success 10. Health 11. Immortality 12. The Key   320 Pages . . . $15.00

THE MAGIC IN YOUR MIND

1. The Hidden Cause of All Things 2. Discovering the Secret Self 3. The Greatest Magic of All 4. Self-Mastery 5. Mind Over Matter 6. Mental Imagery 7. The Power of Choice 8. Overcoming Opposition 9. Developing Skills 10. Creating Your Own Talent 11. How to Use Your Sixth Sense 12. The Mental Attitude That Never Fails

256 Pages . . . $15.00

THE GREATEST POWER IN THE UNIVERSE

1. Discoveries of Cybernetics 2. Brain Waves Made Simple 3. Door to the Subconscious Mind 4. Turning On With Alpha Waves 5. Space and Time Unveiled 6. The Power to Change 7. Inner Ecology 8. The Ecology Diet 9. Outer Psychology 10. Male and Female Forces 11. Sex Ecology 12. The New Ecologists 13. Psychic Power 14. The Brotherhood of Light 15. The Master Mind 16. The Master Self 17. The Master Game 18. The Master Plan   272 Pages . . . $10.00

THE SECRET POWER OF THE PYRAMIDS

You'll want to read *The Secret Power of the Pyramids*, sequel to *The Greatest Power in the Universe*. It relates the further adventures of U.S. Anderson in his quest for the highest truth. *The Greatest Power in the Universe* tells of his discovery of an ancient knowledge which leads to a hidden world. *The Secret Power of the Pyramids* describes his encounter with a brotherhood of adepts who have developed an energy unknown to science.

272 Pages . . . $10.00

SUCCESS-CYBERNETICS

1. Cybernetics: Science of Success. How to Use the new Science of Success Cybernetics. How to Find and Develop Your Greatest Potential. How to Set Your Self-Concept to Switch on Success. 2. The Cybernetics Success-Training Program How to Design Your Own Automatic Success Mechanism. How to Train the Success Mechanism into Your Nervous System. How to Constantly Improve Your Skills and Abilities. 3. The Cybernetics of Solving Problems. How to Rocket Your Brain Power up into Orbit. How to Use the Technique of Imagineering Ideas. How to Find Inside Solutions to Unsolvable Problems. 4. The Cybernetics of Handling People. How to Push-Button People into Fast Action. How to Persuade People to Your Point of View. How to"Dynamite the Success Block Between People's Ears. How to 'Quick-shift Adversity into Achievement. How to Make Yourself into an Opportunity Magnet. How to Use a Great Secret That Brings Lasting Happiness.

272 Pages . . . $10.00

Available at your bookstore or directly fromWilshire Book Company.
Please add $2.00 shipping and handling for each book ordered.

Wilshire Book Company
12015 Sherman Road, No. Hollywood, California 91605

For our complete catalog, visit our Web site at http://www.mpowers.com.

WILSHIRE SELF-IMPROVEMENT LIBRARY

ASTROLOGY

____ASTROLOGY—HOW TO CHART YOUR HOROSCOPE Max Heindel 7.00
____ASTROLOGY AND SEXUAL ANALYSIS Morris C. Goodman 10.00
____ASTROLOGY AND YOU Carroll Righter 5.00
____ASTROLOGY MADE EASY Astarte 7.00
____ASTROLOGY, ROMANCE, YOU AND THE STARS Anthony Norvell 10.00
___MY WORLD OF ASTROLOGY Sydney Omarr 10.00
___THOUGHT DIAL Sydney Omarr 7.00
____WHAT THE STARS REVEAL ABOUT THE MEN IN YOUR LIFE Thelma White 3.00

BRIDGE

____BRIDGE BIDDING MADE EASY Edwin B. Kantar 15.00
____BRIDGE CONVENTIONS Edwin B. Kantar 10.00
____COMPETITIVE BIDDING IN MODERN BRIDGE Edgar Kaplan 7.00
____DEFENSIVE BRIDGE PLAY COMPLETE Edwin B Kantar 20.00
____GAMESMAN BRIDGE—PLAY BETTER WITH KANTAR Edwin B. Kantar 7.00
___HOW TO IMPROVE YOUR BRIDGE Alfred Sheinwold 7.00
____IMPROVING YOUR BIDDING SKILLS Edwin B. Kantar 10.00
___INTRODUCTION TO DECLARER'S PLAY Edwin B. Kantar 10.00
___INTRODUCTION TO DEFENDER'S PLAY Edwin B. Kantar 10.00
____KANTAR FOR THE DEFENSE Edwin B. Kantar 10.00
____KANTAR FOR THE DEFENSE VOLUME 2 Edwin B. Kantar 10.00
___TEST YOUR BRIDGE PLAY Edwin B. Kantar 10.00
___VOLUME 2—TEST YOUR BRIDGE PLAY Edwin B. Kantar 10.00
____WINNING DECLARER PLAY Dorothy Hayden Truscott 10.00

BUSINESS, STUDY & REFERENCE

____BRAINSTORMING Charles Clark 10.00
____CONVERSATION MADE EASY Elliot Russell 5.00
____EXAM SECRET Dennis B. Jackson 7.00
___FIX-IT BOOK Arthur Symons 2.00
___HOW TO DEVELOP A BETTER SPEAKING VOICE M. Hellier 5.00
___HOW TO SAVE 50% ON GAS & CAR EXPENSES Ken Stansbie 5.00
___HOW TO SELF-PUBLISH YOUR BOOK & MAKE IT A BEST SELLER Melvin Powers 20.00
___INCREASE YOUR LEARNING POWER Geoffrey A. Dudley 5.00
___PRACTICAL GUIDE TO BETTER CONCENTRATION Melvin Powers 5.00
___PUBLIC SPEAKING MADE EASY Thomas Montalbo 10.00
___7 DAYS TO FASTER READING William S. Schaill 7.00
___SONGWRITER'S RHYMING DICTIONARY Jane Shaw Whitfield 10.00
___SPELLING MADE EASY Lester D. Basch & Dr. Milton Finkelstein 3.00
___STUDENT'S GUIDE TO BETTER GRADES J.A. Rickard 3.00
___YOUR WILL & WHAT TO DO ABOUT IT Attorney Samuel G. King 7.00

CALLIGRAPHY

___ADVANCED CALLIGRAPHY Katherine Jeffares 7.00
___CALLIGRAPHY—THE ART OF BEAUTIFUL WRITING Katherine Jeffares 7.00
___CALLIGRAPHY FOR FUN & PROFIT Anne Leptich & Jacque Evans 7.00

CHESS & CHECKERS

___BEGINNER'S GUIDE TO WINNING CHESS Fred Reinfeld 10.00
___CHESS IN TEN EASY LESSONS Larry Evans 10.00
___CHESS MADE EASY Milton L. Hanauer 5.00
___CHESS PROBLEMS FOR BEGINNERS Edited by Fred Reinfeld 7.00
___CHESS TACTICS FOR BEGINNERS Edited by Fred Reinfeld 10.00
___HOW TO WIN AT CHECKERS Fred Reinfeld 7.00
___1001 BRILLIANT WAYS TO CHECKMATE Fred Reinfeld 10.00

_____1001 WINNING CHESS SACRIFICES & COMBINATIONS Fred Reinfeld 10.00

COOKERY & HERBS

_____CULPEPER'S HERBAL REMEDIES Dr. Nicholas Culpeper 5.00
_____FAST GOURMET COOKBOOK Poppy Cannon 2.50
_____HEALING POWER OF HERBS May Bethel 5.00
_____HEALING POWER OF NATURAL FOODS May Bethel 7.00
_____HERBS FOR HEALTH—HOW TO GROW & USE THEM Louise Evans Doole 7.00
_____HOME GARDEN COOKBOOK—DELICIOUS NATURAL FOOD RECIPES Ken Kraft 3.00
_____MEATLESS MEAL GUIDE Tomi Ryan & James H. Ryan, M.D. 4.00
_____VEGETABLE GARDENING FOR BEGINNERS Hugh Wilberg 2.00
_____VEGETABLES FOR TODAY'S GARDENS R. Milton Carleton 2.00
_____VEGETARIAN COOKERY Janet Walker 10.00
_____VEGETARIAN COOKING MADE EASY & DELECTABLE Veronica Vezza 3.00

GAMBLING & POKER

_____HOW TO WIN AT POKER Terence Reese & Anthony T. Watkins 10.00
_____SCARNE ON DICE John Scarne 20.00
_____WINNING AT CRAPS Dr. Lloyd T. Commins 10.00
_____WINNING AT GIN Chester Wander & Cy Rice 10.00
_____WINNING AT POKER—AN EXPERT'S GUIDE John Archer 10.00
_____WINNING AT 21—AN EXPERT'S GUIDE John Archer 10.00
_____WINNING POKER SYSTEMS Norman Zadeh 10.00

HEALTH

_____BEE POLLEN Lynda Lyngheim & Jack Scagnetti 5.00
_____COPING WITH ALZHEIMER'S Rose Oliver, Ph.D. & Francis Bock, Ph.D. 10.00
_____HELP YOURSELF TO BETTER SIGHT Margaret Darst Corbett 10.00
_____HOW YOU CAN STOP SMOKING PERMANENTLY Ernest Caldwell 5.00
_____NATURE'S WAY TO NUTRITION & VIBRANT HEALTH Robert J. Scrutton 3.00
_____NEW CARBOHYDRATE DIET COUNTER Patti Lopez-Pereira 2.00
_____REFLEXOLOGY Dr. Maybelle Segal 7.00
_____REFLEXOLOGY FOR GOOD HEALTH Anna Kaye & Don C. Matchan 10.00
_____YOU CAN LEARN TO RELAX Dr. Samuel Gutwirth 5.00

HOBBIES

_____BEACHCOMBING FOR BEGINNERS Norman Hickin 2.00
_____BLACKSTONE'S MODERN CARD TRICKS Harry Blackstone 7.00
_____BLACKSTONE'S SECRETS OF MAGIC Harry Blackstone 7.00
_____COIN COLLECTING FOR BEGINNERS Burton Hobson & Fred Reinfeld 7.00
_____ENTERTAINING WITH ESP Tony 'Doc' Shiels 2.00
_____400 FASCINATING MAGIC TRICKS YOU CAN DO Howard Thurston 10.00
_____HOW I TURN JUNK INTO FUN AND PROFIT Sari 3.00
_____HOW TO WRITE A HIT SONG AND SELL IT Tommy Boyce 10.00
_____MAGIC FOR ALL AGES Walter Gibson 10.00
_____STAMP COLLECTING FOR BEGINNERS Burton Hobson 3.00

HORSE PLAYERS' WINNING GUIDES

_____BETTING HORSES TO WIN Les Conklin 10.00
_____ELIMINATE THE LOSERS Bob McKnight 5.00
_____HOW TO PICK WINNING HORSES Bob McKnight 5.00
_____HOW TO WIN AT THE RACES Sam (The Genius) Lewin 5.00
_____HOW YOU CAN BEAT THE RACES Jack Kavanagh 5.00
_____MAKING MONEY AT THE RACES David Barr 10.00
_____PAYDAY AT THE RACES Les Conklin 7.00
_____SMART HANDICAPPING MADE EASY William Bauman 5.00
_____SUCCESS AT THE HARNESS RACES Barry Meadow 7.00

HUMOR

____HOW TO FLATTEN YOUR TUSH Coach Marge Reardon 2.00
____JOKE TELLER'S HANDBOOK Bob Orben 10.00
____JOKES FOR ALL OCCASIONS Al Schock 10.00
____2,000 NEW LAUGHS FOR SPEAKERS Bob Orben 7.00
____2,400 JOKES TO BRIGHTEN YOUR SPEECHES Robert Orben 10.00
____2,500 JOKES TO START'EM LAUGHING Bob Orben 10.00

HYPNOTISM

____CHILDBIRTH WITH HYPNOSIS William S. Kroger, M.D. 5.00
____HOW YOU CAN BOWL BETTER USING SELF-HYPNOSIS Jack Heise 7.00
____HOW YOU CAN PLAY BETTER GOLF USING SELF-HYPNOSIS Jack Heise 3.00
____HYPNOSIS AND SELF-HYPNOSIS Bernard Hollander, M.D. 7.00
____HYPNOTISM (Originally published 1893) Carl Sextus 5.00
____HYPNOTISM MADE EASY Dr. Ralph Winn 10.00
____HYPNOTISM MADE PRACTICAL Louis Orton 5.00
____MODERN HYPNOSIS Lesley Kuhn & Salvatore Russo, Ph.D. 5.00
____NEW CONCEPTS OF HYPNOSIS Bernard C. Gindes, M.D. 15.00
____NEW SELF-HYPNOSIS Paul Adams 10.00
____POST-HYPNOTIC INSTRUCTIONS—SUGGESTIONS FOR THERAPY Arnold Furst 10.00
____PRACTICAL GUIDE TO SELF-HYPNOSIS Melvin Powers 10.00
____PRACTICAL HYPNOTISM Philip Magonet, M.D. 3.00
____SECRETS OF HYPNOTISM S.J. Van Pelt, M.D. 5.00
____SELF-HYPNOSIS—A CONDITIONED-RESPONSE TECHNIQUE Laurence Sparks 7.00
____SELF-HYPNOSIS—ITS THEORY, TECHNIQUE & APPLICATION Melvin Powers 7.00
____THERAPY THROUGH HYPNOSIS Edited by Raphael H. Rhodes 5.00

JUDAICA

____SERVICE OF THE HEART Evelyn Garfiel, Ph.D. 10.00
____STORY OF ISRAEL IN COINS Jean & Maurice Gould 2.00
____STORY OF ISRAEL IN STAMPS Maxim & Gabriel Shamir 1.00
____TONGUE OF THE PROPHETS Robert St. John 10.00

JUST FOR WOMEN

____COSMOPOLITAN'S GUIDE TO MARVELOUS MEN Foreword by Helen Gurley Brown 3.00
____COSMOPOLITAN'S HANG-UP HANDBOOK Foreword by Helen Gurley Brown 4.00
____COSMOPOLITAN'S LOVE BOOK—A GUIDE TO ECSTASY IN BED 7.00
____COSMOPOLITAN'S NEW ETIQUETTE GUIDE Foreword by Helen Gurley Brown 4.00
____I AM A COMPLEAT WOMAN Doris Hagopian & Karen O'Connor Sweeney 3.00
____JUST FOR WOMEN—A GUIDE TO THE FEMALE BODY Richard E. Sand M.D. 5.00
____NEW APPROACHES TO SEX IN MARRIAGE John E. Eichenlaub, M.D. 3.00
____SEXUALLY ADEQUATE FEMALE Frank S. Caprio, M.D. 3.00
____SEXUALLY FULFILLED WOMAN Dr. Rachel Copelan 5.00

MARRIAGE, SEX & PARENTHOOD

____ABILITY TO LOVE Dr. Allan Fromme 7.00
____GUIDE TO SUCCESSFUL MARRIAGE Drs. Albert Ellis & Robert Harper 10.00
____HOW TO RAISE AN EMOTIONALLY HEALTHY, HAPPY CHILD Albert Ellis, Ph.D. 10.00
____PARENT SURVIVAL TRAINING Marvin Silverman, Ed.D. & David Lustig, Ph.D. 15.00
____SEX WITHOUT GUILT Albert Ellis, Ph.D. 7.00
____SEXUALLY ADEQUATE MALE Frank S. Caprio, M.D. 3.00
____SEXUALLY FULFILLED MAN Dr. Rachel Copelan 5.00
____STAYING IN LOVE Dr. Norton F. Kristy 7.00

MELVIN POWERS MAIL ORDER LIBRARY

____HOW TO GET RICH IN MAIL ORDER Melvin Powers 20.00
____HOW TO SELF-PUBLISH YOUR BOOK Melvin Powers 20.00
____HOW TO WRITE A GOOD ADVERTISEMENT Victor O. Schwab 20.00
____MAIL ORDER MADE EASY J. Frank Brumbaugh 20.00
____MAKING MONEY WITH CLASSIFIED ADS Melvin Powers 20.00

METAPHYSICS & NEW AGE

A Personal Invitation from the Publisher, Melvin Powers...

There is a wonderful, unique book titled *The Knight in Rusty Armor* that is guaranteed to captivate your imagination as you discover the secret of what is most important in life. It is a delightful tale of a desperate knight in search of his true self.

Since we first published *The Knight in Rusty Armor,* we have received an unprecedented number of calls and letters from readers praising its powerful insights and entertaining style. It is a memorable, fun-filled story, rich in wit and humor, that has changed thousands of lives for the better. *The Knight* is one of our most popular titles. It has been published in numerous languages and has become a well-known favorite in many countries. I feel so strongly about this book that personally extending an invitation for you to read it.

The Knight in Rusty Armor

Join the knight as he faces a life-changing dilemma upon discovering that he is trapped in his armor, just as *we* may be trapped in *our* armor—an invisible kind that we use to protect ourselves from others and from various aspects of life.

As the knight searches for a way to free himself, he receives guidance from the wise sage Merlin the Magician, who encourages him to embark on the most difficult crusade of his life. The knight takes up the challenge and travels the Path of Truth, where he meets his real self for the first time and confronts the Universal Truths that govern his life—and ours.

The knight's journey reflects our own, filled with hope and despair, belief and disillusionment, laughter and tears. His insights become our insights as we follow along on his intriguing adventure of self-discovery. Anyone who has ever struggled with the meaning of life and love will discover profound wisdom and truth as this unique fantasy unfolds. *The Knight in Rusty Armor* is an experience that will expand your mind, touch your heart, and nourish your soul.

Available at all bookstores. Or send $5.00 (CA res. $5.41) plus $2.00 S/H to Wilshire Book Company, 12015 Sherman Road, No. Hollywood, CA 91605.

For our complete catalog, visit our Web site at www.mpowers.com.

Books by Melvin Powers

HOW TO GET RICH IN MAIL ORDER

1. How to Develop Your Mail Order Expertise 2. How to Find a Unique Product or Service to Sell 3. How to Make Money with Classified Ads 4. How to Make Money with Display Ads 5. The Unlimited Potential for Making Money with Direct Mail 6. How to Copycat Successful Mail Order Operations 7. How I Created a Bestseller Using the Copycat Technique 8. How to Start and Run a Profitable Mail Order Special Interest Book Business 9. I Enjoy Selling Books by Mail—Some of My Successful Ads 10. Five of My Most Successful Direct Mail Pieces That Sold and Are Selling Millions of Dollars' Worth of Books 11. Melvin Powers's Mail Order Success Strategy—Follow it and You'll Become a Millionaire 12. How to Sell Your Products to Mail Order Companies, Retail Outlets, Jobbers, and Fund Raisers for Maximum Distribution and Profit 13. How to Get Free Display Ads and Publicity that Will Put You on the Road to Riches 14. How to Make Your Advertising Copy Sizzle 15. Questions and Answers to Help You Get Started Making Money 16. A Personal Word from Melvin Powers 17. How to Get Started 18. Selling Products on Television   8½" x 11½" — 352 Pages . . . $20.00

MAKING MONEY WITH CLASSIFIED ADS

1. Getting Started with Classified Ads 2. Everyone Loves to Read Classified Ads 3. How to Find a Money-Making Product 4. How to Write Classified Ads that Make Money 5. What I've Learned from Running Thousands of Classified Ads 6. Classified Ads Can Help You Make Big Money in Multi-Level Programs 7. Two-Step Classified Ads Made Me a Multi-Millionaire—They Can Do the Same for You! 8. One-Inch Display Ads Can Work Wonders 9. Display Ads Can Make You a Fortune Overnight 10. Although I Live in California, I Buy My Grapefruit from Florida 11. Nuts and Bolts of Mail Order Success 12. What if You Can't Get Your Business Running Successfully? What's Wrong? How to Correct it 13. Strategy for Mail Order Success   8½" x 11½" — 240 Pages . . . $20.00

HOW TO SELF-PUBLISH YOUR BOOK AND HAVE THE FUN AND EXCITEMENT OF BEING A BEST-SELLING AUTHOR

1. Who is Melvin Powers? 2. What is the Motivation Behind Your Decision to Publish Your Book? 3. Why You Should Read This Chapter Even if You Already Have an Idea for a Book 4. How to Test the Salability of Your Book Before You Write One Word 5. How I Achieved Sales Totaling $2,000,000 on My Book *How to Get Rich in Mail Order* 6. How to Develop a Second Career by Using Your Expertise 7. How to Choose an Enticing Book Title 8. Marketing Strategy 9. Success Stories 10. How to Copyright Your Book 11. How to Write a Winning Advertisement 12. Advertising that Money Can't Buy 13. Questions and Answers to Help You Get Started 14. Self-Publishing and the Midas Touch

8½" x 11½" — 240 Pages . . . $20.00

A PRACTICAL GUIDE TO SELF-HYPNOSIS

1. What You Should Know about Self-Hypnosis 2. What about the Dangers of Hypnosis? 3. Is Hypnosis the Answer? 4. How Does Self-Hypnosis Work? 5. How to Arouse Yourself From the Self-Hypnotic State 6. How to Attain Self-Hypnosis 7. Deepening the Self-Hypnotic State 8. What You Should Know about Becoming an Excellent Subject 9. Techniques for Reaching the Somnambulistic State 10. A New Approach to Self-Hypnosis 11. Psychological Aids and Their Function 12. Practical Applications of Self-Hypnosis

144 Pages . . . $10.00

Available at your bookstore or directly from Wilshire Book Company.
Please add $2.00 shipping and handling for each book ordered.

Wilshire Book Company
12015 Sherman Road, No. Hollywood, California 91605

For our complete catalog, visit our Web site at www.mpowers.com.